YANKEE COMMANDOS

YANKEE COMMANDOS

*HOW **WILLIAM P. SANDERS***

*LED A **CAVALRY SQUADRON***

*DEEP INTO **CONFEDERATE TERRITORY***

STUART D. BRANDES

The University of Tennessee Press / Knoxville

Library of Congress Cataloging-in-Publication Data

Names: Brandes, Stuart D. (Stuart Dean), 1940- author.

Title: Yankee commandos : how William P. Sanders led a cavalry squadron
  deep into Confederate territory / Stuart D. Brandes.

Description: First edition. | Knoxville : The University of Tennessee
  Press, [2023] | Includes bibliographical references and index. |
  Summary: "In June of 1863, Col. William P. Sanders led a cavalry raid of
  1,300 men from the Union Army of the Ohio through Confederate-held East
  Tennessee. The raid's purpose was to sever the Confederate rail supply
  line from Virginia to the Western Theater, and Sanders and his raiders
  were largely successful. Brandes presents readers with the most complete
  account of the Sanders raid to date using Sanders's official reports,
  East Tennessee diaries and memoirs of the Civil War, and pertinent
  secondary sources. In doing so, Brandes fills an important gap in Civil
  War scholarship and showcases Unionism in a mostly
  Confederate-sympathizing state"—Provided by publisher.

Identifiers: LCCN 2022051946 (print) | LCCN 2022051947 (ebook) | ISBN
  9781621907466 (hardcover) | ISBN 9781621907473 (Adobe PDF)

Subjects: LCSH: Sanders, William Price, 1833–1863. | Unionists (United
  States Civil War)—Tennessee, East—History. | Tennessee,
  East—History—Civil War, 1861–1865. | United States—History—Civil
  War, 1861–1865—Cavalry operations.

Classification: LCC E531 .B736 2023 (print) | LCC E531 (ebook) | DDC
  973.7/34—dc23/eng/20221028

LC record available at https://lccn.loc.gov/2022051946

LC ebook record available at https://lccn.loc.gov/2022051947

Designed and typeset
by Nathan Moehlmann,
Goosepen Studio & Press

CONTENTS

ILLUSTRATIONS

Photos

Maps

Wednesday, June 10

11:00 AM: 720 men leave Camp Somerset, KY, under command of Maj. Tristram Dow, 112th Illinois Mounted Infantry. Midnight, arrive Camp Wildcat, near Mt. Vernon, KY.

Thursday, June 11

Camp Wildcat.

Friday, June 12

Camp Wildcat. Sanders arrives from Lexington, KY.

Saturday, June 13

In camp. Receive orders to march at 6:00 AM on June 14.

Sunday, June 14

Leave Mt. Vernon, KY. March 25 miles on London Road. Camp in woods 5 miles south of London, KY.

Monday, June 15

Early AM: March 25 miles to Williamsburg, KY.

5:00 PM: Hear distant firing to east at Big Creek Gap, TN. Camp early, 3 miles north of Williamsburg, KY. Night's sleep.

Tuesday, June 16

10:00 AM: Depart Williamsburg, KY, with ten days' rations (hard tack) and five days' forage. Ford the Cumberland, proceed southwest along Marsh Creek Road (present-day Hwy 92), turn south.

11:00 PM: Halt to allow horses to feed on grass. Proceeding south, cross into Tennessee.

Wednesday, June 17

1:00 AM: Rest eight miles south of KY/TN border, probably near Oneida, Scott County, TN [Chitwood] Pass three miles west of Huntsville, Scott County, TN. Ford New River, three miles north of Robbins, TN, taking cool bath.

10:00 PM: Halt at Emory Creek, twelve miles north of Wartburg, TN. 48 miles from Williamsburg, KY.

Thursday, June 18

1:00 AM: Arise and proceed south.

Dawn: 1st East Tennessee captures 125 prisoners at Wartburg, TN. Some escape, notify Kingston, Loudon, and Knoxville of raiders' presence. After pause of one hour, evacuate Wartburg. One hour later, Pegram's troops arrive from Monticello, 93 miles northwest.

5:00 PM: Arrive 3 miles from Kingston, TN. Have marched 34 miles. Confederate cavalry have fortified Kingston, drive off Sanders.

Sundown: Knoxville learns of enemy raiders operating west of city, by wire from Richmond.

After dark: Move to Waller's Ford, 8 mi. above Kingston on Clinch River. Five drown.

Friday, June 19

Dawn: Within 3 miles of Loudon, after all-night march, 18 miles. Probe defense ("Loudon fight").

8–10:00 AM: Proceed to Lenoir's Station. Capture 40, 57 rebels. Burn depot.

10:00 AM: Knoxville advised by Richmond that Yankees are headed toward Lenoir's Station.

Noon: March northeast toward Knoxville on Kingston Road. Destroy track and telegraph line at one-mile intervals. Dr. Harvey Baker killed.

2:00 PM: Knoxville learns that Lenoir's Station is burning, raiders are coming.

5:00 PM–12:00 AM: Raiders arrive west side of Knoxville. Circle Knoxville to north.

Saturday, June 20

Daylight: Move toward Knoxville on Tazewell Road. Streets barricaded. One-hour skirmish. Capture two cannon, equipage for one regiment, 80 horses, 31 prisoners. Proceed northeast along railroad to Flat Creek, four miles from Strawberry Plains. Capture 112 prisoners, burn Flat Bridge. Leave railroad three miles below Strawberry Plains, cross Holston River, contact rebels on north bank.

2:00 PM: One-hour skirmish, rebels retreat, leaving 137 enlisted and 2 officers as prisoners. Camp all night at Strawberry Plains, destroying bridge after dark, 14 miles from Knoxville. Night's sleep at Strawberry Plains.

Sunday, June 21

Daylight: March east toward Mossy Creek.

10:00 AM: Capture 120 prisoners and supplies. Burn bridge, and gun factory.

Noon: Leave railroad and march north toward Kentucky. Cross Holston River at Hayworth's Bend. Proceed toward Powder Springs Gap of Clinch Mountain, 28 miles distant.

Monday, June 22

Morning: In retreat. Hunger, thirst, sleeplessness. Enemy in pursuit.

Late afternoon: Reach Powell River, 30-man rear guard holds for one hour. Approach to within $1\frac{1}{2}$ miles of Rogers's Gap, which is found to be blocked and guarded. General Pegram's forces number 2–3,000, [and] have arrived from Monticello, KY, 56 miles west. Abandon artillery and follow wooded path to Childer's Gap. Drive away 5th Georgia Cavalry regiment. Climb mountain after dark. After midnight, reach summit. All thirsty. 170 men become lost and rejoin Sanders in Kentucky.

Tuesday, June 23

In retreat. Noon, last of raiders cross Pine Mountain. Late afternoon, first troops arrive at Boston, KY.

Wednesday, June 24

Sanders arrives at Boston, KY. Sends report. Buckner promises Richmond that railroad will be open in two weeks, on new trestle bridge.

Thursday, June 25

Burnside notified of Sanders's return, sends congratulations to men at London, KY.

Friday, June 26

Sanders and troops reach Mount Vernon, KY. Troopers given a two-week rest.

Sunday, June 28

Sanders returns to Lexington, KY.

Introduction

AT ELEVEN O'CLOCK IN THE MORNING of Wednesday, June 3, 1863, an urgent telegram arrived in Lexington, Kentucky, the field headquarters of the Union Army of the Ohio. The message came from Washington, DC, and carried the signature of Major General Henry W. Halleck, the general-in-chief of the Union Army. The addressee was Major General Ambrose E. Burnside, the commanding officer of the Department of the Ohio, who was in Lexington preparing to lead a force of about 16,000 men, south through Kentucky and into the Confederate Department of East Tennessee. Burnside expected to move out in only four days, but Halleck's message obtruded. "You will immediately," the general-in-chief bluntly ordered, "dispatch 8,000 men to General Grant, at Vicksburg [Mississippi]."[1]

This directive stripped the Army of the Ohio of about half the troops which Burnside counted upon for his East Tennessee foray. With only two divisions remaining, Burnside believed that he was too weak to both mount a general invasion and also to protect his supply line, which stretched nearly 200 miles from Cincinnati, Ohio, to the Kentucky-Tennessee border. Convinced that an invasion was now impracticable, Burnside suspended the operation.

Halleck wanted to maintain pressure on the enemy while the men were absent, so Burnside devised a bold but trimmed-down alternative: a cavalry raid. Within a week the Army of the Ohio began preparing to dispatch a squadron of 1,300 horsemen on a sweep through enemy-occupied East Tennessee. Led by Colonel William P. Sanders, the raiders successfully severed the principal rail artery which connected Confederate troops in Virginia to rebel forces in the West. The safe return of almost the entire squadron made national headlines, but the memory of the feat faded over the years (See Map 1).

There are reasons why the Sanders Raid lost its foothold in the chronicle of the war. Southern historians dominated the history of the Civil War written in the late-nineteenth and early twentieth centuries, and since Sanders's raid was both a Yankee victory and a rebel embarrassment, few were inclined to mention it.

Moreover, several aspects of the event contradicted their notion that Southerners were united in support of disunion. In most of Tennessee, secession was very popular, but in the eastern counties, where the raid took place, a heavy majority of voters disapproved of separation. As a further expression of their loyalty, about 42,000 citizens (or roughly a quarter of the total number of Tennesseans who went to war) preferred to fight for Old Glory. Three-fourths of Tennessee's Union troops hailed from its eastern counties.[2]

Southern writers ignored William P. Sanders as well, although he was a true son of the Old South. Sanders was born in the capital of a border state (Frankfort, Kentucky), but he grew to manhood in the heart of the Cotton Kingdom, Natchez, Mississippi. Sanders's father, a prominent attorney and pro-slavery activist (he owned twenty slaves in 1850), was also a lifelong friend and political ally of Jefferson Davis. Yet, when war erupted, William Sanders swam against the tide. Unlike three of his brothers, who fought for Dixie, he chose to don Union blue. His decision both defied his father's wishes and clashed with the concept of a Solid South.

Northern writers also neglected the Sanders raid, but for different reasons. Most Yankees awarded primary credit for the Union victory to the eastern front, to conventional forces (notably the Army of the

Potomac), and to big battles like Antietam and Gettysburg. Though Northern writers respected the accomplishments of the western armies and did not entirely ignore small-scale operations, they too found no room in their pages for a Southern-born hero and his obscure raid.[3]

The raid remained in limbo until 1963, when the hundredth anniversary of the battle of Knoxville prompted Digby Gordon Seymour, a Knoxville physician and amateur historian, to publish *Divided Loyalties: Fort Sanders and the Civil War in East Tennessee*. Openly pro-Confederate, Seymour touched upon the Sanders raid but allotted it just two pages. Nonetheless, *Divided Loyalties* reigned as the standard history of Civil War Knoxville until 2006 when Robert Tracy McKenzie replaced it with *Lincolnites and Rebels: A Divided Town in the American Civil War*. McKenzie also discussed the Sanders raid but not thoroughly. A more complete account appeared in 2012 when Earl J. Hess published *The Knoxville Campaign: Burnside and Longstreet in East Tennessee*.[4]

Both northern and southern writers relied heavily or exclusively upon Sanders's official reports, which he wrote for a limited purpose—simply to inform his superior officers, not to serve as a lasting history. Sanders described, somewhat dryly, the route traveled, the facilities destroyed, the prisoners captured, the casualties sustained, and so forth.[5]

Yet, while his reports are indispensable to any account of the raid, he omitted much material of interest to future historians. Sanders furnished no information on the enemy's deployments, was unaware of the raid's effect on other campaigns, and was unable even to measure accurately the amount of damage he caused. His reports do not address the political aspects of the raid or speculate on the reasons for his success. Most of all, they leave out the colorful details of a tale of high adventure: a harrowing chase through 250 miles of enemy-occupied territory.

CHAPTER ONE

Stern Measures

Summary justice is necessary to repress Tories.
—Jefferson Davis

EAST TENNESSEE WAS A PRIZE. From the earliest days of the war, both Jefferson Davis and Abraham Lincoln recognized its importance, and both became involved in its affairs. Davis pounced first. Within weeks after fighting broke out in South Carolina on April 12, 1861, rebel militia units occupied Knoxville. In May 1861, Tennessee's legislators voted to join the Confederacy, then submitted their decision to the general electorate. In a statewide referendum held on June 8, 1861, 69.6 percent of Tennessee voters approved of secession. From that point on, and even before, the rebels believed that all of Tennessee was Confederate soil.

From the Union perspective, conversely, although most of Tennessee was enemy territory, East Tennessee was not. Unionists noted that the votes for disunion were distributed unevenly. While the statewide canvass was heavily in support of separation, most of the approving votes came from Middle and West Tennessee. East Tennesseans rejected disunion by a resounding margin.

Nearly seventy percent of the voters in the twenty-nine counties which constituted East Tennessee spurned the secessionists. The secessionists carried only six of the twenty-nine, and in some counties the opponents' winning margin exceeded ninety percent. In Scott

County, for example, voters rejected separation by a margin of 521 to 19 (96.4 percent). Its voters were so estranged from their western neighbors that they took the state's-rights doctrine to its logical limit. They resolved to secede from the state of Tennessee. In place of the old state government, they created a new polity. Henceforth their county would be known as the "Free and Independent State of Scott," and they pointedly named it after the commanding general of the United States Army.

The "State of Scott" never won recognition elsewhere, but East Tennessee was nonetheless largely Unionist territory. That central fact dominated the course of events during its Civil War years. The rebels held East Tennessee for twenty-seven months while Lincoln struggled to pry it loose. The contest in East Tennessee was secondary to the far greater strife in Virginia and the West, but it formed the backdrop of the Sanders raid.

There was ample reason for each side to covet East Tennessee. Tennessee was the second most populous state in the Confederacy, after Virginia,[6] and its easternmost counties counted 355,000 residents in 1860, of whom fewer than ten percent were enslaved.[7] East Tennessee's free population was therefore comparable to that of Mississippi (355,000), larger than that of South Carolina (301,000), and much larger than that of Florida (79,000).[8] Tens of thousands of potential recruits resided in the region.

Besides its pool of manpower, East Tennessee was rich in militarily valuable products. It was a leading wheat producer, and its secessionists boasted that it was "the breadbasket of the Confederacy." Its fields also yielded bountiful crops of corn and hay, while cattle, hogs, horses, and mules thrived there as well.[9]

Confederate copper came primarily from mines near Ducktown, Tennessee, about seventy miles south of Knoxville. Every day the Ducktown smelter produced more than five tons of pure ingots, allowing its young German manager to crow that his castings "can match any copper in the world." With equal pride he noted that his copper "is used immediately for casting cannon, percussion caps, saber hilts, etc."[10] Workshops throughout the South consumed all the copper that

Ducktown could produce and begged for more. East Tennessee was also rich in saltpeter, tin, iron, and lead. There were twenty-nine ironworks, and its contractors supplied the rebel army with guns, tents, uniforms, and shoes.[11]

Food production required enormous quantities of salt. Without salt, meat spoiled, and as much as two-thirds of Confederate salt originated about forty miles east of the Tennessee line, in mines located near Saltville, Virginia.[12] Saltville's mines could meet both civilian and military needs, but owing to salt's weight and bulk, meat packers received adequate supplies only as long as East Tennessee railroads remained in service. In April, 1863, freight tonnage shipped to Richmond from East Tennessee was twice that supplied by any other region outside Virginia.[13] After the closure of the rail connection that summer, both soldiers and civilians suffered from shortages of salted meat. Shipments declined, inventories dipped, and prices climbed.[14] Food riots erupted and disgruntled soldiers deserted their regiments.

While East Tennessee's men and resources were of prime value, its capacity to transport troops was what first caught the eyes of military strategists. The Confederates believed they could overcome their manpower shortage by shuffling troops east and west, as needed. General Robert E. Lee declared that it was futile to aspire "to have a large army at every assailable point in our territory," adding that "We must move our troops from point to point as required."[15]

Belief in mobility was widespread in Dixie. "The rebel forces are acting on interior lines," expounded the *Knoxville Register*, "Consequently, the natural plan of our operations is to concentrate on the different points successively and to defeat the Union troops successfully and in detail before they unite."[16] This basic axiom of Confederate military theory—that survival depended upon superior mobility—required having the capacity to transport troops by train.

But the southern rail grid was built for commerce, not war. No fewer than 113 carriers owned sections of track, and often tracks could not be connected, due to variations in width. The lines which linked Lee's forces to their sources of supply lacked capacity, and the war generated more traffic than their undersized and often worn-out equipment could carry. Confederate railroad managers worked tirelessly to overcome these problems, but despite their wizardry, the Confederate government never mastered its predicament.

Among the newest and best-equipped lines were the two which the Sanders raiders targeted—the East Tennessee & Georgia (completed in 1855) and the East Tennessee & Virginia (completed in 1858). The two firms operated under separate management, but both used the same five-foot track gauge. Their rails were up-to-date and durable, and their locomotives and rolling stock were modern. The East Tennessee & Virginia owned seventeen locomotives, the five largest of which had been built in state-of-the-art foundries and purchased in 1860.[17]

The East Tennessee & Georgia originated in Chattanooga, then ran northeasterly until it met the East Tennessee & Virginia at Knoxville. Together their tracks traversed the entire Valley of Tennessee, along a line that stretched 242 miles from Chattanooga to the Virginia border. Knoxville was ideally situated near the midpoint, and hosted yards and workshops which serviced both firms. After passing into Virginia, the line continued eastward more than 300 miles until it reached the rebel capital. Knoxvillians christened the link "the Richmond route."[18]

East Tennesseans had an independent streak. "The people of the Cumberland Mountains . . . are of a type unto themselves in our land," mused one visitor. "They are marked by a stubbornness of purpose, an independence of action, a fixity of purpose, an Indian-like stoicism."[19]

Elsewhere, slavery was firmly established, but during the 1810s and 1820s East Tennessee was home to a small band of abolitionists, many of whom were Quakers.[20] The abolitionist impulse had faded long before the secession crisis, but only a tenth of East Tennessee families owned a slave. Only one farmer in 500 owned twenty or more.[21]

Support for slavery was tepid. In 1861, each of the Southern states had to decide whether to embrace a government which, if it won its independence, would make human slavery a permanent fixture. Eleven states signed up, the last of which was Tennessee. Yet, Tennessee was unique. It was the only state which held a referendum on its future. As a whole, Tennessee voters upheld separation by a wide margin, but in the eastern counties the Confederate persuasion had little appeal. The eastern region's voters repeatedly snubbed their neighbors' choice.[22]

On May 30, 1861, 500 Unionists rallied in Knoxville in a raucous convention to renounce the rebel call, and some tried to go even further.[23] The Knoxville convention debated whether East Tennesseans should destroy their railroad bridges in order to keep recruits from the Deep South from joining the rebel army. This measure—the first of several proposals to burn the bridges—failed to pass.[24]

The anger reached a peak, a few days later. On June 17, Union supporters convened at Greeneville, Tennessee, the home of United States Senator Andrew Johnson, where they drafted a petition seeking legislative permission to form their own state. To no one's surprise, their request fell on tin ears.[25] East Tennessee was vital to the rebel war effort. If the Confederacy lost East Tennessee, its chance of winning its independence would be weakened. To permit their neighbors to leave in peace was unacceptable.

The Knoxville and Greeneville conventions, the June 8 referendum, and other signs of Unionist strength impelled Jefferson Davis to take preemptive action. Volunteer companies supporting both sides had been drilling on the streets of Knoxville and, sensing that a clash might occur at any time, Davis sent companies and then regiments to take the city.[26] For the next twenty-seven months, Confederate soldiers camped in or near Knoxville, and thousands were available on short notice. Knoxville enrolled and trained recruits, was home to several army hospitals and a military prison, and became the site of a large ordnance depot.

Aware that Unionists were the majority, Davis and Tennessee Governor Isham G. Harris instructed their men to treat dissenters with restraint. To carry out this policy, Davis chose a former United States Representative, Brigadier General Felix K. Zollicoffer, to lead the department. Zollicoffer, a lifelong Whig, tried forbearance without success.[27]

Leniency was not what most Confederates wanted. Confederates reckoned that Unionists were spies or saboteurs and demanded a crackdown. Recalling the lexicon of the American Revolution, they condemned Unionists as "Tories" or "Hessians." The governor of North Carolina went further. He called Unionists "disaffected desperadoes of the worst character, who joining with deserters from our army, form very formidable bands of outlaws, who hide in the fastnesses, waylay the passes, rob, steal, and destroy at leisure."[28]

On August 8, 1861, the Confederate Congress dashed all hopes of tolerance. It approved an "Alien Enemies Act" which required all males over fourteen years of age to take an oath of loyalty, or be subject to arrest. A few weeks later the Congress extended its policy even further. Confederate law now permitted the confiscation and public sale of real and personal property owned by persons deemed to be "Alien Enemies."[29]

In September, the Confederate district attorney in Knoxville charged 109 civilians with the crime of disloyalty. There were few convictions, but the effect was chilling. Anyone who wrote or uttered words of dissent risked arrest. Jail cells swelled with Unionists, and in October the only remaining Unionist newspaper in the Confederacy, the *Knoxville Whig*, closed down. Its editor, the famously caustic "Parson" William G. Brownlow, feared arrest. Brownlow agreed to go to into exile in Kentucky, but the District Attorney rejected the offer. He charged Brownlow with treason and sent him off to jail.[30]

During the next two years, Confederate authorities muzzled, expelled, pursued, and in some cases killed, citizens loyal to the United States.[31] Their tribulations formed the background of the Sanders raid. More than half of the Union soldiers who rode with Sanders were veterans of the fratricidal struggle known as the "Neighbors' War."

Beginning in June, 1861, Senator Andrew Johnson, joined by East Tennessee's U.S. Representative Horace Maynard, implored President Lincoln to send troops to relieve the region.[32] Lincoln was willing, but his generals were not. Brigadier General George H. Thomas bluntly declared that "to make the attempt to rescue them when we are not half prepared is culpable." Brigadier General Albin F. Schoepf promised to advance if so ordered, but added that he thought that such an attack would be "most decidedly imprudent."[33]

The generals cited difficulties presented by East Tennessee's topography. The region was known as "Little Switzerland," owing to its steep slopes. But while the Cumberland Mountains are not as rugged as the Alps, soldiers still found them daunting. A Confederate colonel described "Little Switzerland" as "a tumultuous mass of steep hills, wooded to the top, with execrable roads winding through the ravines and often occupying the beds of water-courses [*sic*]." Union general William T. Sherman bluntly declared that "East Tennessee is my horror."[34]

Logistical issues presented another problem. Knoxville was directly accessible by rail from either the east or west, but not from the north. The western commanders knew that the nearest railroad stations linking Knoxville to the north were in Cincinnati, Ohio, about 250 miles away, or in Lexington, Kentucky, about 170 miles distant. Without good rail access, an invasion force would be short of supplies. The western armies were also short of troops, and many of the men on duty were raw recruits, were poorly equipped, or were sickly. Major General Don Carlos Buell, who commanded the Department of the Ohio, declared in 1861 that an invasion was "simply ridiculous."[35]

While Lincoln's generals brooded, the Unionists of East Tennessee suffered. The September arrests brought a spate of appeals, and Lincoln, eager to gain a victory after the humiliating Union defeat at the battle of Bull Run in July, became determined to help.[36] The president relied for advice on three brothers who were members of an Old Tennessee family: ironmaker James Patton Taylor Carter, clergyman William Blount Carter, and career naval officer Lieutenant Samuel Powhatan Carter USN.[37] All three Carters advocated burning the bridges, but William and Samuel were the most directly involved.[38]

William B. Carter was an ordained member of the Presbyterian pulpit and a slaveholder.[39] Nonetheless, he openly and categorically proclaimed his willingness to forfeit his entire slave property rather than submit to secession.[40] Carter was the first of several men of the cloth who participated in forays against the East Tennessee rail lines.

Reverend Carter wanted relief, and he wanted it promptly. In September he presented President Lincoln with a plan to destroy the railroad bridges of East Tennessee. This scheme won the approval of General William T. Sherman, who judged it to be a useful prelude to a full-scale invasion, which would be carried out by a Kentucky-based force under the command of General George H. Thomas.

Lincoln liked Carter's idea, agreeing with a contemporary who said that Carter was "the very man for such an enterprise—cool, cunning, sagacious, and brave." Lincoln authorized a payment of $2500 in gold—a handsome sum—to cover the Reverend's expenses.[41] Aided by two Union officers, Carter targeted nine bridges located along a 270-mile stretch of track.[42] On the night of November 8, 1861, small bands of Unionists, some of them masked, attacked and burned seven lightly guarded bridges. No lives were lost, but one watchman lost a hand.[43]

Anticipating invasion, some 1,200-1,500 East Tennesseans armed themselves with shotguns, squirrel rifles, and "every conceivable weapon." But enthusiasm was no match for trained troops, and the local men ran "at the first fire." When the news spread that General Thomas had called off the invasion, they returned to their homes. This week-long, almost bloodless episode entered local lore as "the little Rebellion against the big Rebellion," or the "Carter County Rebellion."[44]

The East Tennessee uprising convinced Davis to guard the railroad all the way from Chattanooga to Bristol. Confederate Brigadier General William H. Carroll, in command at Knoxville, formally declared that the "exigencies of the time" required "adoption of the sternest measures." Carroll proclaimed martial law, and squads fanned out to conduct a house-to-house search for Unionists and firearms. Churchgoers were astonished to learn that they needed a written pass issued by the army in order to enter the city to attend Sunday services. Even a simple visit to a doctor's office was impossible without military permission.[45]

Men who actually participated in the bridge burnings were principal targets of the dragnet, but rebel agents also rounded up more than a thousand others who were merely suspected of being Union supporters. Colonel William B. Wood of the 6th Alabama, an ordained minister of the Methodist Episcopal faith, took charge of approximately 150 prisoners. Seeking direction on how to treat the "Tories," Wood asked, "What shall I do with the prisoners?"[46]

Three hundred eighty miles to the east, news of the attack electrified Richmond.[47] Colonel Wood's question landed on Jefferson Davis's desk, and the president assigned his most trusted aide, acting Secretary of War Judah P. Benjamin, to handle the matter. Benjamin, who won acclaim as "the most gifted of the Confederacy's leaders," was a brilliant lawyer who had been the Attorney General. According to William J. Cooper, Davis's biographer, Benjamin enjoyed a "special place" among Davis's aides. "Although President Davis made almost every decision, large and small, he wanted to talk them out before deciding."[48]

Davis was incensed. As a graduate of the United States Military Academy, he shared an opinion held by most professional soldiers—he despised guerrillas. Yet, though Davis was in accord with military thinking, he was in conflict with American practice. Americans employed partisan warfare effectively during the Revolution, and from the very earliest weeks of the Civil War, partisan bands engaged in a variety of operations on behalf of the Rebellion, including the burning of railroad bridges.[49] The Congress of the Confederate States explicitly authorized such warfare under its Partisan Ranger Act, which was in effect from 1862 through 1864. Still, when *Unionists* burned bridges, Davis denounced their tactics as "barbarous."[50]

Davis likened the southern states to a large, extended family, and he seldom permitted dissension within his household.[51] Secretary Benjamin answered Colonel Wood's question. Although the Confederate district court was in session, the district attorney reported that its presiding judge was soft. Benjamin decided to bypass it.[52]

On November 25, 1861, he decreed that bridge burning was a capital crime.[53] "All such [prisoners] as can be identified as having been engaged in bridge burning are to be tried summarily by drum-head court-martial," he ordered. "And if found guilty," he continued, the prisoners were to be "executed on the spot by hanging." Just in case someone missed his message, he added a grisly flourish. "It would be well," he wrote, "to leave their bodies hanging in the vicinity of the burned bridges." He also said that he hoped "to hear they have hung every bridge burner at the end of the burned bridges."[54]

Benjamin's edict was legally weak, however. In 1861 partisan or guerrilla warfare was impermissible under the classical or "Westphalian" code of international warfare adopted at the Congress of Vienna in 1814-15. Under this code, acts of war were illegal if carried out by persons who had not been mustered into an army and who did not appear in uniform. Violent, clandestine actions, such as bridge burning, if not conducted under the auspices of a recognized nation-state, could qualify as criminal acts.[55]

Partisans could be executed if captured while engaging in a criminal act, but if they were apprehended later, they were to be treated as prisoners of war. As records maintained in the National Archives show, the men who participated in the bridge burning of November 8, 1861, were sworn into the Union Army prior to the attacks. They were assailing a legitimate military target (a bridge which carried troop trains) and were doing so as part of a normal military operation (a pending invasion). Moreover, they acted under the auspices of the United States Army.[56]

Though bridge burners were not in uniform (as far as is known), in the Civil War the absence of a uniform did not normally lead to a prisoner's execution.

Jefferson Davis contended that if one of his soldiers was captured, the lack of a uniform should not compromise his status as a prisoner-of-war. But significantly, before demanding executions of the bridge burners, neither Davis nor Benjamin bothered to ask whether the attackers were in uniform, whether they had been duly enlisted into the Union Army, or whether they acted in concert with a larger military operation.

General Carroll hesitated to carry out Benjamin's directive and telegraphed Richmond seeking assurance that President Davis did in fact want the prisoners hanged. Benjamin replied that "the President . . . entirely approves my order to hang every bridge-burner you can catch and convict."[57]

Since Benjamin's name was affixed to the order, historians have assigned him responsibility for the executions and the degradation of the remains.[58] But Jefferson Davis was a lifelong micro-manager and, in the words of historian William C. Davis, he "had an obsession with doing everything himself."[59] Judah Benjamin, conversely, was known for following Davis's orders to the letter. The Confederate president, not his deputy, bears responsibility for hanging the bridge burners. In 1863 Davis's policy remained in effect. "Summary justice is necessary to repress tories [*sic*]," he decreed.[60]

The executions proceeded. On November 30 two prisoners were hanged from a tree within sight of the railroad depot at Greeneville, near where the Unionists had rallied. Since Greeneville's bridge was in ruins, corpses could not be exhibited as directed, but they remained on open display for about twenty-six hours, or until decomposition made the odor too offensive. Passengers passing through Greeneville allegedly expressed their contempt by striking the corpses with canes.

To extend their object lesson even further, the rebels built a gallows near the depot in north Knoxville. They hanged a raider and a week later, two more alleged bridge burners, father and son, were led to the noose. In an unspeakable act of cruelty, the executioners forced the father to watch while his son died. Then they hanged him as well.[61]

One rebel traveler, in a macabre commentary, chortled that "it is a most pleasing reflection that some of the incendiaries have paid the penalty of their treason by dancing on nothing." But he also complained that after the attacks his train had to "move so cautiously" and "with much circumspection." The trains could make ten miles per hour in daytime, but after the attacks on the bridges, they dared not run, at all, in darkness.[62]

The bridge burning left a bitter legacy. Five saboteurs were executed, but most escaped. To protect their identities, Captain David Fry, the Union officer who swore them in, concealed or destroyed the muster roll. Nonetheless, those who escaped remained in great danger (one even hid in his basement for six weeks).[63] Some conspirators kept their names secret for the rest of their lives, and as late as 1899 some feared that they were still in danger. An unknown number joined the Union Army, and some rode with Sanders.[64]

This draconian action was a formative event. Knoxville's scaffold stood in the open as a deterrent to sabotage. But soon after the Army of the Ohio reclaimed the city, Knoxville Unionists showed that they too could remember a revolution. They assailed the gallows "with a fury similar to that which characterized the destruction of the Old Bastille by the populace of Paris."[65]

Despite the hangings, a new spate of sabotage could erupt at any time.[66] Determined to keep the trains running, on April 8, 1862, Davis formally proclaimed East Tennessee to be enemy territory, suspended the writ of *habeas corpus*, and ordered the formation of a military police unit to enforce his edicts. Confederate commanders stationed troops along the line to protect the tracks and bridges.[67]

Although Jefferson Davis needed East Tennesseans, convincing them to enlist had proved to be nearly impossible. Rebel leaders privately conceded that most men who lived in the region wanted no part of the Rebellion and would not willingly serve in the Confederate army.[68] The guards were given an important collateral duty—to keep men from escaping to Kentucky and joining the Union Army. The Confederacy's policies induced about a thousand men to flee to Kentucky by September, 1861, and many more slipped away, over the winter.

In the spring, even more absconded. On April 16 the Confederate Congress approved its first Conscription Act, which required that all men between the ages of eighteen and thirty-five (later forty-five) must report for induction. Within the three weeks at least seven thousand East Tennesseeans fled. Known as "stampeders," they found safe haven at Camp Dick Robinson, a Union post located about 125 miles north of Knoxville. During the summer of 1862 about 150 stampeders arrived daily,[69] and in 1863 a Union colonel reported that, every week, from one to two hundred stampeders were still showing up at his camp.[70]

Stampeders played a leading role in the Sanders raid. Sanders's second-in-command was a stampeder: Colonel Robert King Byrd, a wealthy farmer who resided near Kingston, Tennessee, the seat of thoroughly Unionist Roane County.[71] In the summer of 1861, Byrd gathered his neighbors and formed a band which operated against the rebels, before fleeing to Kentucky. Augmented by other stampeders, they formed a regiment formally designated as the 1st East Tennessee Cavalry USA. With Colonel Byrd in command, the entire regiment was assigned to Sanders's task force, and its 700 men made up more than half of the squadron. Some Tennesseans dubbed the operation the "Byrds and Sanders raid" [sic].[72]

The men of the 1st East Tennessee had scores to settle. Byrd escaped Davis's dragnet, but some of his comrades were caught. Refusal to report for induction could bring a charge of desertion, a capital offense, and some draft dodgers captured on their way to Kentucky were hanged on the spot. Stampeders caught serving in the Union army were also at risk: they could be hanged or shot for treason. As natives of the region, Byrd's men were recognizable and could expect harsh treatment if apprehended.[73]

Many of their family members had suffered as well. Relatives of fugitives from Confederate service were subject to arrest, confiscation of property, and/or banishment to the north (the last was the fate of Byrd's wife). Rebel foraging parties were under orders to confiscate crops and livestock from Unionists first, and sometimes burned their houses. Wives, mothers and sisters, who refused to divulge the hiding places of their husbands, sons or brothers, were at risk of harassment, beatings, or worse. Deaths were reported, and while some accounts were doubtless false or exaggerated, some were true.[74] As a consequence of martial law, political arrests, house-to-house searches, gun confiscation, property seizures, summary executions, and at least one assassination, a deep rage mounted in the hearts of Unionists, including many who would later ride with William P. Sanders.[75]

Knoxville's famed editor, "Parson" William Brownlow, had himself been arrested, imprisoned, and exiled to the North. Dipping his pen in a well of vitriol, Brownlow beseeched President Lincoln for relief: "In God's name," Brownlow wrote, "I call upon President Lincoln, and upon his cabinet and army-officers [sic], to say how long they will suffer a loyal people . . . to suffer in this way. The Union men of East Tennessee . . . have no arms; they are in the jails of the country; they are working on Rebel fortifications, like slaves under the lash, and no Federal force has ever yet been marched into that oppressed and down-trodden country." He demanded assistance, "no matter at what cost in blood and treasure." President Lincoln and the Union army could not in conscience ignore this plea, but neither could they answer it.[76]

"There were many men in the ranks of the 1st Tennessee," wrote one of the raiders, "whose mothers and relatives had been driven from their homes into the mountains, or murdered, because they would not tell where their men were, that they might not be conscripted into the Confederate army." The agents of this persecution were home guards and other shadowy forces who roamed the mountains without restraint. The men of the 1st Tennessee struggled to find words harsh enough to describe the "demons and blood hounds who were scouting the whole country, hanging and whipping and murdering old men and women, the fathers, mothers, sisters and wives of Union men, trying to force them to reveal the hiding places of their fathers, brothers, and sons."[77] The rebel troops who were stationed near Kingston were well aware of the rage that was ingrained in the men of the 1st East Tennessee. One rebel who feared their wrath described the East Tennesseans as "bloodthirsty."[78]

The quiet college town of Strawberry Plains, which nestled on the south bank of the Holston River, had been a battleground since the war began. The rebels correctly regarded Strawberry Plains as a strongly Unionist area, and gave its large and vulnerable railroad bridge special protection.[79] They fortified the brick buildings of the college, and in the summer of 1862, seven companies of "Thomas's Legion," a unit organized by William H. Thomas, a North Carolinian who made his fortune as a slave trader, garrisoned the town.[80]

Thomas's Legion was notorious for its contingent of Cherokee Indians. The Cherokees were excellent trackers, and they chased stampeders, disarmed civilians, impressed property, and compelled citizens to take loyalty oaths. They also served as provost guards and, in September, 1862, scalped several Union prisoners. The extent to which scalping was their usual practice is unresolved, but even a single outrage was enough to inspire a lust for vengeance. The Cherokees were sent away several months before Sanders's troops arrived[81] but, though the Indians were gone, Davis's practices—hangings, shootings, arrests, expulsions, impressment, travel restrictions, and so forth—left ample reason to be wrathful. Byrd's men were heavily armed and when opportunities for reprisal appeared, some took them.

CHAPTER TWO

Lincoln's Wish

President Lincoln's ardent wish to send a column for the relief
of the loyal people of East Tennessee never slumbered.

—*Major General Jacob D. Cox USA*

ON JUNE 1, 1863, WITH THE WAR IN its third year, the
Union armies numbered 461,000 battle-ready soldiers.[82] President
Lincoln contended that such a powerful host could best exploit its
strength by attacking "with superior forces at *different* points, at the
same time." Lincoln split his troops into four main armies, augmented
by several secondary units, and ordered a simultaneous advance.[83] The
combined offensive appeared strong enough to crush the Rebellion, but
defeat and stalemate compelled a change of plans. One of the alternates
became the Sanders raid.

In accordance with Lincoln's schema, in the spring campaign the
Army of the Potomac was to march against Richmond with 95,000
men, while in the West, the Army of the Tennessee, which grew to
60,000 men, was to resume its drive against the great river fortress
at Vicksburg, Mississippi. In the middle theater, twin salients were
poised to strike. The westernmost arm, the Army of the Cumberland
(84,000 men), was to drive into Tennessee and capture the railroad hub
at Chattanooga. Its companion, the Army of the Ohio (38,000 men),
was to seize East Tennessee by occupying Knoxville, its commercial
hub and rail center. The seizure of Chattanooga and Knoxville would
cut the major rail artery of the upper South, would deny the rebels

the men and resources they received from the west, and would bring Tennessee Unionists some much-needed relief.[84]

Lincoln's generals were loath to operate in East Tennessee, but he overrode their objections. Major General Jacob D. Cox recalled how Lincoln persistently expressed his "ardent wish to send a column for the relief of the loyal people of East Tennessee." Cox marveled that Lincoln's determination to help the Unionists of Tennessee "never slumbered."[85]

As Cox realized, East Tennessee retained the president's interest because of its political complexion. Lincoln was a careful student of election returns and knew that more than two-thirds of East Tennessee citizens maintained some degree of loyalty to the Union, and had no intention of aiding the Rebellion.[86]

In his view the merits of supporting them were unmistakable. Despite Davis's numerous attempts to staunch the flow, the region provided a steady supply of recruits for Lincoln's armies. Moreover, every man obtained from a rebel state counted as *two* soldiers—one who wore Union blue, and one who would never wear rebel gray.[87] The Tennessee contingent, which totaled about 42,000 men, or roughly twenty regiments, exceeded the contributions sent to the Union armies by any other secessionist state, and even by ten of the Union states.

Lincoln also felt a personal commitment which stretched back to the first autumn of the war, when he encouraged the Unionists of East Tennessee to rise in rebellion. They rose, lost, and suffered. Lincoln was determined to bring them relief, and while the immediate reason for the Sanders raid was to disrupt inter-regional troop traffic, the attack would also show them support.

In that respect, the Sanders raid differed from operations which lacked its broader purpose. Sanders and his men went to East Tennessee initially to destroy bridges, but also to show the flag, to rally sagging spirits, and to nourish the flow of East Tennesseans into the Union army.

In the winter of 1863 Lincoln reorganized the Army of the Ohio. He replaced its commander, Major General Don Carlos Buell, with Major General Ambrose E. Burnside, who received the post "more from political than from military reasons." Burnside was "acting on an understanding with President Lincoln himself" that he would invade East Tennessee.[88]

Burnside brought his Ninth Corps, 8,600 strong, from Virginia. The Ninth entrained in small groups and made their way under a cloak of secrecy, appearing in Cincinnati even before the rebels detected their departure.[89] The Army of the Ohio now had the strength to proceed as Lincoln desired. In early March, its forward elements advanced to a point near Somerset, Kentucky, a strongly Union town located 165 miles due south of Cincinnati. On March 30, the Yankees drove off a cavalry force under the command of Brigadier General John Pegram CSA, in a clash known as the battle of Dutton's Hill. This was the first western fight in which William P. Sanders participated and also the first time that he won recognition for gallantry while serving with the Army of the Ohio. The Army of the Ohio then paused to consolidate its position in southern Kentucky as it gathered strength for the approaching push into Tennessee.[90]

By early April the other Union columns had also either begun to move or would soon be ready to do so. But, unfortunately for the Union cause, the four-pronged offensive lurched to a halt. The chief failure occurred on May 2-4, when Hooker's advance in Virginia ended in defeat at the battle of Chancellorsville. The western salients were then left to sustain the offensive while Hooker's men regrouped.

Fortunately for the life of the nation, General Grant made progress. On May 14 his men seized Jackson, Mississippi, then moved west to invest Vicksburg. Grant mounted heavy attacks on Vicksburg on May 19 and May 22, but the two assaults showed that its defenses were too strong to carry. The stout rebel defense compelled Grant to halt, surround the city, and place it under siege.

This standstill presented a possibility that Davis would send reinforcements, cut through the encirclement, and save the city. Davis reportedly promised that if the Vicksburg garrison could hold out for fifteen days, he would send 100,000 men to relieve it. Grant thought that unlikely, but nobody was entirely certain that the siege would succeed.[91]

The Union high command debated whether to send reinforcements. The issue was resolved when they received information which indicated that Confederate General Joseph Johnston was "being heavily reinforced." Apparently, as intelligence reports testified, Davis intended to attempt to save Vicksburg. Davis and his top generals were in fact contemplating such a deployment.

After the Chancellorsville victory, rebel leadership faced a fateful decision. They could either detach some of their troops and commence a western venture—which was what they did four months later—or, as General Robert E. Lee had been planning all winter, they could keep the Army of Northern Virginia intact and undertake a new foray into northern territory.[92] The Confederate high command debated the question until May 26, when the president and his Cabinet endorsed Lee's plan with only a single dissenting vote. There would be no additional troops for Tennessee. Instead, Lee would take his men into Pennsylvania.[93]

The Union leaders were unaware of this development. Union Major General Henry W. Halleck believed that Grant needed help, and the Ninth Corps was his best option. When Burnside arrived at his hotel in Lexington, Kentucky, on June 3, he found a telegram waiting. It detached the Ninth Corps and sent it to Mississippi.[94] Burnside protested that this shift would be a departure from the overall strategy, but Halleck reasoned that it was more important to win at Vicksburg than to advance in Tennessee. He told Burnside to send the Ninth Corps west. Burnside despaired that "my plans are all deranged," but he dutifully obeyed.[95]

The transfer strengthened Grant's siege force, but it impeded both Burnside and Rosecrans. Burnside lost half of his army. He now had only about 6,000 infantrymen—fewer troops than the combined Confederate forces in East Tennessee and southwest Virginia. He had sufficient strength to guard eastern Kentucky from rebel probes, but not enough to advance into Tennessee.[96] He had no choice except to switch to a primarily defensive posture.

Rosecrans was also weakened. The Union strategists believed that as Rosecrans's men pushed south, they would gradually become exposed to attack on their eastern flank. The rebel locomotives were known to be slow and rickety by northern standards, but as long as they remained in service, Jefferson Davis owned the capacity to transfer troops to middle Tennessee. Burnside's incapacity did not entirely prohibit the Army of the Cumberland from advancing anyway, but Rosecrans was unwilling to risk another defeat. He chose to sit still.

The Army of the Ohio was now too weak to mount an invasion, but General Halleck ordered Generals Burnside and Rosecrans "to keep a threatening front." Rosecrans refused to risk an advance until his eastern flank was secure, so he and Burnside groped for a way to give their comrades in Mississippi and Virginia some relief. The Union generals knew that the Neighbors' War was exacting a gruesome toll.

In June, 1863, Robert A. Crawford, General Burnside's "Chief of Secret Policy" (or principal intelligence officer), wrote that, based on statements from 200 escapees, Unionist morale in East Tennessee was at a low ebb. "Robery, theft and murder is of daily occurrence [sic]," Crawford reported, explaining that "the men over forty-five years of age of the Secession party have organized themselves into home Guard companies and are prowling over the County searching the Houses of the Union men examining their letters and private papers and taking off such things as they need. The Indians are scattered over Greene & Jefferson Counties, doing the work of Treason, Hell & Secession [sic]."[97] Pressure for action to support the Union loyalists was unrelenting.

A cavalry strike against the Richmond route had been under discussion for weeks, since about 140 miles of its track lay tantalizingly close—only fifty miles from the Kentucky border. The rebels stationed troops at key points, but 140 miles was a long stretch to defend. As the Confederate General Braxton Bragg observed: "It is said to be easy to defend a mountainous country, but mountains hide your foe from you, while they are full of gaps through which he can pounce upon you at any time. A mountain is like the wall of a house full of rat holes. The rat lies hidden at his hole ready to pop out when no one is watching. Who can tell what lies hidden behind that wall?" The trackage at risk was longer by thirty miles than Robert E. Lee's main line of defense in northern Virginia.[98]

The supply of soldiers available for guard duty—never more than a small fraction of Confederate forces in the West—was too few to protect the entire line. The Confederate Army of East Tennessee counted about 16,000 men, but many units were stationed east and northeast of Knoxville, and 2,000 were based in positions stretching into southwest Virginia. About 3,000 cavalry operated north of the mountains in eastern Kentucky, leaving only smaller units of mostly infantry to patrol the mountain gaps and shield the bridges. These garrisons were sufficient to thwart a band of saboteurs, but most would be no match for a squadron of battle-tested cavalry augmented by cannon.[99]

As early as March 23 General Halleck had urged Burnside "to annoy the enemy and threaten his communications by making cavalry raids into East Tennessee." Two weeks later, General Rosecrans sent an aide to confer with Burnside. He reported that Rosecrans's preference was for an attack on the section of railway which ran northeast of Knoxville toward Virginia.

This stretch, however, did not include the fattest target in Tennessee, which was the bridge at Loudon, southwest of the city. Loudon bridge finally became the primary target several weeks later when Rosecrans changed his mind. He decided to enter Tennessee along a route that placed his left flank close to Loudon, and he wanted its great bridge eliminated.

To meet Rosecrans's request, Burnside assigned his most trusted subordinate, Brigadier General Orlando Bolivar Willcox USA, to devise a plan of action. Willcox, who commanded the District of Central Kentucky, proposed to attack the bridge with a task force consisting of 1,500 cavalry augmented by two pieces of artillery. "It is a rail road [sic] bridge some 500 feet long, and its destruction would cut the rail road from Knoxville to Bragg's Army," Willcox noted.[100]

His scheme featured two ruses. "I should first make a move [to the west] towards Monticello and Albany [Kentucky]," Willcox wrote. His second move would be a feint to the east towards Cumberland Gap. Each of the two diversions was to be meticulously gauged "so as to draw off but not to drive them out." "For if driven out of these places," he warned, "they would fall back to Clinton and Kingston [Tennessee] and thus cut off our expedition."

Aware of the advantages of operating in friendly territory, Willcox proposed to send the main body of troopers along a path which led down the "Big South Fork of the Cumberland by the Bridge Road through Montgomery [Tennessee]." "This [central] route leads through Union counties," he emphasized. Though he did not select the shortest distance, Willcox believed that this route was the safest and surest way to get to Loudon bridge.[101]

Willcox thus became the architect of the Sanders raid. At forty, Willcox had been a friend of "Amby" Burnside ever since they were freshly-scrubbed plebes in the West Point Class of 1847.[102] But in 1863 Willcox and Burnside had personal as well as professional grounds for wishing to penetrate the rebel line. They both harbored grudges against Major General Simon Buckner, the Confederate commander in East Tennessee.

Buckner, Burnside, and Willcox had once been good friends. They had much in common. All three met at West Point, though Buckner was a First Classman when the other two joined the Corps. All three were nearly the same age and had fought as lieutenants in Mexico. Both Buckner and Willcox loved poetry and even had the same middle name, "Bolivar," after the famed Venezuelan general.

Though the three had marched together on the Plain, the Civil War ruptured their friendship. Willcox was shot in the arm and captured at the battle of Bull Run in 1861 and then sent to Richmond to convalesce.[103] While on a visit to the city in late August or early September, 1861, Simon Buckner called on his old friend.

Buckner wore a uniform which identified him as a brigadier general in the Kentucky State Guard, a unit formed under the authority of the state of Kentucky, which was officially neutral. Yet, contrary to Kentucky's official position, for months Buckner had secretly conspired to bring the state into the Confederate orbit. His errand in Richmond was to seek arms and men to augment rebel forces in Kentucky.

Concealing his clandestine activities, Buckner assured Willcox that he had no intention of joining the Confederate army unless Kentucky seceded.[104] He broke his word. Shortly after leaving Willcox, Buckner accepted a commission in the Confederate States Army and took command of all Confederate forces in southern Kentucky.[105] Then, just three days after he received his commission, his troops occupied Bowling Green, the city which the Confederate government designated as the provisional capital of the state. But this decision stained Buckner's honor. Kentucky had not seceded, and indeed its lawfully elected legislature never did so.[106]

Willcox never forgot nor ever forgave his dissembling former comrade, nor was he alone in his umbrage. Kentucky Senator John J. Crittenden denounced Simon Buckner as an "unblushing traitor," and the Louisville *Journal* became apoplectic: "Away, parricide! Away, and do penance forever! . . . You are the Benedict Arnold of the day!" In 1863 Willcox and Burnside saw a chance to destroy the railroad which their erstwhile comrade was entrusted to protect. Vengeance was not the reason they conceived the raid, but the raid did offer an opportunity to settle an old score.[107]

Willcox knew that Confederate forces at Loudon varied considerably in strength, but he thought that the raiding force would have an accurate estimate, before making its approach. "We can get information from there at almost any time," he reasoned. "There are said to be six pieces of artillery . . . two to one side and four on the other, and some stockades. The guard is a variable force sometimes small and sometimes as many as three regiments." He estimated that a force of 1,500 would be of optimal size: large enough to overwhelm the enemy defenders, but not so large as to encumber the advance or betray its presence.[108]

Early intelligence reports appeared to confirm Willcox's prediction that the risk would be minimal. Burnside relied upon a network of informants to advise him of enemy activities in general and in particular to furnish estimates of enemy troop dispositions.[109] On March 9 one of Burnside's intelligence officers, a Lieutenant J. R. Edwards, debriefed a spy who had just returned from a lengthy tour of enemy territory.

Lt. Edwards had no reason to doubt the loyalty of his clandestine agent, because she was his own mother. Mrs. Edwards secretly collected data on Confederate troop strength and as a result became the first of several mountain women who abetted the raid. Women could not enlist as uniformed soldiers, but to a few the raid presented an opportunity for covert service. Throughout the episode, loyal Union women accepted the not-inconsiderable risk of acting as a spy, scout or local informant.[110]

Mrs. Edwards's observations indicated that rebel lines were thin. She placed only 150 rebel soldiers at Big Creek Gap, one of the main gateways into the region. This suggested a lightly defended entry point which might be passed without great difficulty. She also estimated that only 800 troops were available to patrol the hundred miles of track between Cleveland and Strawberry Plains. This stretch included several enticing targets, including the bridge at Loudon, the rail yards in Knoxville, and various other combustible structures.[111]

Sources interviewed in subsequent weeks generally supported Mrs. Edwards. Rebel lines appeared to be porous. On April 20 a secret agent reported that Confederate defensive positions in the mountain gaps had been evacuated. A month later an informant asserted that Confederate defenses had been thinned by a transfer of troops from East Tennessee to Mississippi. On May 29, however, a spy known to history only as Mrs. M. B. Lee, notified Burnside that General Buckner had assumed command in Knoxville.[112] Since Buckner was a well-respected officer, his arrival signified that the rebels intended to strengthen their defenses rather than abandon the region.

Mrs. Lee also reported that she had seen Confederate soldiers defending key positions beyond the city. These troops, she said, occupied the principal points of entry, Cumberland Gap and Big Creek Gap, as well as important waypoints at Clinton, Kingston, and Loudon. While generally accurate, the various reports contained contradictions and discrepancies such as are normal in wartime.

Intelligence data is seldom good enough to satisfy a commander, and the Union leadership was perplexed. Doggedly trying to peer through the fog of war, Brigadier General Samuel Carter wrote that

"I am at a loss to know what the rebel force there is." His reports varied from a low of 7,000-8,000 to a high of 20,000 enemy troops. Since the correct number was 16,000, his estimates were not far off the mark, but they lacked the precision that Carter wanted.[113]

Several other factors were matters of concern. The first was whether the Army of the Ohio possessed the capacity to strike at that distance. During the first two years of fighting along the middle border, Union cavalry operated primarily in defensive assignments, while rebel cavaliers were offensive-minded.[114]

Rebel horsemen so ravaged Union supply lines that Rosecrans's predecessor, Major General Don Carlos Buell, grumbled that there was a "great and immediate need of more cavalry in Kentucky and Tennessee." Help had been slow in coming, but by the close of 1862 the western cavalry had shown improvement.[115]

Between December 30, 1862, and January 3, 1863, a mounted force led by General Carter conducted a successful incursion into East Tennessee. In what became known as Carter's Raid, Carter's 980 raiders covered 470 miles, although only about a third of that might be termed enemy territory.[116]

Carter's men accomplished their mission, but with difficulty. The historian Allan Nevins termed the fighting of 1861-62 "The Improvised War," and Carter's raid was indeed improvised.[117] Carter was a naval officer temporarily serving with the army, and his plan reflected his inexperience.[118] Carter's men trudged through snowy, mountainous terrain before finally destroying two smaller bridges which spanned the Holston River. A rebel captain lamented that Carter's men had caused "inestimable trouble, expense & injury to the country," but his fears were overstated.[119]

Rebel carpenters completed repairs by mid-February. Though Carter's operation brought no lasting results, it established the feasibility of employing cavalry in the mountains, and it identified the problems involved in doing so.[120] A more ambitious venture would have to have more men, better forage, and greater firepower than Carter received.[121]

In Nevins's apt words, in the second two years the fighting became "the Organized War." By June, 1863, the cavalry of Army of the Ohio had become a better trained and more professionally led force. When drafting plans for a new raid, its leaders drew lessons from Carter's excursion. They saw that Carter had limited experience, that his troopers were too few and too green, that his squadron ran short of supplies, and that the terrain chosen for his foray was too imposing.[122]

The planners resolved not to repeat these mistakes. The command assignment went to a veteran cavalryman, and he received an ample number of troops.[123] While not all of the mounted troops in the Army of the Ohio had become "veteranized" (to use a soldier's term), a core of seasoned troopers was available. The commanders picked raiders who were known for their stamina, experience, and reliability.

Carter's men had succeeded in crossing the mountains in January, but cavalry operations were generally impractical during winter and early spring. Many of the roads were mere paths in the forest, and snowdrifts clogged them for prolonged (and unpredictable) periods. Since horses had to negotiate steep slopes, slipperiness was a serious impediment, and mud could be expected during the rainy months of April and May. Spring rains also gave commanders pause. Rains could wash out roads, undercut banks, or cause rivers to rise without warning. Unwary riders could be doused, stranded without means of escape, or drowned.[124]

The preferred season for cavalry raiding was in late spring, when roads had dried, foliage gave concealment, and grasses were thick enough to offer forage. June was ideal, though even under dry conditions, some slopes were "so terrible steep and rock that the cannons had to be dragged up by 60 men on a rope."[125] But peak conditions would not last indefinitely. The moon was full on June 1, 1863, and would be full again on July 1. Sanders and his men were fortunate to march under a new moon, which offered some concealment.

The muddy roads of April were impassable, but roads could also become too dry. On a dry road in mid-summer, a thousand horses would kick up a massive cloud of dust. This could betray their presence, and in one raider's words, thick dust could be "very nearly suffocating."[126] And as the Sanders raiders were soon to learn, even well-conditioned horses and riders suffered exhaustion in the heat of a southern summer.

Carter's concern about enemy strength was warranted. Robert A. Crawford, General Burnside's intelligence chief, reported that, as of June 5, "from the best and most reliable information I can get," most of the Confederate troops in East Tennessee had been transferred to Bragg's army near Chattanooga.[127] While this appraisal may have been the best obtainable at the moment, it was nonetheless erroneous. The Confederates had not begun to withdraw in significant numbers. The rebel Army of East Tennessee actually numbered about 16,000 men, although absenteeism, illness, and desertion constantly drained its strength.[128]

Crawford was close to the mark on two points, however. First, he estimated that "there are not 2000 men between Bristol & Knoxville."[129] Indeed, most of Buckner's troops were deployed north and west of Knoxville, positioned to repel a general invasion; comparatively few of them were close to the city protecting the railroad. And even if 2000 men had been scattered along the 112 miles of track between Bristol and Knoxville, no single garrison would pose a serious obstacle to the projected raiding force. Confederate defenses were not as thin as Crawford reported, but if the raiding force concealed its presence and moved quickly, escape would be possible.[130]

Crawford also warned that two heavy cannons had been sent to Loudon to reinforce its battery.[131] This information was ominous because, if the raiders attempted to attack a heavily fortified bridge while armed with only two light guns, they were likely to fail. Burnside and Willcox either ignored Crawford's report or mistook its importance, because they chose not to revise their plan.

That was a mistake. Six cannon were thought to be defending the bridge, so if Crawford's report was accurate, the enemy had added two more.[132] Few commanders would assault a position when out-gunned by a ratio of eight to two, particularly when the emplacement was far behind enemy lines. General Burnside evidently considered Loudon bridge to be a high-value target, or he would not have imperiled a substantial number of his best men to attack it.

Burnside took risks. He liked to gamble on cards, and according to his biographer, as a junior officer he exhibited a "dangerous penchant for increasing the stakes whenever the cards went against him; he would wager again and again, until his last dollar had gone across the table."[133] In June, 1863, Burnside bet heavily.

The great bridge at Loudon towered high above the Tennessee River. Railroads were the vanguard of the Industrial Revolution, and their bridges foretold a bright, prosperous future. The foremost intellectual in East Tennessee was Dr. J. G. M. Ramsey, a banker, farmer, physician, historian, and railroad promoter. Ramsey said of Loudon Bridge that "ever since its erection...it had been one of my idols." He remarked at how it was "strange that inanimate things should become the objects of our idolatry."[134]

Erected at a point where the river was more than three-tenths of a mile wide, the bridge's deck rested on stone pillars. Known as a pier bridge, its tracks were supported by massive, sixteen-inch by sixteen-inch timbers. These beams formed a framework which spanned gaps that were 150 feet wide. The bridge's height, 1,670-foot length, and 24-foot trusses placed it among the most splendid edifices in the South.[135] Opened to traffic only eight years earlier, it was an engineering marvel that was emblematic of a progressive, forward-looking community.[136]

Confederate commanders viewed the bridge as a military asset, but it was of special interest to the invaders. The bridge was part of the East Tennessee & Georgia Railroad, whose managers had chanted praises in support of secession and on behalf of Jefferson Davis's occupation policies.[137] The demise of Loudon bridge would both weaken the rebel army and gladden the hearts of Union supporters.[138] News of its destruction would reach every hearth in East Tennessee.

The forward base of the Army of the Ohio was at Williamsburg, Kentucky. Williamsburg was only twelve miles north of the Tennessee line but a hot, hilly, 125-mile ride away from the target. The distance alone made it risky. The Army of the Ohio could obtain reports on the strength of the bridge's defenses, but the intelligence was never fresh. The attacking force would need to haul heavy loads, since each cannon weighed about 1000 lbs., excluding its ammunition.[139] In the heat of a Southern summer, horses and mules could not pull heavy loads that far without rest.

Cavalrymen could cover flat ground for considerable distances, but not indefinitely. A cavalryman in the Army of the Ohio could ride for twenty hours even on hot, dusty roads, and could cover fifty-five miles per day for an extended period, but a ride all the way to Loudon would sap the strength of men and animals. Veteran troopers acquired an ability to sleep in the saddle, but both men and stock would need to stop and rest for at least part of a night. (One grizzled campaigner described how to take a nap while on horseback: "experienced riders . . . learned to brace themselves in their saddles, rest their hands on the pommel, and catch many a cat-nap while riding. These snatches of sleep were of short duration . . . but often proved more refreshing than might be supposed.")[140] Even if the squadron met no opposition, a ride to Loudon would require at least twenty-five tiring hours, and it would be reckless to send weary troopers directly into action.[141]

No prudent commander would attempt to assault such a target without carefully assessing the risks involved. The bridge was known to be protected by artillery, and there were three redoubts on the west side of the river, plus a redoubt and a stockade on the east end.[142] The rewards would be substantial, but 1,300 soldiers plus their horses, small arms, cannon, and equipment would be placed in jeopardy. Given the distance and the strength of the enemy defenses, some troopers would likely not make it back to Kentucky, and it was entirely possible that none would return.

Since catastrophic failure was a possibility, the general staff took some precautions. Willcox offered a solution to a perennial problem—how to provide forage for the horses. "The stock would have to feed on grass but at the start could take sacks of grain on the horses," he assured. His optimism was well-placed, for by June grasses had grown sufficiently for the livestock to find forage en route.[143]

The primary target remained Loudon bridge, but the plan authorized the field commander to divert the mission if its fortifications were too sturdy. If an attack appeared imprudent, Willcox listed alternatives: "The return route of the expedition would have to depend upon the information they obtained. If Knoxville is stripped of troops they might go up to Strawberry Plains and burn the trestle bridges there some two miles in extent." Thus, Knoxville and Strawberry Plains became Sanders's objectives after Loudon seemed impregnable. The blueprint for the raid thus observed cardinal military principles: clarity of objective, simplicity of plan, and flexibility of approach.

The attacking force would have to be large enough to overcome the garrison at Loudon, but it could not grow so large so as to compromise its agility or impair its escape. Intelligence reports indicated that the garrison at Loudon fluctuated from a few men to as many as three regiments.[144] Since the target of choice was a position of indeterminate strength, the prospect of success would improve significantly if the garrison could be surprised.[145] The officers who planned the Sanders raid were all veterans of the Indian wars.[146] The Plains Indians were masters of mounted warfare, and their way to conduct a raid was to move fast, achieve surprise, strike hard, and be gone before the enemy recovers.[147]

General Burnside endorsed Willcox's proposal, but before Willcox could proceed Burnside sent him to Indianapolis to direct operations against Confederate sympathizers and draft evaders. With Willcox off chasing Copperheads, primary responsibility for organizing the operation shifted to Major General George L. Hartsuff, who had formerly served as chief of staff of the Army of the Cumberland.[148] Powerfully built with a full beard, Hartsuff had twice been severely wounded, first in a skirmish with the Seminole Indians and again at the battle of Antietam. A member of the USMA Class of 1852, Hartsuff joined its faculty and was an instructor when William P. Sanders was a cadet.[149]

Hartsuff assumed command of the Twenty-Third Corps, Army of the Ohio, at its headquarters in Somerset, Kentucky. One of his first tasks was to review the latest version of the proposed attack on Loudon bridge. While there was no question that the target was important and the operation had been carefully planned, there were numerous reasons for a wizened soldier to be leery of the venture.

There was much to commend. The mission had a clear objective and ample flexibility. Steps had been taken to remove the flaws which marred Carter's raid, and efforts had been made to shrink the risks inherent in conducting an operation at such a distance. The raiding force was of optimal size, and its mounts, armaments, and accoutrements would be the best obtainable. Its leader would be a proven officer, and the troopers would be hand-picked. The route led through sympathetic territory, and precautions had been taken to maintain security.

On the other hand, several potentially ruinous circumstances had not been eliminated. The detachment depended upon diversionary probes to disguise its presence. While the *ruse de guerre* has been employed for as long as men have marched, feints often fail to deceive and, in any case, offer only fleeting protection. In Carter's raid the rebel counterattack was clumsy, but the enemy had made improvements. Buckner was a capable, professional soldier who sooner or later would deduce the raiders' intentions. When that happened, the defenders would be able to trace Sanders's position by telegraph and move reinforcements by rail. Interception of the raiding force must be expected, and it could be wiped out even before it reached its target.

Yet despite its hazards, the raid would be a bold, even audacious assault, plus, it fit the wishes of President Lincoln and implemented the orders of General Halleck. Lincoln had sent General Burnside to Cincinnati to lead the Army of the Ohio for the specific purpose of attacking East Tennessee. Now was his time to strike.

The senior officers had extensive experience in mounted warfare and, after analyzing all the risks involved, concluded that the plan had a reasonable chance of success. The remaining steps were to select the commander, assemble the troops, and prepare to depart.

CHAPTER THREE

Bold Cavalier

CONFEDERATE CAVALRY HAD THE upper hand in the Middle Border during the first two years of the war. The new commander of the Army of the Ohio, Major General Ambrose Burnside, concluded that its cavalry arm needed fresh leadership. Burnside had a candidate in mind, a twenty-nine-year-old regular army captain, William P. Sanders.[150]

William Price Sanders entered the world on August 12, 1833, the youngest member of a wealthy, politically connected, Old Kentucky family. The boy was born in Frankfort, the state capital, where his father, Lewis Sanders Jr., 36, served as Kentucky's Secretary of State. His mother was Margaret Price Sanders, 29.

Young William joined a family whose patriarch, Lewis Sanders Sr. (1781–1861), bred cattle, raced thoroughbreds, owned slaves, and had extensive business interests in Lexington. In 1810 an inventory of Lewis Sr.'s property showed a value of $4,875. Although such values are not strictly comparable, two centuries later a person would need perhaps $3 million to enjoy a similar economic position. As a sign of his wealth, Lewis Sr. built an elegant mansion, "Grass Hills" (which still stands), on a 400-acre tract near the village of Ghent, Kentucky, about fifty miles north of Frankfort.[151]

Lewis Sr. adopted an orphaned nephew and renamed him "Lewis Jr.," then raised him as his son.[152] Lewis Jr. (1796–1864) eventually sired ten children. His sixth child and third son was christened "William Price," after a late uncle. The boy was one of those rare individuals who never shed their childhood nicknames. Young William's namesake was a physician, hence he became known as "Doc." As a cadet and even after donning the star of a brigadier general, William Price Sanders was known to friends and fellow officers as "Doc." There was a streak of boyishness in "Doc's" personality which he also never outgrew. His nickname stuck, and he liked it.[153]

Doc's father, Lewis Jr., was a prominent Jacksonian Democrat. After his term as Secretary of State ended, he served a term as the United States Attorney for Kentucky. But after four years in office, Lewis Jr. decided to open a law practice in Natchez, Mississippi.[154] Antebellum Natchez was a cluster of exquisite homes which reigned as "the richest principality in the domain of King Cotton." Its legal business was booming, and Lewis Jr. wanted part of it.[155]

He succeeded. In 1850, after practicing in Natchez for a decade, Lewis Sanders Jr. owned real estate valued at $10,000 and counted twenty slaves as his property. By most benchmarks the Sanders family was very wealthy, but by the gilded standards of Adams County, Mississippi, they stood in the middle rank. At least forty-seven families owned more than fifty slaves, seven owned more than 250, and two owned more than a thousand. Natchez society was stratified by wealth, and the Sanders clan was two cuts beneath the top.[156]

Lewis Jr. remained active in the Democratic Party. In 1844, he favored John C. Calhoun, the most aggressively pro-slavery candidate, for the presidential nomination. In backing Calhoun, he allied with Jefferson Davis, a rising star in Mississippi politics who also stood with Calhoun. Both Sanders and Davis were staunch supporters of slavery and had been friends since boyhood. They were probably related, and they were natural allies.[157]

Sanders and Davis were delegates to the Mississippi Democratic Convention of 1844, with Sanders serving as its vice-president. The Mississippi Democrats declined to endorse Calhoun, but they did proclaim their attachment to the "peculiar institution." The Convention resolved that actions by "abolitionists, or others, made to interfere with the questions of slavery, are calculated to lead to the most dangerous consequences."[158] Though "dangerous consequences" were not defined, the words pointed toward a broken Union or even war. Thus, fully seventeen years before the people of Mississippi actually took up arms, Sanders and Davis had formed an alliance and were anticipating a crisis. Though Lewis Jr. could not realize it at the time, his partnership with Jefferson Davis would have fateful effect upon the life of his eleven-year-old son, "Doc."

Most young Sanders men aspired to attend the United States Military Academy, and two got in.[159] The first was William's older cousin John, who graduated with the class of 1834. John Sanders served in Mexico, winning laurels at the battles of Monterey and Vera Cruz. His young cousin doubtless aspired to follow his path.[160] Lewis Sanders Jr. had influence with Albert Gallatin Brown, a powerful Democratic Congressman and a pro-slavery expansionist. Brown knew of John's heroism, and in 1852 he nominated nineteen-year-old "Doc" Sanders to the Military Academy as a member of the Class of 1856.[161]

William Sanders was typical of a cohort of Southern youths described by a famed rebel cavalryman, Brigadier General Basil W. Duke. Duke said that Southern boys were "very similar in character—reckless, devil-may-care youngsters, always eager for adventure and excitement."[162] "Doc" was born to the saddle. The Sanders clan loved horse racing, and true to his heritage, Lewis Jr. maintained a stable where William and his brothers learned to ride at an early age.[163] In an era when stylishness in the saddle was a much-admired quality, William Sanders stood out.

One envious trooper said of Sanders that he rode "with that perfect grace and ease of horsemanship which characterizes a West Point graduate." "Doc" Sanders stood a full six feet two inches, weighed nearly two hundred pounds, and cut an impressive figure.[164]

But while horsemanship ran deep in the Sanders bloodline, scholarship did not. Southern cadets were known for their spendthrift and carefree habits, not their classroom ability, and Cadet Sanders struggled to meet the Academy's scholastic requirements.[165] About seventy percent of the instruction was reserved for engineering subjects, but the faculty also expected their graduates to be conversant with the best military thinking. In practice, this meant that cadets had to learn French.

However, the department of French was understaffed, and Cadet Sanders stumbled.[166] The superintendent of the Academy during Sanders's first three years was Robert E. Lee, then a brevet colonel. In 1853 Colonel Lee recommended that Cadet Sanders be expelled owing to his deficiency in French.[167] Yet, at that time, army regulations forbade the superintendent to dismiss a cadet without the approval of the Secretary of War.

Cadet Sanders's career might have come to an abrupt halt on the War Secretary's desk except for a stroke of luck. On March 7, 1853, President Franklin Pierce took office. Pierce, a New Englander, selected as his Secretary of War a prominent Southerner—none other than Jefferson Davis. Secretary Davis, of course, was the longtime friend and political ally of Cadet Sanders's father.[168] The new War Secretary listened to "Doc's" story with a sympathetic ear, for he had himself once been a struggling plebe.[169]

Davis gave the French-challenged lad a second chance, but his helpfulness had limits. Shortly after the school year ended, Lewis Sanders Jr. asked Davis to grant Cadet Sanders a furlough so that he could visit his cousin, Major John Sanders. Davis reviewed the request and observed that besides his French deficiency, William had received a total of 193 demerits during the course of the academic year. He was only seven short of the two hundred which made dismissal automatic. Davis denied the furlough and added a pointed reprimand. "You must be aware from the friendship I entertain for your father," Davis warned, "how much distressed I am to ascertain that you are so negligent of the Regulations—and you must permit me in the most friendly manner to urge you to change your course."[170]

Davis's reproof was stern, but not stern enough. In the following year Sanders's grades sank precariously low. This time, his sister, Eliza Sanders Haggin, asked the Secretary to protect her brother in case Colonel Lee again tried to oust him.[171] However, the floundering cadet had come to the Secretary's attention once too often. Davis warned Eliza that if her brother failed a forthcoming examination, he would not get another reprieve. Apparently, Davis's admonition registered, for Sanders passed his test and in due course graduated on schedule.

Sanders's overall performance at West Point was anything but stellar. In the 1850s the Academy ranked cadets according to a composite benchmark called "general merit." Measured by that standard, Sanders stood a dismal forty-first in the forty-nine-member Class of 1856. Yet, while his class rank implies that he was a weak student, the full record tells a different story. Sanders's scholastic marks placed him in the third quartile of his class, and he ranked near the top in both artillery and cavalry tactics. If his place had been assigned according to classwork alone, he should have finished near the middle of his class. But the scores for "general merit" also included each cadet's disciplinary record. When demerits were factored in, Sanders's standing plunged.

Secretary Davis had seen fit to admonish Sanders for his "neglect of the Regulations" after his plebe year, but his first year actually turned out to be his best, though he ranked only eighth from the bottom.[172] The worst was yet to come. In his next three tries, Sanders had the poorest record once, and placed next-to-last twice. In his final year, when the average number of demerits accumulated by a First-Class cadet was 101.9, Sanders received 173, just four shy of last place.

During his four years at the Academy, Sanders accumulated a total of 645 demerits. which meant that he avoided the title of the worst-behaved member of the class of 1856 by just ten points. He flirted with dismissal throughout his years at the Academy. He even managed to get into a fistfight with an upperclassman, the soon-to-be-famous J. E. B. Stuart. (Stuart ended up in the hospital.)[173]

While Sanders's class standing failed to predict his excellence as an officer, his overall record actually foretold his future with fair accuracy. His instructors correctly recognized that his best placement was in a mounted unit, and his collection of infractions revealed a personality trait which surfaced repeatedly: Sanders was fearless to a fault.

Shortly before graduation, his father wrote to his old friend, Jefferson Davis, to ask for another favor. Lewis Jr. wanted his son assigned to California, arguing that the young "Mississippian" could be of value to the pro-slavery cause. California had entered the Union as a free state, but the slave states needed more votes in Congress. Davis and other pro-slavery men believed that the best way to ensure the future of slavery was to legalize slavery in California, and one way to do that was to fill it with pro-slavery men.[174]

Writing from Sacramento, Lewis Jr. warned of an antislavery conspiracy. He grumbled darkly that the Pacific Navigation Company was filling "our shores with northern abolitionists. We want western men [who] become permanent citizens, and help to build up a state, whilst those from New York & Boston prey upon it. I fear there is some design in all this."[175]

Davis hoped to link California to the South by placing the western terminus of the projected transcontinental railroad in San Diego, hence it made sense to station the son of an avid slaveholder nearby. Lieutenant Sanders's first military assignment was thus part of a strategy calculated to open California to slavery by populating it with Southern men. He was ordered to join a detachment of the Second Dragoons in San Diego. The plot backfired, however. Lieutenant Sanders went to California as ordered, but he did not change the Golden State. California changed him. Residence in the West weakened his sense of Southernness.

After a year in San Diego, Sanders transferred to the Second Cavalry at Fort Laramie, Wyoming. This posting was a plum, because Secretary Davis was stocking the Second with the army's most promising officers. The Second's roster reads like a list of illustrious Confederate generals: its colonel was Albert Sidney Johnston, its second-in-command was Robert E. Lee, and other Confederate notables included John Gibbon, William J. Hardee, Henry Heth, John Bell Hood, Edward Johnson, Edmund Kirby Smith, William D. Smith, and Earl Van Dorn.[176] Among Union officers, at least twelve veterans of the Second earned a star.[177]

Duty on the Plains was the perfect placement for a soldier who liked action. Sanders rode with the Second to Utah as a participant in the Mormon expedition of 1857–58. He was appointed a company commander for that operation and remained in Utah as a company commander until the Civil War erupted.

The Second's regimental historian, Major Alfred E, Bates, observed that "regiments, like individuals, have characteristics peculiar to themselves." The Second had its own, distinctive *élan*. Bates likened its personality to that of a cavalier "mounted on his well-groomed horse, . . . sitting as if he would be out of place anywhere else, cap a little on its side, with a twinkle in his eye, and the suspicion of a smile about his mouth." The officers of the Second had the reputation, Bates said, for always remaining poised and confident, "whether in the parlor, in the tavern, or on the field of battle." Sanders, he recalled fondly, was a perfect example of the Second's band of high-living young Hussars. Sanders agreed; he made up his mind that Army life was for him. Henceforth, he described himself as a "lifer."[178]

A close friend who knew him well on the Great Plains was his longtime comrade-in-arms, Brigadier General August V. Kautz, USMA Class of 1852. Kautz remembered Sanders as a buoyant, free-spirited companion, a man who was famously willing to take a chance. "He was careless and devoid of method," Kautz recalled with a touch of Victorian reproof, "but always ready when there was anything to do. He had a tendency to dissipation, and was fond of cards, and generally disposed [of] his pay in one way or another soon after it was drawn."[179] He was a man of action, and he had a high tolerance of risk.

The happy-go-lucky cadet had changed into a devil-may-care junior officer without missing a step. When he finally went to war, his fearlessness remained marked. One comrade characterized him as "gallant and daring" and "brave and skillful." Another who served on the Sanders raid, admired him particularly for his "love of adventure." Sanders, he remembered, "united all the noble qualities of a soldier with the elegant accomplishments of a gentleman. Refined in manner, pleasant in address, fearless in battle, and a faithful, generous friend."[180]

In April, 1861, officers of the United States Army faced a crisis of conscience. Must a career soldier, sworn to defend the Constitution of the United States, honor that pledge under every conceivable circumstance? Or did a higher loyalty compel him to march on behalf of the community in which he came of age? For Sanders, the choice must have been particularly unsettling, because fundamentally the dispute centered upon the life of privilege which the white families of Natchez enjoyed.

Old Natchez was a community of striking contrasts. In 1850, 2,952 white citizens lived in varying degrees of elegance, while, scattered among the mansions and magnolias, there were 13,862 slaves and 255 free blacks. For the black majority, life was but an existence.[181] The inescapable question which faced Lieutenant Sanders was whether he was willing to risk his life to preserve the comforts of white Natchez.[182]

For three out of four young West Pointers from the Deep South, the Confederate Army was the preferred choice. Several factors predicted that William Sanders would join the rebels, as did two of his brothers.[183] But after deliberating for weeks, William chose to retain his commission in the United States Army. His decision was remarkable, in view of his age. Life in the Old Army had a nationalizing effect, and Southern officers who had decades of service were more likely to remain loyal to the national government than were younger men. Sanders had been in the Regular Army for just five years.[184]

Slave ownership was also a strong predictor of loyalty to the Rebellion. Sanders men had owned slaves for generations, and both his father and surrogate grandfather had worked to protect slavery for decades.[185] During Jefferson Davis's rise to national prominence, Davis and Lewis Sanders Jr. corresponded periodically and maintained their political collaboration. At least, until the cannons flamed in April, 1861, William Sanders remained proud of his father's connection to Davis and mentioned it frequently.[186]

By 1861, Sanders had completed five years of military service but was still a second lieutenant. The Southern army presented enticing opportunities for men whose career progress had been stifled by the logjam which clogged the senior grades of the Old Army. The Confederates had no choice except to build their army from scratch, and trained soldiers were spread throughout their regiments. As a family friend of the president of the Confederacy, Sanders would be in line for a choice posting. He was also known to two future chieftains of the Confederate Army, Albert Sidney Johnston and Robert E. Lee.[187]

If he remained in the United States Army, his prospects were not so bright. General Winfield Scott, who commanded the U.S. Army during the early months of the war, refused to allow regular officers to serve in volunteer regiments. Sanders could reasonably expect to be promoted, but only within a regular regiment. During the initial months of the war, moreover, the U.S. Army declined to appoint southern-born officers to high command. For an officer with Sanders's experience and political connections, the Confederate side offered a better chance of advancement.[188]

When the first cannonballs streaked across the Charleston sky, Sanders was in San Francisco. He learned of the clash when a Pony Express courier delivered the news several days later. An old West Point comrade, E. Porter Alexander, was also in the city, and the two lieutenants mulled their plans while dining and playing billiards in the home of Sanders's sister.[189]

As Alexander later remembered their discussions, "Sanders was intensely Southern in all his views." Alexander chose the Confederate side and invited his friend to join him on a steamer that would take them to Richmond where they would report for service. Sanders begged off, explaining that he planned to wind up his affairs in Utah, resign his commission, and then continue east to Richmond on horseback.[190] But for reasons which Alexander never fathomed, and for which Sanders left no written record, he changed his mind. He returned to Camp Floyd, resumed command of Company H, and continued his military service.

Sanders's attachments had shifted. Though he spent a dozen years in Natchez, his life was now the United States Army. Its officer corps was tightly-knit, and Sanders, like nearly half of Southern-born West Pointers, was unwilling to sever the ties which linked him to his comrades. In 1863 he wrote that "I have been twelve years in the U.S. Army and expect to die there." One historian of the antebellum officer corps believes that Lieutenant Sanders was a classic example of how service in the Old Army weakened regional ties and replaced them with a more national identity.[191]

William Sanders's parents and two of his sisters had left Mississippi for good. In August, 1852, when William left Natchez to join the Corps of Cadets, his father was practicing law in Sacramento. William's two older sisters had married two law partners, James Ben Ali Haggin and Lloyd Tevis, who became fabulously wealthy in the California gold fields. When William Sanders decided not to fight for the Confederacy, most of his family had lived in California for a decade. They would never again own slaves or reside in the Deep South.[192]

In any event, "Doc" evidently felt little, if any, affection for Old Natchez. In an introspective letter he penned in 1863, he proclaimed his allegiance clearly and forcefully: "I am a Kentucky man," he wrote. Though he had not visited the Blue Grass State in twenty years, he had fond memories of his childhood and hoped that one day he might marry a Kentucky girl. "I am fond of Blue Grass Farms," he mused.[193]

Sanders rode back to Washington, and on May 10, 1861, won promotion to first lieutenant. In peacetime, five years had passed without promotion, but with the war on, his next advancement came in just four days.[194] Now sporting a captain's bars, in August Sanders reported to the newly organized 6th U.S. Cavalry. Raw cavalry recruits required extensive training (one to two years in peacetime), so Sanders remained in training camp at Washington for the rest of 1861. In March 1862, when the 6th mustered for the Peninsula Campaign, Captain Sanders was in command of two companies.[195]

During the following four months on the Peninsula, the erstwhile rule-breaker revealed a rare gift for leading men. Sanders saw action at Yorktown, Williamsburg, Slatersville, and Hanover Court House, and was several times cited for gallantry. His actions at Williamsburg and Slatersville were particularly noteworthy.

At Williamsburg, two enemy squadrons compelled Sanders and his men to withdraw under fire. While attempting to protect their retreat, his citation read, "Captain Sanders wheeled his company about, charged and repelled the enemy with great gallantry." His regimental commander added that "though every one felt that few would survive . . . not one showed the slightest concern. Captain Sanders showed great prudence and bravery in the timely manner in which he met the enemy, though taken at a disadvantage by superior numbers." As the historian of the 6th summed up the action, "the daring counter-charge of Captain Sanders was the salvation of the rear of the command." At Slatersville, four days later, Sanders "distinguished himself by repeatedly charging superior forces of the enemy's cavalry."[196] When minié balls flew, Sanders kept his wits, faced the enemy, and spurred his mount.

The Army rewarded the rising young officer with appointment as the acting regimental commander. As the leader of the 6th Cavalry, Captain Sanders continued to shine. He was cited for bravery while trying to dislodge the enemy from Sugarloaf Mountain in Maryland on September 10, and again a week later for his service during the battle of Antietam.[197] Then, as the Confederates retreated, Sanders was cited twice more, this time for his performance in skirmishes with Confederate General J. E. B. Stuart's cavalry.[198]

Sanders led the 6th Cavalry in one of the war's epic struggles, the Antietam campaign, and again showed his popularity. One of his officers later wrote, "I question whether any other officer of the 6th Cavalry ever had the esteem and confidence of both officers and men to such an extent as Captain Saunders [sic]." (During the Civil War, the 6th had fifteen different commanders.)

Sanders showed bravery in combat as well. At Williamsburg on May 5, a rebel regiment charged the 6th, and in the ensuing melee, Sanders put the enemy commander out of action with a blow from his saber.[199] Sander's aggressive leadership brought him to the attention of three men who would soon take command of the Army of the Ohio, Generals Ambrose Burnside, Orlando Willcox, and George Hartsuff. They saw Sanders in action, trusted him, and served as his patrons during the 1863 campaign.

During his years in the West, Sanders was a carefree junior officer, but war and responsibility tempered him. His old friend and comrade-in-arms, August V. Kautz, noticed that Sanders had settled down. "For some time he had been quite proper in his habits," Kautz recalled, "which I attributed to the fact that he was engaged to a Kentucky girl."[200] While Kautz's explanation was plausible, in truth Sanders was a lonely soldier with no real prospect of matrimony. In fact, he was actively looking for a suitable "Kentucky girl" until just a few days before he died.[201] He never lost his zest for life, but by the time he was tapped to lead a thrust deep into enemy territory, he had long since grown up.

Illness idled Sanders in late 1862, but he returned to Kentucky in February, 1863, as a staff officer under Brigadier General Quincy A. Gillmore, who commanded the District of Central Kentucky. The U.S. Army had abandoned Scott's policy of prohibiting Regular officers from serving with volunteer units, and in Kentucky there was a pressing need to stiffen the cavalry arm.[202] Sanders was promoted again and designated the colonel of the 5th Kentucky Volunteer Cavalry.[203]

Sanders never commanded the 5th Kentucky in the field, however. Though that was his nominal position, in practice he was the chief of cavalry of the Army of the Ohio.[204] In that capacity, Sanders remained close to the action. On March 30, 1863, he distinguished himself in the battle of Dutton's Hill, three miles north of Somerset, Kentucky. In a classic cavalry *vs.* cavalry melee, Sanders rallied three Ohio companies to repel an attack by enemy horsemen who were charging at full speed. According to his citation, Sanders's men "routed and scattered the Rebel charging columns, capturing from them nearly two hundred prisoners and two battle flags." Pursuing the enemy until dark, Sanders added 250 head of beef cattle to the captured list. Once again, the battle report commended Sanders for displaying "conspicuous bravery" in the field. Sanders's leadership at Dutton's Hill burnished the reputation for aggressiveness.[205]

Sanders's coolness under fire cemented his reputation among his superiors, but he also earned the respect and affection of his men.[206] They routinely described him as "a gallant, generous gentleman." Tall and handsome, and mounted on a snow-white stallion, he was widely admired for his manliness.[207] Noting traits which had long been apparent, his comrades said that he had "quite a vein of humor in his disposition" and that he was "a universal favorite in the army."[208] One of his admirers described him as a "splendid specimen of physical manhood."[209]

Although not yet thirty years old, Sanders had "seen the elephant," to use the contemporary term for having combat experience. His battlefield performance had been acclaimed in encounters large and small on both eastern and western fronts. When an Ohio trooper learned that Sanders would lead the raid, he assured his parents of his safety. They could be confident that their son would return unharmed, he wrote, because his commander was "a brave, dashing officer who was with us at Dutton Hill."[210] And in perhaps his finest compliment, one of his men stated flatly that "we . . . relied upon the brave Kentuckian more than any other officer."[211]

The United States Military Academy had been created to furnish the nation with a corps of trained officers. Its faculty had rated Cadet Sanders as only a mediocre prospect, but his performance in the field voided their judgment. The instructors who thought that demerits were predictive of future success missed the point: here was a man who could fight. The farther Sanders strayed from the spit-and-polish regimen of the Academy, the better he performed. Sanders showed little promise as a cadet, but when the great test of loyalty arrived, he stood fast. When tests mattered little, Sanders barely scraped by, but when they truly counted, he delivered—on the Peninsula, at Antietam, and at Dutton's Hill. When his countrymen needed a leader to take their sons deep into enemy territory, Sanders was ready. His academic demerits were long forgotten when his commanders presented him with a colonel's eagles, a laurel that was fairly won.

Brown-Faced Men

Behold the brown-faced men . . .

—Walt Whitman

THE RAIDING FORCE ASSEMBLED near Somerset, Kentucky, a base which had been in Union hands ever since the Dutton's Hill fight two months earlier. The Somerset outpost served as a defensive position in case the enemy attempted an invasion of Kentucky and also as a staging point for operations against East Tennessee. It was thirty-seven miles north of the Tennessee line and about seventy-five miles north of the headquarters of the Confederate Department of East Tennessee at Knoxville. By June 1, about 6,000 troops of the First Division, Twenty-Third Army Corps, had gathered there. Sanders's raiding force came from seven separate regiments and constituted about a fourth of the First Division's personnel.

The troops had seen little action since Dutton's Hill, and the weeks of idleness weighed heavily. The prospective foray offered relief from boredom, as well as opportunities for advancement. If past practice applied, a colonel who successfully led a squadron deep into enemy territory could expect to wear a general's star, and his subordinates could anticipate similar recognition. Though while laurels awaited if the raid went well, failure would mean discredit, imprisonment, or death.

William P. Sanders liked to wager, but these stakes were higher than any for which he had played. Major General George L. Hartsuff, having recovered from a wound suffered at the battle of Antietam, assumed command of the Twenty-Third Corps on May 28, replacing Major General Orlando B. Willcox, who had been sent north to Indiana.

Having only a week's experience in his post, Hartsuff assigned responsibility for selecting the men to the leader of the previous raid, Brigadier General Samuel Carter. Carter understood perhaps better than anyone else the dangers which the men would encounter.

The composition of the squadron reflected its twin objectives. The First East Tennessee Mounted Infantry furnished six companies (about 700 men), or slightly more than half of the total raiding force.[212] The First Tennessee was under the command of Colonel Robert K. Byrd, 39, a farmer and trader who resided at Kingston, Tennessee, directly along the route which Sanders proposed to follow. Byrd was wealthy; in 1860 he estimated the value of his farmland at $17,700, or about $500,000 in present-day currency. He had fought in Mexico as a 24-year-old First Lieutenant in the 4th Tennessee Infantry, and his loyalty to the Union never wavered.[213]

As a Southerner garbed in blue, Byrd personified the political quarrel which cursed the region. Byrd had scores to settle.[214] In the summer of 1861 he organized a pro-Union militia unit, and he was the foremost surviving member of Lincoln's corps of saboteurs which had attacked the nine railroad bridges on November 8, 1861. These actions so provoked the Confederates that they arrested his wife and confined her in prison on the grounds that her husband was "a dangerous enemy."[215] The Confederate provost-marshal eventually agreed to her release, but only with the stipulation that she must go into exile in Kentucky. Mrs. Byrd, who was still a newlywed, was escorted to the state line under armed guard and released. This expulsion was doubtless insulting to a southern lady, but the rebels' characterization of her husband as a "dangerous enemy" was on the mark.[216]

Byrd's expatriates were a logical selection for the raiding force. Like their commander, many of them also had personal scores to settle with their former neighbors. While five bridge burners were hanged, about three dozen survived. Six months earlier several former bridge burners had eagerly volunteered for Carter's raid, and one was given the honor to strike the match that scorched the first trestle. Byrd's men needed no inducement. Several participated in the Sanders raid, although the precise number is unknown.[217]

Besides the Tennesseans, soldiers from several associated units joined the squadron. There were 534 Ohioans, composed of four companies (200 men) of the Forty-Fourth Ohio Mounted Infantry, two companies (150 men) of the Second Ohio Cavalry, and two companies (150 men) of the Seventh Ohio Cavalry. The 112th Illinois Mounted Infantry sent 200 troopers, and 100 members of the 1st Kentucky Cavalry completed the roster.[218]

The squadron mixed detachments from various states and units, but some had fought shoulder-to-shoulder in prior engagements. A core grouping of 300 or 400 men from the 2nd and 7th Ohio, the 112th Illinois, and the 1st Kentucky had operated together on several previous forays behind enemy lines.

This section already had been stationed along the north bank of the Cumberland River for several weeks, where its mission had been to drive off rebel defenders who were operating along the south bank. The men slipped across the river and captured enemy pickets on at least three occasions. "Our habit was to go up to the river at night, and at daybreak we would drop in between the rebels' reserve picket and their main force, and take them in without firing a shot," remembered a captain.

Since these men were used to operating independently behind enemy lines, Sanders chose them to form his rear guard.[219] This station proved to be the most dangerous position in the column and the men experienced more than their fair share of wild chases, and escapes by a hair's breadth. They also sustained the heaviest casualties of any of Sanders's units.

Battery D of the First Ohio Light Artillery sent a section of thirty-four men led by a popular and capable twenty-five-year-old, Second Lieutenant Henry C. Lloyd. Lloyd was ably assisted by two sergeants, H. C. Grant, twenty-seven, and William J. Patterson, twenty. (Both Grant and Patterson received battlefield commissions following the raid.) Most of the artillerymen were residents of north-central and northeastern Ohio, and had seen extensive action. They were crack shots. With proper equipment, they could hit a house in four shots, at a range of three miles.[220]

The artillery section consisted of two rifled guns, each of which weighed about 900 pounds and had a range of about 1850 yards, or slightly more than a mile. The 3-inch Ordnance Rifle, which featured a tube that was strengthened by a wrought iron band, was the lightest gun then in production. Each cannon fired either a ten-pound solid shot or an anti-personnel shell equipped with a "Schenkl" combination fuse.[221] This device detonated the projectile either when it struck an object or while still in flight (at a time selected by the gunner).

These guns and caissons normally required a team of as many as thirty-one horses, but such a train was not feasible on the steep and rocky slopes of the Cumberlands. To suit the conditions, the cannoneers removed the rear wheels of the gun carriages so that the guns rode on only their forward axles. The caissons were also left behind, which meant that some 800 rounds of ammunition had to be packed onto twelve mules. Occasionally, paths had to be cut through the forest, but with this system the guns could go nearly anywhere that a horse or mule could travel. On the steepest slopes, the guns still had to be manhandled up or down, with ropes. On flat ground, artillery horses moved at about three miles per hour.[222]

The principal reason for bringing the cannon was to destroy railroad bridges, nearly all of which were protected at either end by blockhouses constructed of heavy timbers. These structures were built to deter small bands of saboteurs and worked well for that purpose, but they were no match for a detachment of a thousand riders augmented by cannon. Two three-inch mountain guns could turn a timbered blockhouse into a pile of splinters in minutes, but to their dismay the Sanders men found that the Loudon bridge was protected by earthen emplacements as well as blockhouses. The Union cannon were ineffective against earthworks. The field pieces could be employed as forward assault weapons, but in most scrapes small arms were sufficient.

There was a clear and deliberate intention to send only the most reliable, battle-tested soldiers that could be found. The 112th Illinois

Mounted Infantry selected 200 of its best men, and 100 more from the First Kentucky Cavalry filled out the brigade. First Lieutenant Charles D. Mitchell of the 7th Ohio Cavalry recognized that he was serving with the finest of his command when he wrote that the three officers leading the Ohio detachment were "the best officers in the regiment in rough weather."[223] What was true of the Ohioans applied to their comrades as well; all were the best available, and none ever faltered.

Besides two full colonels, the troop included at least two majors, three captains, and numerous lieutenants. The officers were a mixture of small-town lawyers, journalists, and merchants, while the enlisted rank-and-file intermingled lads from the Appalachian hills with farm boys and tradesmen from the northern prairies and country villages. Since half the detachment were sons of Tennessee and Kentucky, and not a single raider is known to have resided in New England or even on the eastern seaboard, it amused the participants to hear themselves described as "Yankees." Though none of the units hailed from anywhere east of Ohio, nevertheless as "Yankees" they were known.[224]

The principal difference between the raiding force and their opponents was that the defenders were mostly from the lower South. Some of the participants recognized a confusing double irony: first, expatriated Tennesseans garbed in blue uniforms were "invading" their own home counties, and second, the region was being defended primarily by non-Tennesseans. A revealing exchange in this regard took place when a rebel captain from Georgia was captured in East Tennessee. His Union Army captor, a Kentuckian, told the Georgian that Confederates were not true enemies at all.

"We count you only as deluded fellow citizens," the Union man explained, "whom we are compelled to whip back to your allegiance to the best government on earth."

"All we want," shot back the Georgian, "is to be left alone."

"It looks that way," the Kentuckian retorted sarcastically, "when you have come all the way from Georgia here, and are shooting down my men, many of whom are within hearing of their homes." At that point, since there was nothing to be gained from further discussion, the conversation terminated.[225]

Colonel Thomas Jefferson Henderson, the commander of the 112th Illinois, also chose his best men for the raid. Henderson was born in western Tennessee, but his father, who disliked slavery, moved his family to Stark County, in west-central Illinois. Young Thomas had an aptitude for politics and served in the Illinois legislature, where he became known as a staunch ally of Abraham Lincoln. In 1862, he left behind a wife and four children to risk his life for the principles he championed.[226]

Henderson selected Major Tristram Dow, a lawyer and the scion of a wealthy Illinois family, to lead the detachment. At the war's close, Henderson rated Dow as the unit's foremost combat officer. He described Dow as "very brave" and "a quiet, modest man, a thorough disciplinarian of clear and strong intellect and of that perfect self-possession which is proof against misjudgement and terrifying occurrences." As Dow's subordinate, Henderson selected Captain James McCartney, whom Henderson characterized as "an intelligent, brave and reliable officer."[227]

The officers and enlisted men of the troop were not volunteers, but were carefully selected. Approximately ten days before their planned departure, General Burnside ordered that the best horses and healthiest men in the Twenty-Third Corps be withheld from other mounted operations in order to be ready for the raid. Besides energetic physiques, Sanders preferred "light riders" whose weight would not task the stamina of their horses. During the ten-day preparation period the men were refreshed and the horses rested, groomed, fed, and shod. A favorite pastime of horse soldiers was racing their mounts, often with substantial sums and considerable regimental pride at stake. To preserve the horses' strength and restrain his high-spirited troops, Henderson prohibited all "fast riding or even trotting public horses except by special orders."[228]

Besides the best mounts, Sanders equipped his men with the most technically advanced weapons available. Civil War horse soldiers prized the portability and rapid firing rate of Colt's revolvers, often electing to carry several at once, and avoid reloading under fire. The Sanders raiders were equipped with a newer, more compact design known as Colt's Model 1861, which had a .44-caliber cylinder on a .36-caliber frame. This model was lighter and easier for a horseman to handle than the Model 1860, which was favored by infantrymen. Illinois troopers who were not taking part in the raid loaned their best pistols to Byrd's Tennesseans.[229]

About six weeks before the raid, the 2nd Ohio had been issued Colt's Revolving Rifles, which were a shoulder-mounted version of the famous pistol. This weapon was more accurate than the standard hand-gun and could fire much faster than a single-shot rifle. The Illinoisans carried "Burnside" carbines, a single-shot, .54-caliber model which had been invented by their commanding general. Although it was not repeating, the "Burnside" featured a rotating block which eased the insertion of a percussion cartridge. Soldiers loved the "Burney," as they called it, for its fast-firing rate—eight rounds per minute—and its superior accuracy. Both the Colt and the Burnside handled better than the muzzle-loading Springfields which most infantrymen carried, and they could be reloaded while on horseback or lying down—a distinct advantage.[230]

According to the rules of the Army of the Ohio in effect at that time, a cavalryman in "light marching order" packed one hundred rounds of ammunition, and some brought more. Each man also car-ried a blanket, a poncho, one change of underclothes, and a pair of horseshoes with nails. The brigade augmented its weaponry with an assortment of sabers, scabbards, cartridge belts, gun slings, and bayo-nets. Following the customary practice of soldiers, the raiders packed more equipment than regulations required, hence, man-for-man they were better-equipped than their enemies.[231]

The troopers learned that they were preparing for "special service." The officers revealed only that "the expedition is secret and no one knows their destination."[232] Such elaborate preparations would alone elicit speculation, but the veil of secrecy aroused lively conjecture about the probable target. The boys of the 7th Ohio delighted in repeat-ing the prognostications of two imaginary "camp followers," whom they christened *"Rumor"* and *"Report."* In their minds, *Rumor* was a congenial comrade, "a vagabond, coming from nowhere, but going everywhere, ... a companionable sort of fellow, he is welcome at every campfire." *Report*, on the other hand, was only "shabbily respectable ... at best an aristocratic tattler."[233]

With both *Rumor* and *Report* circulating busily, and with no reliable information to correct them, the guesswork was shaky. On the eve of the impending action Lieutenant Mitchell of the 7th Ohio could only sigh that "though camp rumors are rife, nothing has leaked out as to destination." The best conjecture among rank-and-file troopers was that the general destination was East Tennessee. While proved to be correct, it was hardly clairvoyant. When the campfire prognosticators tried to pinpoint the actual point of entry, they missed by fifty miles. A better but still nearly worthless prophecy was that of a trooper who predicted that "We are sure of hard riding, anyway."[234]

By June 8 the men and horses were poised and only awaited the order to march. On that day General Burnside advised General Rosecrans that he proposed to attack Loudon and Strawberry Plains and asked for Rosecrans's concurrence. Burnside reported correctly that the men would be ready to leave by June 10, but he erred when he said that the raid would take only two or three days. The men received only three days rations, plus four days forage for the horses. This supply, the customary amount given when the men were in "light marching order," would take them to Loudon, but it was not enough for a longer mission.[235]

There was little doubt about how Rosecrans would reply. As early as March 23 Burnside had been urged by General Halleck "to annoy the enemy and threaten his communications by making cavalry raids into East Tennessee." A month later Rosecrans had sent an aide to confer with Burnside, specifically to advocate an attack on the railroad line northeast of Knoxville. The railroad bridge at Loudon was then designated as the secondary target, but on May 8 Rosecrans asked that it be made the primary target. The reason for this switch was to protect Rosecrans's left flank as he advanced toward Tullahoma. Since the question was not *whether* to attack but *where,* it came as no surprise when on June 9 General Rosecrans replied enthusiastically

to Burnside's query. "By all means destroy the railroad as extensively and thoroughly as you possibly can," Rosecrans wrote.[236]

Burnside's plan envisioned a second probe in coordination with Sanders's incursion. Brigadier General Julius White, another former Illinois state legislator, commanded 1300 men in the district of eastern Kentucky, headquartered at Louisa. Burnside directed White to advance from Louisa, demolish a saltworks at Abingdon, Virginia, and then destroy the railroad in southwestern Virginia and northeastern Tennessee.

After striking these targets, White was supposed to march southwest along the East Tennessee & Virginia railway, until he linked up with Sanders. White tested the Confederate line, but the roads were too poor, the forage too meager, and the enemy too numerous for his force to proceed. With Burnside's permission, he suspended the operation.[237]

The rumor floating around the Yankee bivouac was that there were 40,000 Confederate soldiers in East Tennessee. This was twice as many as the Union generals estimated, but nobody in the Union rank-and-file knew that the actual number was only a little more than 16,000.[238] Still, with a force of only 1,300 men and two small cannon, the intruders knew that they would be heavily outnumbered.

CHAPTER FIVE

To the Silvery River

Behold the silvery river, in it the splashing
horses loitering, stop to drink . . .
—*Walt Whitman*

Day 1–Day 7, June 10–June 16

THE ADVENTURE COMMENCED on Wednesday, June 10. On the first day, the leading contingent of 720 Ohio, Illinois, and Kentucky troopers plodded for thirteen hours through a soaking drizzle, finally pitching camp at midnight, about a mile west of the village of Mount Vernon, Kentucky. Having no tents, they spent a cold, wet, miserable night beneath some scrubby cedars. Having ridden twenty-seven miles, they slept well despite the rain, but one trooper mused that the boys were "thankful for rubber blankets."[239]

Wet conditions prevailed throughout their journey. The rainfall of June, 1863, reached a level expected only once in 500 years, creating difficulties that challenged description, though one lad tried. He said the roads resembled "mirey quicksand" [*sic*]. He added that he felt sorry for the "poor mules [who] are wallowing along through bogs which would at other times be considered wholly impassable." Another maintained that "in some places, mules perished in the mud, unable to extricate themselves."[240]

The deluges were in some respects an advantage for the raiders. The drizzle served as concealment, and muddy roads settled the dust, protecting them from pursuit. In addition, many of the enemy had fallen ill. Captain Andy Morris of the 65th Georgia Infantry was on guard duty at Loudon and observed that "a great many of our Regt is sick owing to the wet weather and being without tents." A sergeant in the 65th remembered that "at this time our army was in miserable health. About half the men had chronic diarrhea and a lot of our men died." The wet conditions affected rebel morale as well, because their diet staples of corn meal and peas spoiled quickly.[241]

On the second day, June 11, the first group reached Camp Wildcat, about ten miles east of Mount Vernon, where they waited for their colonel, who arrived on the next evening. On Saturday the 13th, the men rode twenty-six miles to Laurel Creek, about ten miles south of London, Kentucky.[242] The distance covered that day was typical of a day's ride while on friendly soil, but in enemy territory they would need to move faster and rest less frequently.

June 14th was another soaking-wet day. Some of the troopers rode twenty-eight muddy miles before camping in a "dense, dripping pine woods." Since they still had no tents, they passed another miserable night amidst another heavy downpour. Drenched but not daunted, they left at dawn of the 15th and rode twenty-four miles to Williamsburg, Kentucky. The rain finally abated, but then the day became cruelly hot. Water was scarce, and both men and mounts suffered from thirst.[243] The troop pitched camp just two miles north of the Cumberland River.

The first arrivals had to wait for four days while the rest caught up. A soldier's life has always been a blend of tedium and terror, and since these were their last tranquil moments, the troopers gratified their penchant for griping. After only two days, one bored soldier grumbled that "Time drags heavily in this uninhabited country." Pining for Ohio, another homesick soldier christened their bivouac "Camp Desolation." He whined that "we can not see the sky without looking straight up, and I think there is no human habitation in this region."[244]

While still in Kentucky, the raiders were accompanied by a train of wagons drawn by mules. Since the wagons could not cross deep water, the mules would have to carry the supplies. But the mules disliked having pack-saddles filled with cannon balls strapped to their backs. Their discomfort was a welcome diversion. "The pack-mules—raw recruits—furnish everybody amusement in their efforts to rid themselves of their burdens," mused a trooper.[245]

The Cumberland River below Williamsburg, Kentucky, formed the informal dividing line between Union and Confederate forces, so the men camped in safety above Williamsburg. Once the showers abated and they dried out, they "passed a pleasant evening." Those who showed signs of weariness were sent back to Somerset, which winnowed the squadron to about 1,300 men. Recognizing that men and horses would need more rations than were permitted when in "light marching order," the remaining troopers drew ten days' rations for themselves and five days' forage for their horses. This would have to last until they returned to Union lines.[246]

The Cumberland presented a naturally strong defensive position. After rising in the mountains east of Williamsburg, the river meanders in a generally westerly direction for about fifty miles, generally paralleling the Kentucky-Tennessee border. In its original channel, the river rose very rapidly following a deluge and became "a boiling flood" that could trap an invading force. A flash flood could block an escape route or prevent reinforcement.[247]

The Sanders men had to expect that their coming would be smoother than their parting. The Confederates knew very well that June was ideal for cavalry operations—indeed, rebel horsemen were preparing for a raid of their own. Tennessee had been probed by Carter's raiders six months earlier, so the rebels might have taken steps to prevent a recurrence. In any case, an incursion by 1,300 mounted soldiers in blue uniforms could not be kept secret for very long.

While their entry into Confederate territory might not be noticed, once the news spread that a squadron had crossed the Cumberland, the enemy would swarm. Sanders's men could not know everything that lay before them, but they could be assured of one grim truth. In war, all are expendable. Given the hazards that lay ahead, it was highly likely that some of them, and perhaps even all of them, would be lost.

Their mood as they began their journey was a blend of high excitement and gnawing fear. Yet, in the grand tradition of men going into action, the troopers masked their fright and soldiered on. "We placed in our pockets the picture of a mother, wife, or sweetheart," one rider recalled, "and bidding good-bye to our friends, with a last look toward the north, we plunged our horses into the Cumberland River and waded and swam to its southern shore."[248]

CHAPTER SIX

Watching and Waiting

June 5–16

ON THE SOUTH BANK OF THE Cumberland, rebels waited warily. Their main adversary, the Army of the Ohio, had swollen in size. With the addition of the Ninth Corps, the Army of the Ohio outnumbered the Confederate Department of East Tennessee by better than two to one. The new Union commander, Major General Ambrose Burnside, had a reputation for aggressiveness, and he established his headquarters on a line directly north of Knoxville.

Indications of an enemy offensive were unmistakable. Burnside assumed command on March 25, and soon the Army of the Ohio began to move into southern Kentucky. By late May it had established a base at Somerset, only about forty miles north of the Tennessee line. Its forward elements were even closer. They camped on the north bank of the Cumberland River, only about a dozen miles from Tennessee.

The Cumberland was a defensive advantage, however. It was swift and turbulent near Somerset, and the only available means of crossing it was by a crude ferry. Cables anchored to trees on either side of the river allowed a boat to be hauled across, but on one occasion, a line parted, the ferry capsized, and ninety men drowned. The ferry could carry an artillery piece and its caisson, but only if the trace horses were detached and made to swim alongside. The rope ferry was not a practical way to transport an entire army, but a pontoon bridge would make the crossing quick and comparatively safe. On June 1, a train of wagons arrived in Somerset carrying pontoons.[249]

The Union commanders made no attempt to conceal the bulky equipment. This led to much speculation concerning when the bridge would be completed and how it would be used. A Union officer wrote that "much conjecture prevails as to the destination of the contemplated movement." Besides the pontoons, many of the northerners received orders to prepare for an eight-day excursion and could be seen busily assembling their equipment.[250]

All of this activity did not go undetected. Even if the loose talk failed to reach enemy ears, the pontoon boats suggested an early departure. On the evening of June 2, a resident of a household frequented by Union officers disappeared without notice. Colonel August V. Kautz wrote that "the evidence goes to show that he was a spy and has gone to the enemy with information that the pontoon train has arrived and that we propose to advance."[251]

While there is no proof that Kautz's acquaintance was the source of the disclosure, Confederate agents were watching for signs that Union forces were about to move. When they observed pontoons and reinforcements in Somerset, they notified General Buckner promptly. By June 5 the Confederates knew that a large number of Yankees had assembled and that they were equipped with pontoons.

Buckner interpreted this development to mean that a "general forward movement" into Tennessee was imminent. On June 5, just five days after the pontoons reached Somerset, he sent three separate telegrams to warn his fellow commanders. He also advised them that the purpose of the "general advance" that was coming was to relieve the pressure upon General Grant.[252]

The southerners had known for months that an invasion was likely and had taken steps to mend their fences. One problem was that they had not established a stable command structure. In twenty-four months, nine different officers commanded the Department of East Tennessee.[253] None of these commanders, with the exception of the last, would be included in any listing of the Confederate Army's most capable officers.[254] Although the command of the Army of East Tennessee was unsettled, it implemented Davis's policies satisfactorily. Although the rebels did not win the loyalty of the civilian population, rail traffic kept flowing and there was no open insurrection. In April 1863 the penultimate commander, Major General Daniel S. Donelson, succumbed while on duty. Donelson, the adopted son of Andrew Jackson, had run for vice-president on the Know-Nothing (American) party ticket in 1856, but he was sixty-two years old, and withered by chronic diarrhea. Recognizing that invasion threatened, Davis replaced him with Major General Simon B. Buckner, a younger, professional officer who had formerly led the District of the Gulf.[255]

Buckner's zone of responsibility was enormous. The borders of the "Department of East Tennessee" approximated an uneven polygon with sides measuring 200 miles by 100 miles, or about 20,000 square miles in total. While Buckner's domain was a fraction of the area that Davis oversaw, it was as large as the states of New Hampshire or New Jersey, and larger than the Netherlands.[256]

Buckner faced multiple threats. East Tennessee's 210-mile railroad corridor was an invitation to saboteurs, and he had a mountainous, 190-mile border to keep sealed against escaping draft-dodgers and deserters. He was also responsible for a warren of mountains, forests, caves, and ravines which offered ample concealment to brigands and bushwhackers. As if these problems were not enough to vex a commander, another cavalry probe such as Carter's raid was always a possibility.[257]

General Buckner's greatest concern, however, was a full-scale invasion. There were three main portals—Jacksborough Gap, Big Creek Gap, and Cumberland Gap—that were the most likely avenues of attack. These were of great concern because no natural barrier stood between them and Knoxville. If the Yankees burst through one of the gaps, their path to the city would be smooth and straight.[258] Buckner's initial troop deployments reflected that overriding danger, as did the decisions he made once he became convinced that a major Union invasion was underway.

The Department of East Tennessee had been part of the vast command of General Joseph E. Johnston, which extended from the Mississippi River to the Appalachian Mountains. General Johnston chose to preside in person over the defense of Mississippi, but before leaving for the southwest he crafted a master plan intended to shield Tennessee from invasion.

Knowing that his men could never match the size of the Union forces, Johnston relied upon Tennessee's natural defenses. If Tennessee was supported by a highly mobile strike force, he reasoned, its rivers and ridges could repel an invader. To implement this concept, Johnston created a combined cavalry command, composed of as many as 16,000 mounted troops. This unit could fall upon the supply train of any Union commander who dared to set foot upon Tennessee soil. Centrally located in Middle Tennessee, Johnston's cavalry force could exploit the advantage of interior lines upon which the Confederates relied.

Johnston's plan was sensible but not flawless. Since it required his mounted units to concentrate in Middle Tennessee, Johnston ordered General Buckner to transfer some mounted troops from East to Middle Tennessee. The practical effect of this decision was to thin out the garrisons which protected the railroad bridges.

The garrisons east of Knoxville remained large enough to fend off saboteurs, but they were no match for a brigade of thirteen hundred hand-picked veterans. Reinforcements could be brought in from southwestern Virginia, but such a movement demanded deft timing. Buckner's force was thus too widely dispersed to protect all of East Tennessee against a fast-moving strike force. Johnston's deployment was designed to ward off a powerful but plodding army, hence it was ill-suited to counter a swiftly moving cavalry probe. Buckner expected a blow from a broadsword, but Burnside struck with a dagger.[259]

On June 6, General Buckner reported that "indications are very decided" that Union troops were about to advance from Somerset, Kentucky. Buckner correctly predicted that the primary Union thrust would come well to the west of Cumberland Gap, but he also assured Richmond that "I am arranging my troops for speedy concentration as soon as [Burnside's] movements are developed."[260] Once the path of the Yankee advance became clear, Buckner planned to shift his forces to counter the main threat. He predicted that this would be at either Wartburg, Tennessee, or at Jacksborough Gap, though Cumberland Gap was a possibility. According to the master plan, troops in southwestern Virginia were to be ready, and assist if necessary.[261]

The Union generals did indeed intend to help Grant, but not in the manner which Buckner foresaw. At 11:00 in the morning of June 3, General Burnside received an order to send the 9,000-man Ninth Corps to Mississippi to reinforce Grant's siege force.[262] Though this meant that the general invasion of East Tennessee had to be postponed, Burnside followed his order.

Moving as quietly as possible, the 9th Corps left for Vicksburg that very night. Colonel August V. Kautz, who as a brigade commander had reason to know of their departure, was caught unawares. "The 9th Army Corps took their departure suddenly in the night last night," wrote the surprised and puzzled colonel when he awoke on the following morning.[263]

Kautz was not the only one deceived. The Union high command also successfully concealed the change of plans from the rebels. For almost two weeks, the Confederates did not learn that the Ninth Corps had sneaked out of Cincinnati. In fact, General Buckner remained convinced that a general invasion was impending.

Since the sightings of the pontoons were tangible evidence of a forthcoming invasion, Buckner spread the alarm. He told four different generals that the arrival of pontoon trains meant that "Burnside [is] advancing upon us." He also directed a brigade commander to "hold your command in readiness to march at any moment to the rescue of the threatened point, which may be either Big Creek Gap, Wartburg, Kingston, or Loudon."[264]

Confederate intelligence estimates overstated the scale of the Union foray and missed its point of entry, but they were correct about three of the four sites which they marked as probable targets: Loudon, Kingston, and Wartburg. Confederate officers mistook the size and form of the incursion, but they nonetheless gave their troops some warning of the movement.

On June 10, still anticipating a major invasion, Buckner reported the enemy "in same threatening attitude."[265] He estimated the Union forces south of Somerset at not less than 12,000 soldiers. Buckner received a report that the Ninth Corps had been transferred to Mississippi on June 16, but as late as June 23 he was still uncertain of Burnside's intentions. He forwarded to Richmond a captured document, which he described as "without doubt genuine," indicating that Burnside was going to be assigned to the defense of Washington. The fog of war was thick and dense in East Tennessee that spring.[266]

While Buckner and his staff were puzzling over the Yankees' likely point-of-attack, they were warned to be ready for yet another threat. On June 10, Secretary of War James A. Seddon notified Buckner by telegram that "marauding bands of deserters" were active in western North Carolina, and they were supported by "brigand collections" in East Tennessee.[267]

For Buckner, this was not news. He knew very well that bushwhackers were threatening the railroad near Greeneville, and he had previously advised Richmond that a "large number" of draft evaders were hiding in the forests and caves near Knoxville. Indeed, advertisements offering rewards of $30 for fugitives from military service were routinely published in Knoxville newspapers.[268] Seddon admitted that while Buckner was doubtless preoccupied with the forthcoming invasion, he nonetheless directed him to enforce "appropriate measures of repression" against the "brigands."[269]

With an invasion in the offing, protecting every bridge against bushwhackers would be nearly impossible. The partisans were a problem which Richmond did not fully appreciate. The partisans burned barns and houses, stole cattle, horses, and hogs, and appropriated more or less everything else "within their reach."[270] They liked to attack foraging wagons, seizing the cargo and killing the teamsters. "They seldom fought," one rebel officer recalled, "but they cut off small parties and took no prisoners."[271] Buckner, despairing that "the civil arm is paralyzed," intended to carry out Seddon's directive by forming companies of local volunteers, arming them with shotguns and squirrel rifles, and employing them as bridge guards.[272]

While the rebels were chasing bushwhackers and preparing for a general invasion, the actual incursion commenced with a feint. In the late afternoon of June 8, Sanders's old friend, Colonel August Kautz, crossed the Cumberland with 800 cavalrymen from the Third Brigade, Twenty-Third Army Corps.[273] On the following day he advanced to within one mile of Mill Springs, where he learned from an informant that five rebel regiments of 3,000 men under Brigadier General John Pegram were stationed a few miles down the road near Monticello, Kentucky.

Although outnumbered by at least three to one, Kautz marched toward Monticello, hoping to convince Pegram that he was being attacked by the main Union invasion force. Kautz met Pegram's men about five miles north of the town, where they fought a "desperate and bloody" skirmish. Kautz then retired to the north.[274]

The ruse worked. Thinking that Kautz had an entire division, Pegram abandoned Monticello. But when he saw that the Yankees had not pursued, he realized his mistake and countermarched. Kautz took fifty troopers, formed a rear guard, and kept Pegram at bay until darkness fell. Having suffered about thirty-five casualties, Kautz returned to Somerset, while Pegram retired to his base near Jamestown, Tennessee. Kautz saw plenty of action in a lifetime of military service, and he ranked the Monticello skirmish as one of the fiercest fights he experienced. One Ohio boy timed the cannon fire and reported hearing about one hundred rounds, shot at intervals of four to twelve seconds, while another told his brother that Monticello "was as hard a fight as I care about being in."[275]

* * * * * * * * * * * * * * * * *

In one of many ironies buried in the tangle of June, 1863, if Kautz and Pegram had met face-to-face they would have had much about which to reminisce. Officially, they were now sworn enemies, but they had met as cadets at West Point and remained warm personal friends. Kautz, a distinguished combat commander, was described by an admiring subordinate as "a philosopher, a man who solved a problem at a glance, a man of indomitable courage, loyal to his country, and proud of his profession."[276] Pegram was not so uniformly respected. Mary Chesnut, the famously tart rebel diarist, sneered that Pegram "is promoted regularly after every one of his defeats."[277]

After their graduation in 1852, Kautz and Pegram toured Europe together before reporting for their first duty assignments. Kautz later remembered how the classmates said good-bye at the Metropolitan Hotel in New York City, with John leaving to join the 2nd Dragoons in New Mexico, and August departing for an assignment in Washington Territory.[278] Eleven years later, when they faced each other again, they were battling for control of the keystone of the Confederacy.

In another subplot, the opposing generals, Ambrose E. Burnside and Simon B. Buckner, were also old friends. They too had first met at the Academy, where Buckner, a member of the Class of 1844, had been an instructor while Burnside was a cadet. Both had served in Mexico, Buckner in infantry and Burnside in artillery.[279]

For two peacetime years, 1858–60, both were in private business in Chicago. Burnside took a position with the land department of the Illinois Central Railroad, while Buckner managed real estate properties which his wife had inherited.[280] When war erupted, Burnside intervened with President Lincoln in hopes of persuading his friend to join the Union Army. Lincoln offered Buckner a choice position, but he declined to accept.[281]

In June, 1863, Kautz, Pegram, Buckner, and Burnside were soldiers in the field, and thoughts of reconciliation were shelved. Friendships might resume one day, but in the meantime Kautz and Burnside were attempting to seize positions which Pegram and Buckner held. The two rebels, on the other hand, were straining to detect the place and purpose of the incursion which their former comrades had conceived.

CHAPTER SEVEN

From Williamsburg, Kentucky, to Wartburg, Tennessee

Day 7–8, June 16—17

THE MOST DIRECT ROUTES from Somerset into East Tennessee passed through Jacksborough Gap or Big Creek Gap. Both openings were about thirty-five miles due south of Williamsburg, near Jacksborough, Tennessee. The best wagon road went through Jacksborough Gap, while Big Creek Gap had a second-class path. Since both were probable invasion routes, Sanders's planners presumed that they would be heavily guarded.

The rebels stationed five regiments (about 3,000 men) at a third encampment located about fifty miles farther west near Jamestown, Tennessee. These were General Pegram's troops. Since that garrison could overpower Sanders's force, the planners selected a middle route, one which would pass about thirty-two miles west of Big Creek Gap and about eighteen miles east of Pegram's camp.

This road was rough but still preferable to a forest trail, and it followed the closest approximation to a straight line leading from the squadron's staging point near Union-held Williamsburg, Kentucky, to their main target, Loudon bridge. It also ran through counties where Union-leaning citizens could render aid. The Union generals were searching for a weak point, and they understood that a good place to find one is the seam where two zones of responsibility are joined.

Fortunately for the intruders, the rebels had made no attempt to close the corridor or to station sentinels there. Sanders's men followed not only the shortest path to the target, but also the safest.

The troop left Williamsburg before sunrise on June 14, then rode up and down hills and through dense forest, all day. Tennessee scouts led the raiding force west and south through Whitley County, Kentucky, along a pathway then known as the Marsh Creek Road. The troopers wended their way past Jellicoe Mountain, turned south, and left Kentucky. Secrecy was complete: most of the troopers "knew nothing of where we were going or what we were going to do."[282]

When they crossed the state line, they entered Scott County, Tennessee. They were nominally within the Confederacy, but this was friendly territory. Scott County, named after Winfield Scott, the commanding general of the United States Army, was the most heavily pro-Union district in Tennessee.

In the special election held on June 8, 1861, 96.4 percent of Scott County voters chose to reject separation from the United States. Angry citizens of Scott County then defiantly voted to secede from the state of Tennessee. Asked whether a county could lawfully split away, one testy farmer allegedly replied, "If the g*dd**n State of Tennessee can secede from the Union, then Scott County can secede from the State of Tennessee." Scott County "secessionists" then formed a polity of their own, named the "Free and Independent State of Scott." That plan failed, but Scott County became a haven for Unionist bushwhackers.[283]

The Sanders men were confident that the people of Scott County would not betray them, for they found the Tennesseans to be "truly loyal." Yet, while their loyalty was strong, their roads were appalling, and there was also almost no forage to be found in the county.[284] One raider complained that "the road is poor and the country barren." Another remembered that "we made our way quietly by by-ways and narrow paths . . . and camped in a lonely valley at the foot of the mountains." The men pitched camp at dark along a slow-moving stream near a settlement known then as "Chitwood." Their first campsite was about eight miles south of the state line, and, as one Ohioan put it, they were "again fairly in the enemy's country."[285]

Up to this point, the march had been "quite leisurely," but their measured pace was brief. That night would be their best night's sleep for five nights, and even that was cut short.[286] The sky was still dark when the men rose at 4:00 AM on June 17, and they "went up and down hills through the woods all day." The purpose of their mission was still a well-kept secret, so they continued to speculate about their destination—their old friends *Rumor* and *Report* rode with them still. "Of course we knew nothing of where we were going or what we were going to do, but observation told us that we were going through the lines of the enemy toward the south upon some desperate purpose." Excitement and apprehension built with every mile.[287]

The Confederates were also confused. General Hartsuff had staged a second feint intended to mask the route of the invaders. Colonel Samuel A. Gilbert, an Ohioan in command of the Second Brigade of the 23rd Army Corps, received the assignment. Gilbert's brigade of 800 men was made up of his own 44th Ohio Mounted Infantry and the 9th Ohio Cavalry, led by thirty-one-year-old Scottish immigrant, Major William Douglas Hamilton. Gilbert advanced due south along the Cumberland River, crossed it, and pointed toward Big Creek Gap. Hamilton then proceeded through Pine Mountain Gap while Gilbert followed a different route.[288]

Hamilton's Ohioans reached the foot of Pine Mountain about 10:00 AM. Hamilton dismounted his men in an orchard and fed his horses. He then took fifty men and climbed the hill, dividing his group into two units of twenty-five each. There was a station built in the gap as a resting place for travelers. Hamilton advanced with one group directly toward the station, directing the other to circle around behind it. The noise of a soldier stepping on a stick betrayed the latter group, but the defenders inferred that they must be surrounded. They fled down the mountain, leaving Pine Mountain Gap open to the Yankee advance.[289]

The northerners pushed through Pine Mountain Gap, intending to give the impression that they were heading for Big Creek Gap. They were led by a Tennessee sergeant named Fullington, whose wife and two children had been killed when Home Guards burned the family cabin. Fullington had vengeance on his mind, and when he approached the rebel positions his former neighbors hailed him scornfully, shouting "There's ol Fullington, God d___m his soul! [*sic*]" This indignity brought the intrepid guide's blood to a boil, and, forming two columns, he hustled his comrades forward, driving the enemy back toward their prepared positions.[290]

About five o'clock on the afternoon of the 16th, Sanders's men heard distant firing as Gilbert's brigade engaged the Confederate pickets. Gilbert's troopers pursued the fleeing rebels and camped for the night below the brow of a hill which overlooked the enemy campground. As a ruse, his men build campfires large enough to cook supper for a force of twice their size, and their subterfuge worked. By morning, the Confederates had not left their barricades, so Sanders's men would not be interrupted as they advanced. Gilbert's troops spent all of June 17 threatening an attack on the Confederate defenses, and on the 18th retired to Kentucky.

Earlier Sergeant Fullington had expressed, in his country way, a feeling shared among the mountain people. "We're a hopin'," he said, "the war wont let up till we c'n git some little satisfaction fer whut's been done to us." [*sic*][291] When the sergeant and his comrades retired to Kentucky, they could feel gratified that they had exacted at least some recompense.

The squadron paused for just two hours on the night of June 17. "At about eleven o'clock at night," a raider remembered, "we halted in a beautiful meadow, and holding our horses by their bridles, let them feed on the grass until one o'clock in the morning." Riding on for the rest of the night, the troop proceeded almost directly southward along a route which passed about three miles west of Huntsville, Tennessee. In 1863 the road was "only a trail through laurel and scrubby pine," as a raider described it.[292]

After a march of another twelve miles, the vanguard arrived early in the morning of their ninth day at the village of Montgomery, then the seat of Morgan County, Tennessee. Sanders learned that a small company of Confederates was stationed just one mile to the east of Montgomery, in the village of Wartburg. Without pausing in

Montgomery, Sanders led his men directly to Wartburg in hope of surprising its garrison. At Wartburg the raiders saw their first action.[293]

Wartburg was a picturesque, Swiss-American settlement which gave substance to East Tennessee's proud nickname, "Little Switzerland." One Southern boy, charmed by its Old-World ambiance, rhapsodized that the village was "a Swiss colony on the summit, where everything looked as described in histories of the Fatherland and we could almost imagine we were soldiering in the mountains of Switzerland." But unlike its namesake (which actually is in Germany), Wartburg was anything but a peaceful village perched on a mountainside. It was the main commissary and supply depot for Pegram's troops.[294]

Sanders and his men had little interest in the settlement's personality. Wartburg was their initial contact with the enemy, and it was the first time that Sanders displayed his tactical skill. Sanders first selected four hundred men of Colonel Robert Byrd's First East Tennessee Mounted Infantry, then augmented them with troopers from Ohio and Illinois, and sent the group ahead with a simple but shrewd plan. Sanders deployed one detachment on the east side of the settlement and the other on the west. Then both advanced at once.[295]

The rebels were busy preparing breakfast. A two-pronged attack by 400 enemy soldiers shocked them, and they offered almost no resistance. "The surprise was complete," Sanders observed dryly. Somewhat more pithily, an Illinois comrade recalled that "they were so much astonished at seeing us that they forgot their guns and we took them prisoners without firing a gun."

The skirmish was not entirely bloodless—two horses were killed and one Ohioan received a ball through the hand—but some 102 enlisted men along with two officers surrendered. They confirmed that the various Yankee ruses had worked. "They just opened their mouths and stared at us while we took their guns and equipment away from them," an incredulous Yankee remembered.

After paroling the prisoners, the raiders destroyed sixty boxes of artillery ammunition, 500 spades, and one hundred picks. Several thousand pounds of bacon, flour, salt, and corn were either destroyed or distributed to the loyal citizens of the surrounding countryside. This was the first time the raiders expropriated property and distributed it to Union loyalists. The Wartburg engagement was a quick and nearly bloodless victory and, as one raider crowed, "the boys are jubilant."[296]

Their exultation was brief. While the prisoners were being paroled, the men stretched out and allowed their horses to graze. They had rested during the previous night, but they had ridden more than sixty miles. Yet, after only an hour's rest, the buglers blew "boots and saddles."[297]

Danger lurked throughout the excursion, but on this day their luck held. In the first of several instances in which loyal private citizens saved the Sanders troops, local informants warned Sanders that they expected a heavy force under General Pegram to arrive any minute. Sanders eluded Pegram's men, but a few Confederates escaped on horseback. Their messages which the Confederate commanders received constituted the first reliable estimates of the size and composition of the Sanders force. Since the couriers were en route to headquarters, from that point on, an attack on the raiders was possible at any moment.

The next destination was Kingston, Tennessee, twenty-seven miles south of Wartburg and thirty-six miles due west of Knoxville. The troopers kept up a good pace throughout the day but were still three miles away at five o'clock in the afternoon. Scouts who rode ahead reported that a brigade of cavalry under the command of Colonel John S. Scott of the 1st Louisiana Cavalry held the town, supported by a battery of artillery. Scott positioned his guns so as to shield a shallow ford in the otherwise deep and dangerous Clinch River. Sanders veered to the east, away from the enemy cannon, choosing to cross the Clinch at Waller's Ford, some eight miles above the rebel positions.[298]

Kingston was the home of Robert King Byrd, colonel of the 1st East Tennessee USA. Many of his men also resided in the area, and for a lucky few the Sanders raid was a unique opportunity—they were able to mix a combat operation with a family visit. Sanders's main force marched steadily forward throughout the warm evening, but some raiders slipped off to surprise their families. "Many a lonely cabin and farmhouse is visited tonight," wrote one joyful trooper, "and mothers, wives and sweethearts made glad. God be praised if they are!"[299]

The "furlough" was very brief—perhaps an hour. The flurry of emotions stirred by such a visit is more easily imagined than described, but one raider made an attempt: "Ah, how brief his stay! In an hour he had to remount his steed and gallop on to overtake the moving column." There were strong temptations to remain behind, but every furloughed soldier rejoined his unit.[300]

An intrepid mountaineer, Sergeant William S. "Stud" Reynolds, of Co. A, 1st Tennessee Infantry USA, guided the troop that night. Reynolds knew the topography of East Tennessee thoroughly, which led to his selection as Sanders's chief scout. Reynolds was a farm laborer who, at age forty-four, left his wife and two children to enlist for three years in the Army of the Ohio. "Stud" Reynolds could neither read nor write, and spoke in an idiom that puzzled all but his fellow mountaineers. He was a great favorite of the men—the kind of non-commissioned officer whose leadership forms the strength of every great army. Sergeant Reynolds was twice cited for leading the troop to safety, and it is no exaggeration to say that without his guidance the mission would have ended in failure.[301]

Reynolds led the way to Waller's Ford down a "circuitous route" which his comrades mocked as little better than a "hog path." The river was swollen by heavy rains, and at least one flatlander blanched when he saw it. The Clinch seemed "deep and dangerous" to boys who were raised beside the meandering streams of the Illinois and Ohio prairies.[302]

The main body of troopers reached Waller's Ford in daylight and were able to cross without incident, but the rear guard did not arrive until well after dark. Sanders was unaware of how far behind the rear guard lagged, and he neglected to leave guides to show them where the river was shallow enough to cross. This was a fatal mistake, because the night was pitch black and the river was "a boiling flood."[303]

Captain James McCartney of the 112th Illinois was in command of the rear guard. McCartney was looking for guides who could show him where to ford the river, when two men dressed as Union soldiers suddenly appeared. "We found here two men on the bank, in blue uniforms, who said they were left to guide us across," Captain McCartney recalled, "Instead of doing so, however, they told us the water was only knee-deep to our horses and to go straight across–there was no danger, and they would follow us."

The Clinch appeared to be about a quarter of a mile wide at that point, which made it seem shallow. McCartney waded in, followed by First Sergeant Eli K. Mauck of Galva, Illinois, and about sixty men. "When we had reached about the middle of the river," McCartney continued, "our horses suddenly plunged into water at least twenty feet deep, the whole line of men and horses following close after us. Instantly the water was filled with plunging horses and struggling men. We had some seven or eight days' rations of hard tack slung in sacks around our necks, besides ammunition, guns, horse-feed, and many other weighty articles. My brave little gray mare, on whose back I had crossed so many rivers, carried me safely to shore, until just before we reached it her fore foot struck a tree lying lengthwise to the river. This threw her over on her back with me underneath; but I threw my arms around her neck and she soon righted herself and carried me safely out."

Safe on the bank, McCartney peered into the gloom in hope of locating his comrades. Eventually, he discerned "a round form crawling along the bank that looked like an immense mud turtle. After coughing, blowing, sneezing and swearing awhile, I found it was tough, reliable Jack Looney, whose horse had struck the same obstacle mine had; but Jack had lost his hold and fallen off; with the weight of ammunition, gun and other things he had slung to him, he went straight to the bottom, some fifteen feet down. However, as he knew the direction he had been going, he just walked ahead along the bottom of the river and came out all right, but very mad."

"Jack never liked to get out of ammunition," McCartney marveled, "and he always did an immense amount of shooting in every engagement.... He probably had a double allowance of cartridges along with him and had picked up a few other things as he went along. We only stopped long enough on the bank of the river to pour the water out of our boots, when we mounted and away again to overtake the main column. We soon joined it, and marched on all night."[304]

The crossing of the Clinch proved to be the most terrifying and memorable experience of the entire raid, perhaps of their entire lives. An Illinois trooper told his mother that "we crossed in the night and lost a few men. Just before our company crossed they commenced drowning. We could hear them calling for help. Then you better believe my hair raises my hat. I expect to go down. I had a little horse and about seventy-five pounds besides my weight for her to swim with, but she took me across straight as a string." An Ohio boy said of that black night, "[it] will be deeply impressed on me, as I barely escape drowning. My horse founders on a submerged rock, rears and falls backwards. In some accidental way as I fell under him, I caught his tail, and on righting he dragged me ashore; but for this my heavy accoutrements would have sunk me like lead. My only loss is my hat. We lose most rations."[305]

Isaiah C. Dye, of the First Kentucky, who survived the war and became a well-liked physician in Middleburg, Kentucky, had an even more horrific experience. "The river appeared wide, and we could not tell the best route to take," Dye remembered. "We found a broken ambulance at the edge of the ford, and we struck in a little below it. I was mounted on a horse on which I had swum the Cumberland River on several occasions. In ten feet after entering, we struck swimming water. My horse swam some distance and struck what I afterward learned from some citizens to be a big boulder, and my horse scrambled upon it, and secured a foothold."

While Dye and his horse were perched safely on a boulder in mid-stream, disaster struck. "Almost immediately after entering the water my comrades' horses commenced plunging and struggling, and the men in pathetic tones began calling for help." But there was nothing Dye could do. "After my horse got somewhat steady on the boulder, I began calling to the men who were in distress, in order to give them the best directions I could, but their voices had become hushed, and to my repeated calls I received no answer. I could hear their horses swimming off down below, and I heard some of them leave the water, as their footsteps sounded plainly on the gravel-beds at the edge of the river. . . ."

His friends had drowned, and Dye found himself marooned on a rock at mid-river with no other choice except to swim. "After making preparations, cutting my forage sack loose, and disposing of other articles to lighten my horse, I spurred him off the rock, and he took me safe to the opposite bank. Not knowing the proper place to land, I struck something like quicksand, and dismounted. I held to the branches on the bank, and led my horse upstream, until I reached the road leading to the ford, mounted, and rode fast for several miles, when I overtook the command and reported what had occurred to Colonel Sanders."

When McCartney and the other surviving members finally found the main force, they learned that no escorts had been left for them, proving that the two mysterious "guides" were indeed imposters.[306] Sanders realized that sending a rescue team was pointless and would compromise the mission, so he made arrangements with loyal citizens to recover and bury the remains of the five brave men who lost their lives on that dark night.[307] The churning waters also soaked ammunition and ruined hard bread, both essentials which could not be replaced in the field.

Meanwhile, back at Army headquarters in Cincinnati, General Burnside fretted. A fresh intelligence report warned him that the enemy garrison at Loudon had grown substantially—it was now much too strong for Sanders's two light guns. Burnside directed that a courier deliver an advisory "as rapidly as possible." Burnside told Sanders "to move cautiously and not be caught."[308]

There is no record that the message reached Sanders, but Burnside tried two other ploys. His first was a feint: he ordered Colonel August Kautz to conduct a reconnaissance in force toward Jamestown, Tennessee, where General Pegram's command was based. Burnside hoped that Kautz would draw Pegram away from Sanders, but by the time that Kautz reached the rebel encampment, it was too late. Pegram was long gone. Leaving only a squad of cavalry behind, Pegram took his main force and went in pursuit of Sanders.

Burnside's second step was a rescue mission. He ordered General Samuel Carter to prepare to march early on the next morning. Carter's assignment was to save Sanders if the enemy attacked him at Loudon—a rescue mission. But Sanders pressed on, blithely unaware that Pegram was after him, and still hoping to demolish his primary target.[309]

CHAPTER EIGHT

A Fateful Choice

Day 10, Friday Morning, June 19

THE RAIDERS WERE WITHIN three miles of Loudon bridge when the sun crept over the horizon on Friday, June 19. They had met their schedule, but local informants reported that the rebels had strengthened the fortifications protecting the bridge. The rebels had spent two weeks building a heavy blockhouse and digging rifle pits, leading a traveler who passed through Loudon to remark (to his surprise) that "everybody was in the ditches."[310]

The Loudon earthworks supported eight or ten pieces of artillery, and the garrison had also been augmented. Colonel John S. Scott of the First Louisiana Cavalry stood in Sanders's way near Kingston, but his detachment was too weak to stop the intruders. One of Scott's men explained that "[since] our force was but 600 men and two mountain howitzers, we did not like to tackle him in the open . . . so we fell back to the breastworks at Loudon, hoping for reinforcements or a right good chance to run away."[311] With the addition of the Louisianans, three regiments now held the Confederate position, or as many as two thousand men.[312]

The defenders outnumbered Sanders's force by as many as three to two, and their advantage in firepower was even greater: four or even five to one. Only a reckless commander would attempt to carry an entrenched position with the men and guns that Sanders had available. Sanders acknowledged his predicament but demanded proof. He sent a small detachment to test the defenses, and this detail briefly mixed it up with Scott's men.

The rebels chased the Yankees away without difficulty. "Colonel Scott decided to give them a lesson and prepared to charge them," one recalled. "Our howitzers began to throw shells among them and worked so fast and furious that their line was soon demoralized, when over we went after them with that 'rebel yell' and they didn't stop to see us, but mounting their horses, struck out, every fellow for himself, like the old harry was after them, throwing away everything that encombered [sic]. We mounted and chased them into the mountains."[313]

The "Loudon fight" was a rout. The great bridge remained intact while Sanders's men fled.[314] Sanders was now at a crossroads—militarily, personally, and literally. The choice he faced was troubling. Should he admit failure, cut his losses, and abort the mission? Or should he soldier on, expose his men to further risk, and attempt to save the day?

The safest option was to return to Kentucky and admit failure. To make the best of the situation, Sanders could play up the number of prisoners captured, the mileage of track destroyed, and the few casualties sustained. He could also report that he had partially accomplished his mission—he had severed the rail line, if only briefly. If questions arose about his inability to destroy the bridge, he could blame his failure on faulty intelligence.[315]

That was the easy choice. The second carried great risk. If he dared, he could follow the railway another thirty miles east, burning rails and twisting track as he went. He would have to bypass the rebel headquarters at Knoxville, and then make his way another twenty miles in order to attack bridges at Flat Creek and Strawberry Plains.

This route would give the enemy extra time to bolster their defenses and mobilize a chase force. Sanders's men would have to ride nearly one-hundred miles further, and be exposed to capture for several more days. There was a possibility that the enemy had also reinforced the works protecting the eastern bridges. In view of these contingencies, a reasonable case could be made against exposing his men to such danger. The military advantage that would be gained depended upon the length of time during which the Richmond Route would be out of service, and this was unclear.

There was another possible benefit, however. Although Sanders's hope of destroying Loudon bridge had disappeared, he was having some success in achieving his subordinate goals, namely, to show the flag and rekindle Unionist morale. The Loudon area was known for its Unionism, and its loyal citizens hailed the Union soldiers as they rode by.[316]

One Ohioan marveled at the scene: "the people look at us in astonishment, but with such manifestations of Union sentiment as has perhaps not been witnessed since the war began. They shout for joy, and thank God for our coming."[317] The northern troops could not remain, but their appearance gladdened many loyal hearts, if only momentarily.

Sanders was a man of action, not reflection. There is no evidence that he gave serious consideration to the possibility of returning directly to base. He was bold even to a fault, and to fall back in the presence of the enemy was alien to his disposition. He gave the order to advance.

The "Loudon fight" with Scott's men went unmentioned in northern chronicles, doubtless because the Confederates won the day.[318] Despite having been thwarted, Sanders turned east in search of better targets. Leaving ninety men of the 112th Illinois to bring up the rear once more, the squadron pushed on to the next eastbound stop on the East Tennessee & Georgia, a hamlet known then as "Lenoir's Station."

Nestled only six miles up the line, this village had prospered since trains first arrived eight years earlier. Sporting a "fine brick" depot that was a source of much civic pride, the settlement was a complex of mercantile and manufacturing enterprises owned and operated by the wealthy Lenoir family. The controlling partners were a forty-two-year-old physician, Dr. Benjamin Ballard Lenoir, and his two brothers, William, 50, and Israel, 38. The Lenoir brothers grew wheat, raised livestock, and sold produce on a handsome plantation that encompassed more than four square miles. To work their land and cook their meals, the brothers held twenty-nine persons in bondage.

The Lenoir brothers were active disunionists whose plans for the future extended well beyond farming.[319] The railway was opening up potentially lucrative markets, and they believed that they had an ideal location from which to tap them. In fact, the enterprises which the brothers were building were a model of the New South which some visionaries hoped to construct, once an independent, slavery-oriented government was established. The Lenoir businesses included, in addition to Dr. Lenoir's medical practice, a bank, a general store, a sawmill, a flour mill, and their showpiece, a cotton mill with a storage capacity of up to 500 bales. In 1860, census takers estimated the value of the mill, land, and slaves to be $151,000, divided about evenly among the three men. An admiring guest rated their enterprises as, "in some respects . . . the most valuable property in Tennessee or the West."[320]

The Yankee raid placed their holdings in jeopardy. Sanders and his men reached Lenoir's Station at about eight o'clock on their fourth morning in hostile territory. The Yankees appeared just thirty minutes after a rebel regiment, the 54th Virginia, hurried off to defend Knoxville. The Virginians, who had been ordered to link up with Buckner's command, left behind only a small detachment of artillery to protect the village.[321]

In a reprise of his maneuver at Wartburg, Sanders placed half of his men on either side of the settlement and then closed the pincer. The appearance of blue-clad horsemen startled the rebel artillerymen, who put up almost no resistance—not a dozen shots were fired. An Ohioan described their attack as "quick and quiet," and one of the rebels conceded that Sanders's arrival was "a perfect surprise." He confessed that he was quietly sitting at a spring when Yankee cavalry "suddenly rode up and caused his surrender." The Sanders men added to their bag eight officers and fifty-seven enlisted men. Again, the Union victory was bloodless.[322]

The Lenoir brothers had ruled the community as their fiefdom, but when the artillerymen surrendered the family's authority faded. The national standard now flew over Lenoir's Station, signifying that, for the moment, the Lenoir brothers were no longer in charge. Their lives and property were in the hands of an angry enemy, and the price they would pay for their support of the Rebellion was yet to be decided.

A young matron, Henrietta Ramsey Lenoir, faced the first test. She was the wife of Dr. Benjamin Lenoir and was as surprised as anyone when a group of horsemen in blue uniforms rode up to her gate that morning. She mistook them for friendly troops.

Henrietta was a daughter of a prominent Knoxville banker and physician, Dr. J. G. M. Ramsey, who had been visiting. Dr. Ramsey was an official custodian of Confederate currency, and when the raiders approached, he rushed back to Knoxville to hide the money. Henrietta reckoned that all rebel funds might be at risk, so she looked for a way to keep her family's cash out of enemy hands.[323]

Her residence, on the main thoroughfare running through the village, stood directly across from the Lenoir general store. As she later told the story, she watched several troopers dismount and enter the building. To her dismay, she remembered that when she opened the store that morning, she unlocked the safe and then left the key in the lock! She knew that she must try to hide the money, but doing so was complicated because several of the unexpected visitors were former customers. She also recognized Colonel Byrd, whom she knew from before the war. These Yankees might well know where she kept the money.

To mask her face, Henrietta donned a long-billed sunbonnet, the type popular among women who wanted protection from the hot sun. Trying to cloak her nervousness, she casually crossed the road and entered the store, pretending to be an ordinary shopper. She opened the safe, gathered up several parcels of currency, and held the cash in the crook of her arm. She then pulled several hanks of yarn from an open bale and used them to cover her "purchase." Still trying to look like a normal customer, she retraced her steps and squirrelled her booty under a hedge in her garden.[324]

Mrs. Lenoir may have outwitted the Yankees as she described, but her exploit probably resulted more from forbearance than from lack of vigilance. The Civil War was a chronicle of destruction and hatred, but it was fought with a restrained, Victorian ethos. Officers thought of themselves as gentlemen and aspired to observe an unwritten code of chivalry. Women were seldom searched, because to inspect a woman's person was to imply that she might be concealing contraband. This was an impermissible affront to her honor. The code required that women, children, and the elderly remain undisturbed, and many, like Henrietta Lenoir and Sanders's spies, took full advantage of its protection.[325]

After the raiders retired, Mrs. Lenoir complimented their politeness.[326] It was fortunate that they had good manners, because if they had checked her carefully, they would have found contraband concealed on her person, a violation of the 56th Article of War [1806].[327] Although Mrs. Lenoir was evidently able to capitalize upon her immunity, the patience of Union officers with Tennessee women was by no means inexhaustible.[328]

Men at arms have long struggled with such questions. William Sanders and Robert Byrd were men of the pre-industrial South, but now an enemy manufacturing facility had fallen into their hands. Southern manufacturing was not very far along, particularly in the west, but wartime needs compelled them to build up their industry. In this sparse field the Lenoir Cotton Mill stood out. The *Richmond Daily Dispatch* portrayed it as a "mammoth factory."[329] By the standards of 1863, it was that, indeed.

Sanders and Byrd had invaded Tennessee in order to destroy its railroads, but now a manufacturing facility was theirs. Sanders and Byrd were among the first American officers to consider whether or not to demolish a factory. Decades later such a question would require little if any discussion, but in 1863, warfare against enemy industry was a novel concept.

Sanders ordered a survey of the town's resources, and his men quickly discovered a cache of war matériel stored in the town's railway depot. The depot was packed with cannon shells, musket cartridges, five artillery pieces, harnesses, saddles, and a stand of 2,500 small arms. Since these items were of considerable military value, the depot's fate was sealed. The Sanders men hauled several lengths of railroad track into the building, estimating that if the fire burned as hot as expected, the rails would bend under their own weight and be useless.

The raiders next inspected the mill and warehouse where the Lenoirs stored cotton bales. The goods within these buildings were of only marginal military value—spools of thread and bolts of cloth. These could be made into uniforms, but uniforms were not lethal weapons. Sanders therefore had to decide whether his force should destroy only items of immediate military use, or cast its net more broadly, and seize comparatively benign goods such as cloth and currency. Furthermore, should secessionists pay for their support of the rebellion by losing their property?

Before leaving Lenoir's Station, the raiders would have further opportunity to display restraint. The Lenoir mill spun thread and made cloth, both of which were used in uniforms. Under the laws of war Sanders would have been justified if he chose to destroy it, but the mill survived intact.[330]

In matters having a political dimension, Sanders relied on the advice of his second-in-command, Colonel Byrd, a lifelong resident of the area.[331] Byrd knew Lenoir's Station well and asked Sanders not to burn the building. His expressed reason was that the town was heavily Unionist and its mill furnished employment to many loyal women.[332] While Byrd's recommendation was doubtless the determining factor, saving jobs was probably not why he spared the building.

Oral tradition maintains that Lenoir appealed to a deeper, clandestine loyalty. Allegedly, Lenoir and the Union commanders were members of the Masonic Order, and that bond governed their decision. But unfortunately for this theory, there is no evidence that Sanders was either a Mason or had any other connection to the Order.[333] Yet despite that flaw, the "Masonic" explanation is almost certainly correct. Masonic records reveal that Robert King Byrd was indeed a deeply devoted lifelong member of the Order, as was Dr. Lenoir.

The bonds of Masonic brotherhood frequently superseded wartime enmity.[334] Under the laws of the order, Byrd was required to listen receptively to the plea of a Mason who was in trouble and, if duty permitted, to comply with his request.[335] At the time of the raid, Byrd was a past Master of a large and active Masonic Lodge in Kingston, the seat of Roane County.[336] Through holding that office, Byrd would have been familiar with Lenoir, a Mason who lived just eleven miles away.

So, as the oft-told story insists, Byrd probably did persuade Sanders to spare Lenoir's livelihood. In any event, that was Lenoir's understanding. As Lenoir recounted the incident, he stood beside the building, frantically flashing recognizably Masonic signs, and this saved it from the torch. While his account is probably accurate, Sanders's story was not. Sanders reported that the fire spread "by mistake or accident," and destroyed both the mill and rail station. But in fact while the station went up in flames, the mill survived.[337]

Sanders spared the mill but ordered his men to burn the depot, though none of them had ever before blown up an ammunition-filled building. High-explosives were yet to be invented, and the technology of demolition was still in its youth. One trooper, in his words, got the honor "to play incendiary." He struck his match and touched off thunderous explosions. "When the flames reach the shells I can only think of throwing stones through a hornets' nest," the trooper exulted. "They seem to perforate the roof and sides of the building with ease, while the sound is deafening. We hurry away to escape danger." Another trooper was amazed when "a lighted match . . . caused an explosion which tore the building to atoms."[338]

Virtually every recollection of the raid, even one published a half-century later, mentioned the magnitude of the explosions.[339] Most of the men played with firecrackers in their youth, but the Lenoir blast was larger than any of them had ever seen. "All wars are boyish," Herman Melville once observed, "and are fought by boys."[340] While explosions are exciting, the Sanders men stood too close. "We had to get out of the way for the bricks were flying through the air," one remembered. "It was a brick building but there was hardly one stone left upon another," another trooper marveled.[341]

With shells bursting and powder kegs exploding, the marauders made a hasty exit. Recognizing the danger if hundreds ran for the road at once, their officers gave an order which, given the circumstances, was probably unnecessary. "Take to the fields!" they commanded.[342]

While traveling off-road, one squad came upon a farmer who was cultivating his corn, using a very fine mule. The farmer paused, gestured at the columns of smoke rising in the distance, and sneered, "That one of your Yankee tricks, is it?" "Yes," bristled one of the troopers, "and I will show you another!" The Yankee had several well-armed companions nearby, so he threw his saddle on the mule's back and rode away. Like many farmers whose pasture bordered a road where the Sanders men passed by, this acid-tongued fellow was left with nothing with which to pull his plow except a worn-out saddle horse.[343]

Most livestock owners received no compensation whatsoever. Close by was a showpiece, the Lenoir family plantation, which one raider described as a "beautiful farm." The Lenoir spread featured "fields of golden wheat, standing thick and high, just ready for the harvest." This property alone made the Lenoirs wealthy men, as was evident to the raiders. The raiders had neither the time nor the means to strip the crops, but at least one of them helped himself to a mule. With his own horse in tow, he rode his long-eared steed all the way to Knoxville.[344]

Sanders's men routinely scoured the countryside in search of fresh stock. Whenever they found a horse or mule that appeared to be stronger or faster than their current mount, they traded up. If the owner was known to be a rebel sympathizer, they impressed the animal into the national service at gunpoint. Mules were particularly prized because, in the heat of summer, they could pull a cannon or carry a rider better than a horse.[345]

After the war, several farmers sought reimbursement for livestock commandeered by the Sanders men, and a few succeeded. Owners were required to prove that they had never been disloyal to the Union in any way. If even on one occasion a farmer sold a few bushels of grain to a rebel quartermaster—and U.S. agents combed the records carefully—his claim would be denied.[346]

The rules for lost animals were different for Confederates. Rebel officers rode off to war on their own mounts, many of which were lost. Four weeks after the Sanders raid, 1st Lieutenant James C. Luttrell Jr. submitted a request for reimbursement for the loss of a horse "unavoidably captured" by the Sanders men near Lenoir's Station.[347] Lt. Luttrell estimated his horse to be worth $400. His claim was endorsed by three fellow officers, including his regimental commander, who certified that his horse "was actually lost by being captured." Most importantly, his comrades attested that the animal was "fully worth the amount charged." Whether the hapless lieutenant ever got his money is unknown, but seven months later he was still asking to be paid.[348]

The Confederate resistance at Lenoir's Station amounted to almost nothing, but before the garrison capitulated, its telegrapher tapped out a message. Some of the Sanders men revealed that their next destination was Knoxville, and before the telegraph could be silenced, a warning crackled up the wire. The Yankees, Knoxville discovered, were on the way.[349]

The main body of marauders followed a wagon lane that ran northeast toward Knoxville, twenty-one miles away. Known locally as the "Kingston Road," it was originally an Indian trail but since 1822 had been a stage-road. Just thirty feet wide in places, it was known to be dangerous. One segment was home to so many highwaymen that it was dubbed "Murderers' Hollow."[350]

Most of Sanders's men followed the Kingston Road, but one detail paused to wreck the East Tennessee & Georgia Railroad, whose tracks, about a mile south, ran parallel to the wagon road. One Ohioan remembered how captured rebels had "prognosticated all sorts of dire things for us." "But we kept on up the line, tearing up track, kinking rails with fire, and destroying water tanks." The demolition detail burned bridges, smashed culverts, tore up track, and burned ties at one-mile intervals.[351]

About three miles from Lenoir's Station the main body came upon a vacated campsite. Only a few hours earlier, two rebel regiments and an artillery battery abandoned the camp and retired toward Kingston. In their haste, they left behind three "splendid mounted field guns." The Sanders men spiked the cannon, wrecked the caissons, turned their horses to the east, and prepared to strike Knoxville, just twenty miles away.

Hanging of Fry and Hensie near the railroad, by Colonel Leadbetter. (Page 311.)

On November 8, 1861, bands of Unionists struck nine Tennessee railroad bridges, burning five. In retaliation, Jefferson Davis ordered Attorney General Judah P. Benjamin to have the culprits hanged and to have their remains placed on display near the ruined bridges. Harper's Weekly reported that southern travelers abused the corpses. (Library of Congress.)

Railroad accident caused by rebels. Civil War soldiers could be moved faster than ever before, but a few saboteurs could impede a major operation. Locomotive engineers reduced speed or refused to operate at night, but governments took more drastic steps. Davis hanged bridge-burners, while Lincoln imprisoned them without trial. (Andrew Joseph Russell, 1862; Photo History of the Civil War, v. 2.*)*

Major General Simon Bolivar Buckner, CSA. An 1844 graduate of the USMA, Buckner surrendered Confederate forces at Fort Donelson in 1862. After serving five months as a prisoner-of-war, he assumed command of the Department of East Tennessee on May 12, 1863. Just one month later, he organized the defense against the Sanders raiders.

Brigadier General Orlando Bolivar Willcox, USA. A native of Detroit, Willcox graduated from the USMA in 1847. Wounded and captured at First Bull Run, Willcox remained a prisoner for more than a year. In 1895 he received the Congressional Medal of Honor in recognition of his gallantry at Bull Run. A close comrade of Ambrose Burnside, Willcox planned the Sanders raid.

Colonel August Valentine
Kautz, USA. Born in Germany,
Kautz enlisted as a private
in the Mexican War, then
graduated from the USMA in
1852. He served with Sanders
in the Sixth US Cavalry, then
became Colonel of the 2d Ohio
Vol. Cavalry. To protect the
Sanders raiders, Kautz led the
2d in a successful diversionary
attack on Big Creek Gap.

Major General
Ambrose E. Burnside,
USA. Despite his weak
performance as com-
mander of the Army of
the Potomac, Lincoln
chose Burnside to
lead the Army of the
Ohio in the Knoxville
campaign of 1863.

Brigadier General William P. Sanders. Sanders was named a general at only thirty years of age.

Colonel Jesse Johnson Finley, CSA. Finley served as a captain in the Second Seminole War (1836), then as a Florida judge, before entering the Confederate army in 1862. He became colonel of the 6th Florida Infantry, was twice wounded, and represented Florida as a member of the U.S. Congress after the war (pictured).

From the cupola of Old College, high above Kingston Pike, a lookout could see riders approaching from afar. The hill was barren when this photograph was made, but when the Sanders men appeared in June 1863, the land would have been vegetated. The camera stood on the south bank of the Holston River, facing north. The Sanders raiders approached the hill from the west (left) and paused. Under cover of darkness, they circled the city, paralleling the ridge in the deep background (moving from left to right).

The land on which Old College stood now forms part of the campus of the University of Tennessee (Ayres Hall is its replacement). The horses, riders, and wagons in the foreground of this 1864 photo belonged to the Army of the Ohio.

Modern-day photo of the Baker Mansion, built by Dr. Harvey Baker in 1830. The building is now owned by Dr. Larry Tragesser.

After being pursued by Union soldiers, Dr. Baker fled upstairs to his bedroom where he succumbed to his wounds.

Bullet hole in the Baker Mansion.

The Lenoir mill produced uniforms for the Confederate armies, but Sanders spared it, almost certainly because the Lenoir brothers and Col. Robert K. Byrd were fellow members of the Masonic Order. Parts of its walls remain standing today.

Remnants of the Lenoir mill, modern day. (Photo by the author.)

Loudon Railroad Bridge, 1864. (National Archives.)

Bridge at Strawberry Plains, twenty miles northeast of Knoxville, 1864.
(Library of Congress.)

Brigadier General John Pegram, CSA. The scion of a prominent Virginia family, Pegram graduated from West Point in 1854. He entered the Confederate Army in 1861 and became the first professional officer captured. (Ironically, he was exchanged for Orlando B. Willcox, the planner of the Sanders raid.) When the Sanders raiders crossed into Tennessee, Pegram commanded a forward section of the rebel line, but he failed to detect them. This was one of several examples of his dubious military skill. His marriage in January 1865 was the highlight of Richmond's social season, but less than three weeks later he was killed in action.

First Sergeant Larkin German, 65th Georgia Infantry, CSA. German was a twenty-six-year-old farm hand from Pierceville, GA.

Stone wall surrounding the Stringfield family cemetery, Strawberry Plains. The raiders heavily outnumbered the Confederate garrison at Strawberry Plains. A few rebels escaped, but others took cover behind the stone wall shown here, which encloses the Stringfield cemetery. The defenders exchanged fire with the raiders for a brief period, then surrendered. No lives were lost. (Photo by Barbara Parsons.)

CHAPTER NINE

The Killing of
Harvey Baker

MURDERERS' HOLLOW HAD dense thickets and convenient escape routes and had long been infested by highwaymen and others of the outlaw persuasion. Civil War bushwhackers also needed concealment, and soon after Sanders's men returned to Kingston Pike, miniè balls hissed through the trees. Private James Patten, a twenty-seven-year-old farmer from Illinois, was struck in both hands. Though the snipers may not have cared, they stirred a hornet's nest. Patten's comrades loathed skulkers.[352]

As the raiders moved into more open country, firing continued sporadically. The Confederate garrison at Knoxville had only a few cavalrymen, but they sent out what men were available, which was Company G of the 1st Tennessee Cavalry CSA. This unit was under the command of Captain A. P. Wiggs, a twenty-three-year-old lawyer from Thornstown, Indiana. (Wiggs, a Tennessee native, had represented Thornstown in the Indiana state legislature until he was expelled due to his pro-Southern views.)

Company G numbered only about forty men, but most were East Tennesseans who had some knowledge of the countryside west of Knoxville. Wiggs's orders were to fight a delaying action in order to gain time for the men in Knoxville to prepare the city's defenses.

The rebel horsemen skirmished with the advancing intruders through-out the day, firing from concealed positions.[353]

After riding about ten miles down Kingston Pike, the Sanders troopers got a chance to retaliate. They shot and killed Dr. Harvey Baker, one of the foremost rebels in East Tennessee. The full story of the Baker case will never be known, but the episode became the most contentious incident of the Sanders raid. Baker's death led to an official investigation by the Provost Marshal of the Army of the Ohio, followed by decades of dissension. Some justified the killing as an act of war, others called it murder.[354]

The news was shocking, and Knoxville's newspapermen raced to tell the story. First off the mark was Jacob A. Sperry, editor of the *Knoxville Register*, the city's largest paper. Sperry's reports were the most detailed, but none were fully reliable. Sperry understood the circulation value of a sensational story and had a tendency to flex the truth. Soon after the shooting, he ran a front-page story purport-ing to describe how a band of savage desperadoes gunned down and bayoneted an innocent citizen, who expired in his own bedroom in the presence of his wife and daughters. Sperry's bias shows throughout his writing, and he titled his major story, *The Murder of Doctor Harvey Baker by the Yankees*.[355]

The details of the Baker case are blurred by partisanship, but cer-tain basic facts are reasonably clear. Harvey Baker, 52, resided with his wife Agnes, 33, and their four daughters in a handsome brick mansion which faces Kingston Pike, about ten miles west of Knoxville. Their home was a familiar landmark which indicated the halfway point between Lenoir's Station and Knoxville.

The building's spaciousness signaled to every passer-by that Baker was a man of means, and indeed he was. In 1860 he owned land valued at $50,000, his medical practice was thriving, and he held twenty-one slaves, valued at $29,000. An admiring neighbor described him as "one of our most enterprising farmers, and one of our cleverest men." Baker's lifestyle personified an antebellum version of the American Dream.[356]

Not surprisingly, Baker was a staunch advocate of the Confederate "revolution." He spoke in favor of secession (which by itself branded him a traitor in the minds of many Unionists), and he backed his words with deeds: he sold grain to the rebel army and rented pasturage for its livestock (at a rate of 20¢ per animal per day).[357] He was especially proud that his only son, Abner, 19, a trooper in the 2nd Tennessee Cavalry CSA, was among the first young men in Knox County to enter Confederate service.[358]

On the morning of June 19, 1863, Harvey Baker was at home with his wife and daughters. The family had no inkling that the nineteenth would be anything other than an ordinary summer Friday. The first hint suggesting that the day would be different may have been the sound of distant gunfire, but the danger became very evident when a messenger—probably Captain Wiggs or one of his men—arrived to warn the family that a band of Yankee cavalry was approaching from the west. The courier also advised Dr. Baker that Confederate troops were gathering in Knoxville in expectation of an attack.

Baker had to make a decision. One choice was to disappear into the forest, though that would seem cowardly. He could also choose to remain in his house, but that risked capture and he had ample reason to stay out of Yankee hands. In any event, he chose a third option. He told his wife that he "could do no good staying at home, adding that he was going to Knoxville, "where he might be of some assistance in its defense."[359]

According to Sperry's account, Baker armed himself and was making preparations to leave for Knoxville, when a Union soldier rode up to his yard. Allegedly, Baker "told him not to shoot, that he was a citizen and did not belong to the army." The soldier then "raised his gun to his face to take sight, and fired, Dr. B[aker] firing at about the same time."[360] Though it is uncertain who shot first, the situation unraveled quickly.

"Dr. B[aker] then went into his house and locked the doors," the *Register* continued, "sending his family upstairs. His wife insisted he should go upstairs with them, which he did soon after. In a short time the soldier who had fired at Dr. Baker brought up a large number of men who surrounded the house and commenced firing through the windows on both sides, demanding that the men in the house should surrender. Mrs. Baker came to the window and told them there was no man in the house but her husband, and if they would cease firing he would surrender—[but] they continued firing and Doctor Baker came to the window once or twice and told them there was no man in the house but himself and if they would cease firing he would surrender."

"But whenever [Baker] presented himself at the window, they fired on him, and he returned the fire with his pistol. In a few minutes a number of them broke open the lower doors and entered the house and commenced firing through the ceiling into the room where Dr. Baker and his family were. They then went up the stairway and demanded that the men should come out and surrender. Mrs. Baker came out and told them there was no man in the house except Dr. Baker, and if they would not fire on him he would come out.

They ordered her to go away from the door or they would shoot her. Dr. Baker then pulled his wife in the room and threw the door open. They fired upon him with their guns and he returned fire with his pistols. A number of Yankee reinforcements then came up with loaded guns and fired a volley at him inflicting two mortal wounds. Dr. B[aker] said to his wife 'They have killed me,' and fell; his wife, in endeavoring to support him, fell with him. The Yankees then entered the room—one of them who had his bayonet on his gun, jabbed him in the mouth with the muzzle of his gun another ran his bayonet through his cheek—then struck him on the head—one ruffian pushed Mrs. Baker aside from her husband with his bayonet [*sic*]."

Desperate gunfights make good melodrama but not good history. Evidently Sperry was little concerned about the plausibility of his story. He maintained that Baker and his wife were surrounded, with no chance of escape, making surrender their only hope. Sperry then claimed that when Baker allegedly made three attempts to give up, each was ignored. Yet, readers were also told that the Yankees, at least twice, demanded his surrender. Sperry failed to explain why the Yankees would reject three offers to submit after having twice demanded that he do so. Agnes Baker supposedly placed her own life at risk by appearing in an open window to relay her husband's willingness to cease fire. But, if Baker did indeed wish to capitulate, there were safer ways to signify his intention. He might have thrown down his weapons, raised his arms, or waved a white cloth.

Sperry further strained credulity when he reported that a soldier, having expended all of his ammunition, threw a bayoneted rifle at his protagonist and had it thrown back—all while inside a house. The deathbed scene was also retouched. Supposedly, a Yankee stabbed the wounded doctor until he succumbed. But would a dying man, having suffered mortal wounds and having had his cheek run through by a bayonet, use his last words to scold his killers at-length?

And in perhaps the most thinly-veiled attempt to fan the flames of outrage, Sperry avowed that the Union soldiers were not only vile murderers but also contemptible thieves. "After the cowardly scoundrels had murdered her husband," Sperry declared, "they commenced robbing his wife of her jewelry and carried off everything they could find of value that was easy to be concealed. Among other things they took a breast pin containing a miniature likeness of Dr. Baker set in gold." A final dubious allegation was that two Yankees were wounded and nonetheless commended Baker for his pluck. Union records do not mention a casualty occurring in the fracas.[361]

Not to be outdone by the *Register,* the editor of the *Holston Journal* thundered that the Sanders raiders committed "one of the most atrocious and diabolical acts of this war." These accounts insisted that a monstrous crime had been committed and that the killers were still at large. Baker's "murder" became a fixture in the rebel memory of the raid.[362]

The rebel version stood unchallenged until 1885, when a Union veteran, Captain Bradford F. Thompson, late of the 112th Illinois Mounted Infantry, published a response. Thompson, who had not participated in the raid personally, interviewed several men who were there. His informants told him that they knew exactly who shot Baker, but they refused to disclose their names. The story, according to Thompson's sources, began when a small detachment of rebel cavalry (Company G) attempted to delay their progress as they were advancing toward Knoxville. Rebel pickets hid near Baker's mansion and fired upon the approaching Yankees.[363] When the Sanders men reached the Baker place, Thompson said, "Dr. Baker, a noted rebel of East Tennessee, came around his house, a short distance from the road, and deliberately raising his rifle, fired at the column then quietly passing along the public road."

The northerners contended that Baker got what he deserved. "He fired at the wrong time, for it was a detachment of the 1st [East] Tennessee mounted infantry upon which he had fired, many of whom knew Dr. Baker of old, and knew him to be a man who had done more, perhaps than any other citizen of East Tennessee, to urge on the demons and bloodhounds who were scouting the whole country, hanging and whipping and murdering old men and women, the fathers, mothers, sisters and wives of Union men, trying to force them to reveal the hiding places of their fathers, brothers, and sons."[364]

The Illinoisans absolved their comrades of any breach of the laws of war, but also hinted that their motives were not strictly military. "There were many men in the ranks of the 1st Tennessee whose mothers and relatives had been driven from their homes into the mountains, or murdered, because they would not tell where their men were, that they might be conscripted into the Confederate army. Dr. Baker had shown his devotion to the Confederacy by being the leading spirit in all these outrages, and he made a great mistake when he fired upon these men when they passed quietly by his house. Before the smoke had cleared away from the muzzle of his gun, he was surrounded by at least fifty men and twenty musket balls passed through his body." One rebel who feared the East Tennesseans said they were "bloodthirsty."[365]

The northern version placed Baker outside his house, holding a weapon, when troopers in blue uniforms rode by. There was no mistaken identity. He shouldered his rifle, aimed, and pulled the trigger. Several riders saw him shoot, and knowing who he was, seized the chance to punish him. The Yankee version omitted the unpleasant fact that Sanders's men pursued Baker into his house, then dispatched him in his bedroom, in the presence of his family. Baker allegedly was struck by multiple gunshots, with as many as fifty Union soldiers present.

Conflicting accounts of Baker's demise will never be reconciled entirely, but surviving records yield some clarity. The available evidence makes it reasonably certain that Harvey Baker was shot by members of the 1st East Tennessee Mounted Infantry, who rode at the head of the Sanders column.[366] The Union men saw Baker standing in his yard, near the source of the gunfire, and observed that he was bearing arms. This has led historians to infer either that the Yankees "assumed he was part of the [rebel] group," or he *"may* have joined in the attack."[367] But regardless of whether Baker actually shot at the Yankee column, or merely gave the impression of doing so, his death could not be described as a simple murder. Baker appeared on the field, under arms, while a military engagement was in active progress. His display of arms jeopardized his status as a civilian noncombatant, and when he shouldered his piece he became a participant. He could hardly expect to reclaim his civilian standing simply by fleeing indoors. Taking his life under these circumstances was a legitimate act of war according to the rules of engagement then in effect, the Lieber code.

Nonetheless, despite its legality, the Baker killing did have a sinister element. Baker was not in uniform, was not serving in an army, and succumbed in his own bedroom. The reason he was followed into his house cannot be known with certainty, but the weight of the evidence indicates that his killers knew who he was, knew what he had done, and pursued him relentlessly.[368] Bullet holes may still be seen in the door to Baker's bedroom, and their size and shape indicate that the chase happened essentially as was described in the rebel press. The Yankees chased Baker into his house, pursued him up the main staircase, and finished him off in his bedroom.

The war had become hardened. Baker exemplified the slaveholding aristocracy, whom Union soldiers blamed for starting it.[369] Southern-born Union troopers deemed anyone who spoke in favor of the Rebellion to be guilty of treason, but Baker's actions went well beyond seditious language, alone. Confederate army livestock grazed in his pastures for anyone to see.[370] While Baker may have been mistaken for a bushwhacker, it is more likely that he was killed, as the witnesses from Illinois testified, because his neighbors believed that he betrayed his country. They saw a chance to eliminate a traitor, and they took it. Baker was killed not only for what he did, but also for who he was.

The controversy lingered long after Baker's killers disappeared in the distance. The rebels screamed, and to a certain extent, the Yankees listened. Only ten weeks later, the Army of the Ohio seized control of East Tennessee, and General Burnside assigned Brigadier General Samuel P. Carter to serve as its Provost Marshal. Carter, a native of Elizabethton, Tennessee, in the far northeastern corner of the state, was well-suited for the post because, according to one historian, he was "politically shrewd and generally fair."[371]

The Army of the Ohio was engaged in heavy fighting during much of the autumn of 1863, but during the winter of 1864 General Carter conducted an investigation to determine whether a crime had been committed. Carter's inquiry was itself notable, since the concept of an army accepting criminal liability for a wartime death was comparatively new. The term "war crime" had not been coined, but Carter clearly understood its meaning.[372]

Carter's investigation was careful. Either Carter or one of his assistants obtained affidavits from several witnesses and, in what proved to be the decisive piece of evidence, Carter interviewed Dr. William J. Baker, Harvey Baker's older brother. The Baker brothers lived next door to each other, were partners in farming operations, and maintained medical practices.[373] After reviewing all of the relevant affidavits and interviews, Carter advised the U.S. Army's Provost Marshal General of his conclusion: "From the written affidavits and the verbal statements of the brother of the deceased I am fully satisfied that the killing of Dr. Baker was justifiable by the laws of war."[374]

General Carter was certainly not a neutral party, and he was judging his own men. The inquiry was victor's justice, but it must not be casually dismissed. William Baker was by all accounts a credible witness, and when an older brother, next-door neighbor, and business partner, declares a person to be culpable, his testimony must be respected. Secondly, the U.S. Army did not rely solely upon the opinion of its officer in the field. General Carter was required to submit his evidence to the Provost Marshal General, which assured that his determination would be subject to institutional review.

Finally, in the middle of the Civil War, it was impossible anywhere in America, to convene an unbiased panel on a matter as contentious as Baker's death. General Carter, the only man ever to serve both as a general in the U.S. Army and an admiral in the U.S. Navy, was qualified to serve as an arbiter. The judgment he rendered—"justifiable under the laws of war"—was fair.

Of course, the rebels disagreed. They treated Baker's death as a crime prosecutable under civil law. In a letter sent under a flag of truce, General Buckner demanded that the Yankees turn over for trial the men who had "foully murdered" the doctor. The angry general fumed that unless the killers were surrendered forthwith, "the vengeance of the whole Confederacy would fall upon the heads" of Colonel Byrd and his men. Since Byrd was absent, a subordinate replied on his behalf. The officer acknowledged that he knew the names of Baker's slayers and said that they were still serving in the Army of the Ohio and were "enjoying reasonably good health." Then, with tongue planted firmly in cheek, he pledged to assist the enemy general in his quest to bring the killers to the bar of justice. But, he regretted, he "was too busy just then to send them." So, he offered a second option: "if he [General Buckner] would call and get them he might have them." Relating the story on countless occasions thereafter, he noted that "Simon never called."[375]

In another odd aftershock, the outrage of Confederate Tennesseans nearly cost the lives of some twenty Union prisoners. The prisoners were from Illinois and were captured in November, 1863, a few miles west of Knoxville. They were then marched along Kingston Pike to a point near Dr. Baker's mansion, where one Illinoisan foolishly announced that he had been there before—he admitted that he had witnessed the killing of Dr. Baker. "This brought upon us a storm of abuse and curses," remembered a frightened prisoner. "One officer especially, cursed loud and deep, and heaped all manner of vile epithets upon the heads of the 'd—blue b—d Yankees' for killing 'the best citizen in East

Tennessee.'" The prisoners were so startled that they thought they might be executed on the spot, but upon careful reflection, the angry commander elected to spare their lives. He decided that since his men needed new boots, he could punish Baker's "murderers" sufficiently if he simply commandeered their footwear. The hapless prisoners from Illinois then marched off to face an uncertain future in a rebel stockade. They were alive but barefoot.[376]

CHAPTER TEN

The Cumberland Wall

MOSTLY UNAWARE OF THE SHOOT-OUT at the Baker estate, the Sanders men continued along Kingston Pike until they reached the western environs of Knoxville late in the afternoon of Friday, June 19. The leading elements drove the Confederate pickets back to within a mile of the city, but at dusk the rear guard was still twelve miles behind. The main body lingered in the outskirts of town until darkness fell, while in the meantime their gunners fired a few shots toward the rebel position at College Hill, on the west side of the city.

The purpose of this cannonade was to create an impression, both that an attack was imminent, and that it would come from the west. Morale in the Union ranks was high, but the expedition up to this point was a disappointment. "So far the raid had not gone well," Sanders later recalled, "for capturing a few pieces of artillery and burning an unimportant depot had not harmed the Confederates." But Knoxville, the hub of East Tennessee, presented a new opportunity. On the following morning the raid entered a new and decisive phase, and the young colonel executed his most brilliant stratagem.[377]

The Confederate leaders had known since Thursday (about thirty-six hours) that a Union cavalry detachment was operating west of Knoxville. However, they had struggled to deduce its intention. An attack on the city at first seemed unlikely, since for two years the Army of the Ohio had not dared to strike from such a distance. The rebels thought that the Yankees lacked "audacity."[378]

If not Knoxville, the leading possibilities were a strike against Loudon bridge, or a diversion to disguise the forthcoming invasion. If Loudon Bridge was the objective, there was little need for action. General Buckner had beefed up its defenses, and once the raiders discovered its strength they would withdraw. That left the possibility of a ruse. A cavalry probe might be intended to make Buckner think that his headquarters was in danger and recall troops to protect the city. This would give Yankee invaders a smooth path through the mountains. Union attempts to disguise the purpose of Sanders's drive had worked.[379]

General Buckner had been expecting a general invasion for weeks, and with that thought in mind, he was easily deceived. He took several steps consistent with the conclusion that a general invasion was underway. He first told Brigadier General John W. Frazer to "march at once" to Jacksborough Gap, where he could repel any Union column which entered through that portal. Buckner next sought reinforcements from Brigadier General Archibald Gracie, Jr., who commanded the garrison at Cumberland Gap. Gracie, a New Yorker who graduated from West Point, had moved to Alabama and embraced the Confederate cause. Buckner directed him to "march tonight" to link up with Frazer.[380]

Buckner's final deployment offered the strongest evidence yet, of his belief that a major invasion was underway. Buckner arrived at Confederate headquarters in the Bell House in downtown Knoxville, early on Friday morning, June 19.[381] He was moving "hurriedly" and was "excited." He advised a Treasury agent, whose responsibility was to protect Confederate currency, that "he could not get out of Knoxville too soon." At about 10:00 AM Buckner left as well. Escorted by a detachment of bodyguards, the commanding general rode smartly out of town, taking all available artillery with him.[382]

A short rail spur, the East Tennessee & Kentucky Rail Road connected Knoxville to Clinton, Tennessee, a village nestled in the foothills seventeen miles northwest.[383] Buckner transferred his headquarters to a point on the Clinch River near Clinton. The new command post was thirty miles south of the Kentucky border and about fifteen miles equidistant from the two westernmost points of entry, Jacksborough Gap and Big Creek Gap. From Clinton, Buckner would be in telegraphic communication with both Knoxville and Richmond, and he would be able to direct the defense of the invasion routes, in person.

Though Buckner acted as if a major invasion was underway, he had conflicting information. On Tuesday, June 16, Major General Samuel Jones, who was stationed just across the Virginia border in Dublin, sent word that "a large part" of Burnside's men had been sent to Mississippi. Jones advised him that there was no need to worry about "any invasion of East Tennessee on a large scale." Again, on Wednesday the 17th, Confederate army headquarters in Richmond wired an advisory indicating that "nearly all" of General Burnside's troops had been sent to Vicksburg.[384] If the news emanating from Dublin and Richmond proved to be correct, there was little reason for concern. Union troops transferred to Mississippi were no threat.

Unfortunately for the General's peace of mind, local agents muddied the scene. On Thursday, June 18, the scouts who escaped from the Yankees at Wartburg warned Buckner that the northern perimeter had been breached. However, the size, purpose, and probable destination of the enemy squadron were left to conjecture. If "a large part" or "nearly all" of Burnside's men were on their way to Mississippi, as Gracie and Richmond said, then who was in Wartburg? And why were they there?

The reports from afar were, of course, correct. The 9th Corps had indeed left for Mississippi, and Burnside could not risk a general invasion until they were returned. (The 9th Corps was transferred so frequently, its men joked that they were enrolled in "Burnside's Geography Class.")[385]

But fragments of information obtained locally indicated that a general invasion was already underway. Which to believe? A commander in the field can scarcely disregard fresh local information and instead act on dispatches sent from a distant source. And, as of the early morning of June 19, the purpose of the Sanders squadron was still unresolved. The force appeared to be a small-scale probe, but it might also have been the harbinger of a major incursion. This uncertainty hindered Buckner. A prudent commander should always remain prepared to counter the greatest threat to his command—in this case, a general invasion. Buckner had no intention of weakening the Cumberland wall.

Buckner chose to guard against an invasion and deployed his troops accordingly. He transferred his headquarters, a significant number of troops, and nearly all of his available artillery to Clinton. He prepared to parry the greatest peril that he faced, but in the process, he weakened the garrison in Knoxville. Rather than thinning out his northern garrisons, he sent troops to strengthen them. He was not willing to leave the hub of his department defenseless, however, so he left behind two infantry regiments and summoned reinforcements from nearby outposts.

Buckner gambled that two regiments, augmented by as many auxiliary troops as could be brought in or scrounged up, would be enough to hold the city. The combined force would number only about 800 men and would be short in training, artillery, and cavalry.[386] Since some reports estimated the Yankee force at 4-5,000 men, the city was in peril, but if Knoxville's defense held, he would save the city while simultaneously shoring up his mountain redoubts.[387]

The defensive strategy called for shifting army headquarters to Clinton. When Buckner executed this switch, he rode through Knoxville escorted by a train of teams towing cannon and caissons. His departure set the rumor mill spinning. Knoxville's secessionists had long been jittery about whether their troops would actually stand and fight, and now they were rattled.[388] They wanted to know why General Buckner left, why he was in such a hurry, and where he went. Answers were not forthcoming.

Gradually the nature of the threat began to take form. The first rumor circulated well before Buckner left. On the evening of Thursday, June 18, "about sundown," the public learned that Yankee cavalry had been sighted near Loudon.[389] This dispatch placed the Yankee force at 2,000 men, a third too many, but did not warn that it could be a threat to Knoxville. That changed abruptly about ten o'clock on the following morning, Friday the 19th. At that moment an advisory arrived from Richmond with the disturbing news that "for some cause" the Yankee force had changed direction and was now moving east toward Lenoir's Station.[390] This helped to explain why the commanding general made his departure.

The excitement came to a boil in the early afternoon. Passengers aboard a two o'clock train from Chattanooga reported that Lenoir's Station was aflame, that marauders were on the way, and that Knoxville was their next stop. The passengers overestimated the enemy force at 2,000 men but correctly foresaw its destination.[391] The prospect of an attack inspired visions of the city in flames, of citizens in prison, or even, conceivably, ascending the gallows. Knoxville's rebels asked whether General Buckner left enough forces to defend the city.

The city bustled with activity. Men worked feverishly throughout the afternoon and evening to prepare for the attack. Reverend David Sullins, who served the largest Methodist congregation in Knoxville, witnessed the scene. Thirty-six at the time of the Sanders raid, and a former major in the Confederate Army, Reverend Sullins stood well over six feet in height, "with a great shock of cold black hair on his head, blue-grey eyes that kindled when he talked to you, and a voice that could be as caressing as a mother's and as martial as a general's on the field of battle."[392]

A half-century later, Sullins remembered the day vividly. The 19th, he said, was "a day of great excitement when we learned that the enemy were coming sure enough. Of course the whole town, soldiers and citizens, white and black, were excited; everybody hurrying here and there, and all asking questions that no one could answer."[393]

When Buckner and his staff rode away, the raiders were still some twenty-five miles from the city. Nobody could be certain about how many hours remained before the enemy struck, but the clock was ticking. Besides deciding to move his headquarters, Buckner named the officers who would be in charge of Knoxville's defense, designated the regiments which would form its shield, and ordered all nearby stations to send reinforcements as quickly as possible. Buckner's strategy was to give the city the best officers that he had, all the troops that he could spare, send for help, and hope for the best.

Buckner ordered his Chief of Staff, Lieutenant Colonel Victor von Sheliha, to remain as his agent. Von Sheliha was the right man for the job. Born in Poland, he had served as a lieutenant in the Prussian Army. Described as a "highly accomplished, distinguished officer" during his service in Prussia, von Sheliha was trained in both infantry and artillery, and was also a skilled architect. Most of all, he was a model of Prussian efficiency.[394]

Colonel von Sheliha's first move was to notify Richmond by telegram that "a raid on Knoxville is not improbable." While the news was not a complete surprise, it was unsettling. Hoping to soothe worried nerves, von Sheliha assured his superiors that "proper measures for the protection of the place are being taken."[395] This promise could hardly have offered much relief, since von Sheliha declined to explain what he meant by "proper measures." His omission was doubtless for the best, because if the high command had been fully apprised of the situation, there would have been dismay. The truth was that the Department of East Tennessee had done nothing to prepare Knoxville for a cavalry probe.[396] The War Department would have learned that, rather than invoking an organized defensive plan, Buckner was relying upon whatever he could find at the last minute.

Fortunately for Buckner, he had capable subordinates. Colonel von Sheliha was the best-trained, most broadly proficient officer present, but he was too junior to be given overall command of the city.[397] Von Sheliha relayed the commanding general's instructions, but three others managed the deployments. Knoxville's commanding triumvirate were all wealthy attorneys who were early supporters of secession. They either owned slaves personally or came from a slave-owning family.

The Confederate Army did not send its finest officers to East Tennessee, but the three who led the defense of Knoxville were competent soldiers.[398]

Overall command went to the senior officer in the field, Knoxville's post commander, Colonel Robert Craig Trigg. A native of

Christiansburg, Virginia, Trigg finished dead last in his class in each of his four years at the Virginia Military Institute—the poorest record possible, short of expulsion. Yet though he began as a dull student, his combat record showed ability. As colonel of the 54th Virginia Infantry, he was "brave, cool, and exercised fine judgment at critical moments.... He was a great disciplinarian, though not very popular in camp."[399] At thirty-four, Trigg was by a wide margin the youngest of the three leaders.

Colonel Jesse Johnson Finley, also an infantry officer, was second in command. A veteran of the Seminole War, Finley, at 50, was an able politician who at various times was elected to public office in Arkansas, Tennessee, and Florida.[400] An avid secessionist, he wanted independence without inconvenience. His men grumbled that while they slept on the ground, cooked over campfires, and ate from mess kits, their colonel could usually be found "in Knoxville boarding at the tavern." While Finley avoided the vicissitudes of the field, his courage was beyond question. He was wounded twice in the Atlanta campaign, first at Resaca and again at Jonesboro.[401]

Since the infantry were heavily outnumbered, only firepower could save the city if the enemy attempted to seize it. General Buckner ordered Lieutenant Colonel Milton A. Haynes, chief of the Tennessee Corps of Artillery, to procure cannon and site the batteries. Haynes's role was consequential because success depended upon finding heavy guns quickly and working them effectively. On this day, artillery proved to be the most important branch.

Haynes was a flawed man. He began as a professional soldier, having finished eighteenth of forty-five members of the USMA class of 1838, a group which produced thirteen generals.[402] He saw action in Florida, commanded a company in Mexico, and directed rebel artillery batteries during the siege of Fort Donelson in 1862.[403]

Haynes served in the Confederate Army throughout the war but later said that he was only a half-hearted rebel. He maintained that he remained loyal to the United States until the Tennessee General Assembly voted to secede, at which point there was "no other alternative left for him" except to join the Confederate Army.[404] But while he later claimed to have been deeply conflicted, he actually accepted his commission fully three weeks before Tennessee's decision became final. On the day that Tennessee voters approved the legislature's resolution, Haynes was already in uniform. He served faithfully for four years.[405] Haynes became the commander of Tennessee's "Corps of Artillery" and held other important posts. Nonetheless, at war's end, his collar still displayed the same insignia which he received on the day he was commissioned—the stars of a lieutenant colonel.[406]

Haynes failed to win promotion because while serving as "commandant of Post" at Knoxville, he was arrested and charged with four counts of "Habitual Intoxication" and two counts of "Conduct unbecoming an officer and a gentleman." The warrant accused him of having been inebriated while at the Lamar House, at the Franklin House, at his office, and "at divers times while on duty."[407] The indictment further specified that he cursed and abused one R. Waddell "in an outrageous manner."[408] A General Court Martial dismissed five of the charges but found him guilty of being intoxicated while on duty. The Court stripped him of his command, suspended him for three months without pay, and restricted him to Knoxville while under court sanction.[409]

Haynes complied with the terms of his sentence, but his conviction extinguished his prospects for promotion. When the Sanders troop approached Knoxville, Haynes was in disgrace, but the forthcoming fight presented an opportunity to cleanse his record. Not surprisingly, friction developed between the besotted and shamed veteran of the Old Army and his younger commanding officer, the lackluster VMI graduate who also hungered for distinction and promotion.[410]

The gulf was broad, but there was little time for squabbling. The Yankees were coming. Trigg sent all of his cavalry, only thirty-seven men, to intercept the enemy in hopes of buying time to strengthen Knoxville's defenses.[411] But at three o'clock in the afternoon a messenger brought more disturbing news: leading elements of the enemy squadron were now only five miles from the city. The raiding force was approaching from the west, so Trigg placed most of his men on College Hill, which overlooked Kingston Pike. The principal building on College Hill housed the University of East Tennessee. Its cupola rose high above Kingston Pike, so under ideal conditions approaching horsemen could be seen for miles.[412] Trigg deployed his own 54th Virginia on College Hill, and he also stationed part of Finley's regiment, the 7th Florida Infantry, along the city's western boundary. Several other units of the 7th Florida manned positions closer to the city center.[413]

Meanwhile, messages went out by telegram and courier directing all units within marching distance to send troops at once.[414] In effect, Buckner elected to thin out the garrisons which protected the railroad in order to save the hub of his Department—which included warehouses, depots, training grounds, and repair facilities. But recalling troops from afar left thirty miles of the East Tennessee & Virginia open to attack. Its trackage, depots, water tanks, and rolling stock were only lightly guarded.

Buckner dared not recall all of the troops from the distant outposts, for that would leave the bridges open to sabotage. His plan was a calculated risk. He gambled that he could leave the periphery shorthanded until the threat to Knoxville passed. The distant garrisons had earthworks and blockhouses which offered protection from small-arms fire, but wooden structures could not deflect cannonballs. The bridge guards were too few and too spread out to hold off the Sanders squadron, so it was prudent to move most of them back to Knoxville. In the city they would escape capture and could assist in its defense. Concentrating his forces offered Buckner his best chance of keeping the enemy at bay.

At 4:00 PM three companies of the 7th Florida Infantry received orders to march from Strawberry Plains to Knoxville. The Floridians had at one time been members of the Florida Volunteer Coast Guard, but they had been transferred to infantry duty and sent to Strawberry Plains to guard its bridge. The seagoing Floridians disliked Strawberry Plains because in their opinion the town was full of "Lincolnites."[415]

Upon arriving in Knoxville, two of the Florida companies set immediately to work digging rifle pits and strengthening a breastworks erected on Summit Hill in the center of the city. The third, Company K, commanded by 1st Lieutenant Walter C. Maloney, went to the riverfront to guard the two ferries tied up at its dock.[416] At midnight, hearing firing on the northern periphery of the city, Lt. Maloney and his men abandoned the wharf, trotted through the business district, and took up a position defending Summit Hill. Even decades later the Reverend Sullins found the excitement to be unforgettable. "The infantry, at 'double-quick,' hurried through the streets to form a line of battle on 'reservoir hill,' out-of-town then," he remembered. The night was very dark.[417]

Late on Friday, a second messenger overtook a detachment of the 9th Georgia Artillery as they were preparing to pitch camp about twenty-five miles east of Knoxville.[418] The 9th Georgia was under the command of Major William A. Leyden, and he ordered Captain Benjamin Franklin Wyly, a twenty-eight-year-old son of a wealthy Georgia planter, to take his E company back to the city posthaste. Wyly and his cannoneers, most of whom resided in the Atlanta area, were weary from having marched over rough roads all day, as were their horses. But as steadfast soldiers, they faced about and counter-marched for nine hours. They were back in Knoxville by seven o'clock the next morning. They had not slept in nearly twenty-four hours.[419]

The Georgians expected to be met by only a few sentries when they approached Knoxville, so they were surprised when they came upon "a large force of cavalry and infantry drawn up in a line of battle between them and the city." This was baffling, since neither the demeanor of the riders nor the color of their uniforms clearly identified their loyalty (their blue jackets were probably bleached by the sun or dusty, or both). To compound the confusion, "several officers in the rear politely saluted the battery with their swords, and Captain Wyly was at a loss to know whether they were friends or foes." As the wary Georgian pondered what could be a life-or-death decision, better information came to hand. "A young man in the company drew a white handkerchief and rode boldly up to the officers and ascertained that they were the raiders."

Wyly gathered from this impromptu "flag of truce" that he was looking down enemy barrels. After marching all night, his company, which numbered no more than fifty, had chanced upon the staging area of a thousand-man strike force. Wyly reacted quickly and shrewdly. He told his men to roll their guns into firing position and take aim as if they intended to shoot. As he hoped, the enemy officers responded to this gambit by making ready to return fire. While the Yankees were unlimbering their guns, Wyly's men waited their chance and then dashed for safety. They flew past a full Union regiment and reached friendly lines unscathed.

Wyly's men were evidently not the only ones confused by this ploy, because, as he later complained, his men "were fired on by our pickets, who mistook them in their headlong entree for the enemy."[420] Nonetheless, this was a lucky day for Georgia. In the space of half an hour Wyly and his men managed to elude the concentrated fire of two armies without sustaining a casualty. It was a good story, which Wyly told and re-told for half a century.[421]

A third Buckner dispatch also arrived on Friday evening, but with a less satisfactory result. Captain H. Grant, commanding H company, 5th Missouri Infantry CSA, was escorting a detachment of paroled Missouri troops back to their units. The Missourians were aboard a train headed westward toward Knoxville when they received Buckner's order to proceed directly to the city. The train continued to roll forward until it was within earshot of the musketry, about three miles from the outskirts. At that point its conductor received a counter-order from John R. Branner, president of the railroad, admonishing him to bring the train back to safety. Branner supported the Rebellion, but with a limit. He would not bring his rolling stock any closer than three miles from the fighting.

As he was told, the engineer reversed gears and retreated to McMillan's Station, where the soldiers and crew spent the night.[422] At daylight they made a second attempt to reach Knoxville, but again the conductor refused to come any closer than three miles. About one hundred Missourians had weapons and chose to walk the last distance, but by the time they arrived the fight was already underway. Finding themselves caught between raiders and rebels, they detoured to the south, circled the Yankees' position at double-quick time, and entered rebel lines near Mabry's Hill. They were delayed by friendly fire along the way and did not reach position in time to be of much help.[423]

Although the infantry was in position, preparations were far from complete. Reinforcements had not yet arrived and the cannon were not ready. Haynes reviewed the artillery placement and grasped its failings. A search of the inventory turned up eight field pieces, but the ammunition chests were empty and there was no harness for towing guns or caissons. Haynes acted quickly. He requisitioned seventy horses and mules, along with drivers, then asked the quartermaster to fill the ammunition chests and find harness for the animals. When preparations were complete, Haynes set out to position his guns.

Knoxville, resting on a high plateau among seven hills, was not heavily wooded. With its steep topography, clear sight lines, wide streets, and compact business area, it presented a naturally defensible position. The most exposed point, College Hill on the west side of the city, initially received the largest detachment of artillery. This battery, which supported the 54th Virginia, was under the command of Major H. Baker, a veteran officer who had commanded cannon at the battle of Shiloh.[424]

Haynes's second placement was on the north side of the city, along an east/west ridge which protected the civic center. This battery was part of "McClung's Company" of the Tennessee Light Artillery and was under the command of Captain Hugh L. W. McClung, member of a socially prominent, Old Knoxville family.[425] Captain McClung had organized this unit in Knoxville in October, 1861, and became its commander by popular election. McClung's men were combat-tested, having also fought at Shiloh. McClung's battery employed bronze, smoothbore, Model 1841 field guns, commonly known as "six-pounders." Named after the solid shot which the gun normally fired, a six-pounder could also fire an anti-personnel round known as "spherical case." This projectile was a hollow shell filled with small lead balls and an explosive charge. The standard Model 1841 had a maximum effective range of about 400 yards, although this range was insufficient to reach most of the Union positions at Knoxville on June 20.[426]

"Six-pounders" were obsolete but still in the rebel service (including those used against the Sanders raiders) because better equipment was unavailable. The 1st Ohio Light Artillery USA also used six-
pounders, but the Yankee guns had been modernized. U.S. arsenals
rifled the barrels of some M1841s, and these pieces could fire an elon-
gated percussion shell with significantly greater range and accuracy
than the older model.[427] The rebel batteries outnumbered Sanders's
guns by four to one, but the Union cannon were newer and deadlier.

Two rebel batteries stood upon "Summit Hill," an east/west prominence which forms the northern boundary of central Knoxville's street
grid. These batteries overlooked the railway depots and workshops and
were under the command of First Lieutenant John J. Burroughs CSA.
Burroughs normally commanded a company of artillery assigned to
Cumberland Gap, but on this occasion, he happened to be in Knoxville
while recuperating from an illness.[428]

Summit Hill became something of a community project. Reverend
Sullins recalled that "hastily, on the summit, where the Catholic church
now stands, we made some slight breast-works of a few cotton bales,
and brought a small gun, a four- or six-pounder, there."[429] The artillery companies led by Captain McClung and Lt. Burroughs numbered
about fifty to eighty men, each. The men had fought side-by-side on
several occasions, but on this day the batteries were undermanned and
Burroughs and McClung had no choice except to employ untrained
replacements—men from Maryland and Kentucky, convalescents, and
local citizens.[430] Colonel Haynes placed his guns carefully and tried to
man them with practiced gunners, but men with artillery experience
were hard to find.

Summit Hill is steep and furnished an unobstructed line-of-fire
for guns targeting an enemy approaching from the north. Its natural
strength became evident six months later, when the battle of Knoxville
reversed the roles of attacker and defender. By then, Knoxville had
fallen to Burnside's Army of the Ohio, while a much larger force under
the command of Confederate Lieutenant General James Longstreet
sought to recapture it. Longstreet reconnoitered the north side of the

city, accompanied by his artillery chief, Colonel E. Porter Alexander, who two years earlier was William P. Sanders's billiards partner in San Francisco. Longstreet and Alexander looked for a weak point in the Union line, but after one glance at the "formidable breast works" on Summit Hill, they withdrew. Alexander observed that the Summit Hill position was so obviously strong that the decision to attack elsewhere "required no discussion."[431]

Recognizing that the shortage of men was grave, Colonel von Sheliha proposed to recruit an emergency defense unit. Colonel Trigg promptly circulated an order directing all able-bodied citizens and all convalescent soldiers to report to Colonel Edward D. Blake, the chief of the Conscript Bureau.[432]

Observing an ancient tradition, dozens answered the call to arms. The war was well into its third year, but Knoxvillians remained divided. Some were avid disciples of secession, some were neutral, and others were bitter opponents.[433] But all shared a common curiosity. Everyone wanted to see which, and how many, of their neighbors would actually put their lives on the line to save Old Dixie.

Reverend Sullins, an impassioned secessionist as well as a devout Methodist, offered an insider's appraisal. "Knoxville was much mixed on the question of secession," he wrote. "There were many Union men, all in sympathy with the Federals. Many of them were good and reputable citizens, who would have scorned to do an ignoble thing; but the atmosphere was such that bitter, bad men came to the front, and made war worse than war. The Church Street congregation, which I served in Knoxville, was in full sympathy with the Confederacy; but it was composed largely of thoughtful, pious, conservative men and women, who kept politics out of their religion."

Rebel authorities had ruled for two years, giving them ample opportunity to persuade their neighbors of the righteousness of the Cause. But had they won them over? The Yankee challenge forced a showdown, and now proponents of Southern independence were obliged to match their words with deeds. Would the "thoughtful, pious, conservatives" who had warbled the rebel hymn now stand to arms? Or would they step aside and risk being exposed as moral cowards?[434]

Unionists were eager to identify which of their neighbors would take up arms against the United States, since such action might be grounds to prosecute them for treason. At least one arch-secessionist also welcomed the test of devotion. Lawyer William Gibbs McAdoo was a wealthy planter who had long been active in public affairs.[435] A veteran of the Mexican War, McAdoo had become so deeply alienated, that he once wrote of the Fourth of July, "I curse the day, as Job did the day on which he was born."[436]

McAdoo venerated the principles of the Rebellion, but he had no use for its local spokesmen. He considered them traitors to the Cause, and when he learned of the probable Yankee attack his reaction was caustic. "I hope they will take Knoxville," he told his diary. Referring to lukewarm Confederates, he added, "I wish some of the corrupt traitors there who have been pretending to be Southern [will have] to show their real colors."[437]

East Tennessee was Unionist territory, as was Knox County, but the best modern estimate holds that nearly half of the residents of Knoxville proper welcomed secession to some degree. While this would suggest that the town contained a reservoir of manpower available for emergency service, this was not the case.

Prior to the war, the entire population of the city numbered at most 2,500 males, and only half were pro-Confederate. Since most of those who were of military age were already in uniform, new recruits must come from the few not yet called—the very young, the overage, the infirm, and the deferred—or from the pool of new residents who had moved into the city since the war began.[438]

In June, 1863, Confederate law exempted men under age eighteen, over age forty-five, and in numerous trades and professions. The number of potential recruits was small, but it was not zero. Scattered sources identify some sixty men as having reported for duty.[439] Information has been located for thirty-seven names. The special detachment drew from occupations typically found in Southern communities— yeoman farmers, merchants, artisans, and professionals—though not in equal proportion. Confederate conscription rules granted exemptions to a broad assortment of occupational specialties. Tradesmen and almost all professional men found relief, and men from these walks-of-life were well-represented among those who mustered.[440]

About a quarter (nine) were farmers or farm laborers, while about a fifth (seven) were artisans: three machinists, a butcher, a cabinet-maker, a carpenter, and a cooper. About a ninth (four) were merchants, including a bookseller and a dry goods dealer. The emergency detachment's most striking feature, however, was that fifteen professional men mustered. This group, which made up nearly half of the known participants, included two physicians, a dentist, an editor, a professor, three clergymen, and no fewer than five lawyers. There were also three public servants, including the postmaster and a Confederate States Senator.[441] (See Appendix 3.)

A Knoxville Unionist, Samuel Morrow, sneered at the volunteers for being members of *"the first families"* of the city.[442] Yet while Morrow spoke with contempt, he also spoke the truth. The corps of volunteers included much of Knoxville's remaining social, financial, and religious élite.[443] In 1860 sixteen of the Knoxville volunteers estimated their net worth to exceed $1,000, or more than twice enough to place them in the upper half of the city's households. Six claimed more than $10,000, and the wealthiest possessed $172,500.[444] (See Appendix 3.)

The Confederate revolution was often mocked as "a rich man's war and a poor man's fight." While there was much truth in that proposition, the war's *raison d'etre* was the defense of slaveholders, and in this brawl sixteen men of wealth placed their lives at risk. The volunteers represented the city's political leadership (with the exception of its mayor and its absent Unionists). The most prominent Knoxvillians who mustered represented Tennessee in the Confederate Senate. Descended from an old and respected South Carolina family, Senator Landon Carter Haynes had been a Methodist minister, lawyer, and farmer.[445] He had been a Confederate supporter since early 1861, maintaining that East Tennessee would have a bright future as a manufacturing center if the South gained its independence. At the time of the Sanders raid he was forty-six and known as a "spellbinding orator."[446]

Two others had also been early and enthusiastic secessionists. Attorney William H. Sneed was a former Whig congressman who had married a wealthy, slaveholding heiress. On February 2, 1861, Sneed announced his candidacy to serve as a delegate to Tennessee's secessionist convention, promising that if elected he would do all in his power to take Tennessee out of the Union. Bank president and attorney John H. Crozier, at fifty-one years old, had also been a zealous exponent of secession. Both liked to display their wealth in spacious homes: Crozier's was described as a "large, fine mansion" with a "magnificent" library. Both buildings were later commandeered by Union officers.[447]

Knoxville's *ad hoc* warriors could also stake a claim to its moral leadership. Members of "First Families" usually joined mainstream Protestant congregations, and several Knoxville volunteers were weighty voices in the Protestant pulpit. The Reverend David Sullins was arguably the foremost Methodist in the city, and equally prominent was thirty-seven-year-old Joseph H. Martin, a graduate of the prestigious Union Theological Seminary. A slaveholder himself, Martin led Knoxville's Second Presbyterian Church for fourteen stormy years, during which he encouraged his congregation to break away from the General Assembly of the Presbyterian church as a protest against its stand on slavery. Martin helped to form a new Presbyterian synod whose theology taught that it was morally permissible for a Presbyterian to own slaves. Organized in 1858, the United Synod was, in effect, a Presbyterian Confederacy.[448]

Thirty-four-year-old Lucien B. Woolfolk, a native of Kentucky, was the pastor of the First Baptist Church of Knoxville. Woolfolk had trained for the pulpit in New England, at Yale College and Brown University, but he now saw northerners as enemies.[449] In 1863 he volunteered to shoulder a musket to help drive them off, and to take their lives if that proved necessary.

Pastors Sullins, Martin, and Woolfolk were by no means anomalies. Avid support for secession was common in the Southern pulpit, and many clergymen took up arms in defense of the South and slavery.[450] Sullins, Martin, and Woolfolk normally confined themselves to offering pastoral support to troops in camp or in the field, but when an attack on their city loomed, they resolved to use force on behalf of the "First

Families" who formed their congregations. Since more than half of Sanders's raiders were East Tennesseans of the middling classes, the clash in Knoxville represented a most unusual episode. As the historian James Campbell has observed, "the term 'Civil War' was probably more applicable to what took place in East Tennessee than to any other phase of the war."[451] In any case, the concept of the American "Civil War" acquired a deeper meaning on Saturday morning, June 20, 1863.

CHAPTER ELEVEN

A Dark Night in Knoxville

Day 11–12, 5:00 pm, June 19 – 8:00 am, June 20

SANDERS'S FORWARD UNITS reached the outskirts of Knoxville in the late afternoon of Friday, June 19. Sanders's scouts again proved themselves invaluable. Their knowledge of the local back roads shaped his next moves. Sanders had served for years on the Great Plains, where native chieftains were known for attacking where least expected. Sanders's plan to strike Knoxville was simple and clever. The Holston River protected the city against attack from the south, and a line of low ridges running from east to west shielded it against attack from the north. Watching from the cupola of the University of East Tennessee, high above Kingston Pike on the west side of the city, observers could see the Yankees approaching. Sanders wanted to create an impression that he would strike from the west.

Sanders delayed his appearance in the city's outskirts until evening, when there would be too little daylight remaining to mount an attack. He ordered fires lit where their glow would be visible from the city. The fires were meant to show that his men had settled down for the night and to suggest that an attack would come from the west on the following morning. If the rebel commanders took the bait, they would place most of their men and guns in position to defend the city's western approach.[452]

Sanders's real intention was to strike from the north. He proposed to move his men secretly to a point north of the city. This maneuver was feasible because Sanders's scouts knew of a wooded, unnamed trail which ran generally from west to east along the city's northern periphery. This path connected to the "Tazewell Road," a north-south thoroughfare which linked the settlements of Tazewell and Cumberland Gap to Knoxville, fifty-seven miles away.[453]

If the squadron could reach the Tazewell Road without discovery, the men could approach the city from the north and the strike could come as a surprise. This road was particularly appealing because it passed within 250 yards of Knoxville's rail facilities. Sanders was careful not to attack from the direction which the enemy expected, nor at the moment they anticipated.

Sanders planned to pound the rebel positions with his mountain guns. This barrage was supposed to appear to presage an assault by dismounted troopers and would encourage the rebels to fire back. After the enemy guns became fully engaged, Sanders's men would break off the attack and proceed east along the track of the East Tennessee & Virginia Rail Road toward the village of Strawberry Plains. As they had done previously, they would tear up track, burn ties, twist rails, and especially, destroy bridges. The rails, water towers, culverts, bridges, and other collateral facilities belonging to the East Tennessee & Virginia were of greater military value than were its depots, workshops, and roundhouse located within Knoxville.

To execute this plan, Sanders first assigned the 112th Illinois and the 1st Kentucky to serve once more as his rear guard. He posted the Illinoisans and Kentuckians near the flickering campfires on the west side of the city, with orders to hold their position while the rest of his men sneaked north, around the city. This ploy would maintain the impression that the Yankees were bivouacked and would attack from the west in the morning.

After darkness fell, the main force began to creep around to the northern fringe of the city. The sky was very dark that night and the men moved stealthily. The trail was rough, and the northerners, who habitually sneered at southern roads, dismissed the route as hardly a road at all but merely an "unfrequented path." The vanguard encountered a scattering of pickets along the trail, and at about two o'clock there was an exchange of gunfire. The Yankees drove off the pickets without difficulty, but the rebels learned that at least some of the enemy were moving around the city. Nonetheless, the southerners failed to ascertain the size of the movement nor did they deduce its purpose.[454]

Moving 1,300 men on horseback eight miles on a very dark night was slow work. Their destination was a grove of woods located just east of the Tazewell Road and about one mile north of the East Tennessee & Virginia railway. By the time that the first troops arrived, it was well past midnight. Sanders ordered a halt for the night.[455] His plan was to feed and rest the horses, get some sleep, and wait for the rear guard to catch up. To conceal their position, Sanders forbade campfires and warned the men to keep silent. The teams pulling cannon were kept in harness and fed from nosebags. Men and animals then settled down in a copse of scrub oaks, ready to march at a moment's notice. With his preparations complete, Sanders spread his blanket under a white oak and went to sleep.[456]

The rear guard held their position until just after midnight. When they finally moved out, they had to grope their way through the darkness, attempting to follow the path which their comrades had taken. Eventually they came to an unmarked fork in the trail, where they found that their commander had again neglected to leave a guide to point the way. Either confused by the unfamiliarity of the trail or by the moonless void, the stragglers guessed wrong. Thinking that they were proceeding eastward toward the rendezvous point, they turned south and followed a path which descended downhill toward the city center. Rather than maintaining a safe distance from the enemy, they were straying directly into their lines.

First Lieutenant James Humphrey of Company A, First Kentucky Cavalry USA, had the first brush with disaster. Attempting to determine his position, the twenty-three-year-old lieutenant walked toward the city accompanied only by "Red," his African-American "wait man."

Their noise in the shadows spooked the rebel pickets, who fired wildly toward the sound. Seconds before calamity struck, Lt. Humphrey and Red made a quick about-face and hurried back to their company.[457]

The rest of the rear guard continued to feel their way, searching for the right trail, until eventually it became obvious that they were hopelessly lost. Stumbling through the woods was treacherous, so they picked the nearest grove which seemed to offer concealment and lay down, keeping a firm grasp on their horses' reins. The troopers were exhausted after days in the saddle "and in five minutes were all fast asleep."[458]

They slept soundly, but not well. As the first streaks of gray began to lighten the sky, a drummer disturbed their rest. Drumming at dawn was a signal to awaken troops, but the Sanders squadron had no drums. A drumbeat could only come from the enemy. The beat of a drum within earshot meant that the enemy forces were very close and would soon be stirring.[459]

Some discreet reconnoitering revealed that they had strayed into the edge of the city and had slept within two hundred yards of an enemy hospital! As soon as they could see, they rode directly away from the sound of the drum. They turned east, crossed the Tazewell Road, and eventually found the main body of the force, who were sound asleep. The rear guard caught up to their comrades just in time to catch an hour's sleep, before they were summoned to their next adventure.[460]

* * * * * * * * * * * * * * * * *

The gloom of that morning caused yet another harrowing escape. After halting for the night, one Illinoisan fell asleep without remembering to tether his horse. The animal wandered off, leaving his rider fifty miles away from friendly lines and with no means of reaching safety. Desperate to find his mount, he followed a trail leading downhill. He met several troopers, but nobody had seen a stray. Finally, he came to a campfire where several men were gathered. Still anxious, he strode purposefully toward the fire, but in the dim firelight he was almost upon them before he could see that their uniforms were gray. Needless to say, his drowsiness cleared quickly. Grasping his plight with a clarity born of peril, he sauntered over to the soldier who was furthest from the light. As calmly as he could, he asked for a plug of tobacco. His luck held, for the rebel neither noticed his blue uniform nor recognized an unfamiliar accent. He simply gave the stranger a chew. The lucky guest wandered away, being careful not to hurry. He gave up the search and returned to his unit.[461]

*   *   *   *   *   *   *   *   *   *   *   *   *   *   *   *   *

Daybreak found the squadron concealed in the copse of oaks but within sight of both the East Tennessee & Virginia tracks and the north-south tracks of the Knoxville & Kentucky. The men cooked breakfast, grazed their animals, and kept out of sight. Meanwhile, just a mile to the south, Confederates worked feverishly. Trains brought troops into the city and carried civilians away. Sanders made no attempt to interfere with the reinforcements or evacuations, because he wanted the city to fill up with men and artillery. He knew that he could not be chased by train, since he intended to burn rails and twist track as he went. He would be pursued, but he would be hard to catch. Just twenty-eight miles further to the east, the larger prize awaited—the fine bridge at Strawberry Plains.

CHAPTER TWELVE

The Feint

Day 12, 8:00 am – Noon, June 20

POSING AS A FARMER, Colonel Haynes reconnoitered the Yankee positions during the late evening of Friday, June 19. Haynes hoped to lure the intruders into an ambush, so he told some Yankees that "they could march into Knoxville without the loss of a man." After reaching a point where his subterfuge might be detected, he returned to the city around midnight. His scouting persuaded him that his gun emplacements on College Hill, Summit Hill, and McGhee's Hill were sound.[462] He warned each battery to expect the Yankees to attack early in the morning. At about seven o'clock the next morning, while the Yankees were still preparing to strike, four additional cannon arrived, sent by General Buckner. Haynes ordered these guns held in the rear as a reserve.[463]

Throughout the night and early morning, Sanders and his men remained concealed in their thicket, resting and watching the enemy reinforcements pour into the city. They also noticed wagons carrying "a vast amount" of supplies leave the city, evidently in order to prevent its capture in case Sanders took the town. The Union plan was to carry out a short bombardment, then proceed eastward down the railroad track toward their preferred target, the bridge at Strawberry Plains. As one Ohioan explained the ruse, we "threw a few shells over the town and made a feint of giving battle." Sanders deliberately ignored the reinforcement of the garrison and the evacuation of supplies, recognizing that the concentration of enemy troops in the city worked to his advantage. When the raiders headed toward their real objective, their foes would be in their rear, trying to catch up, rather than in their path, blocking their way.[464]

They were in no hurry. Many commanders preferred to attack at dawn, but that morning Sanders was content to watch while rebel troops continued to flow into the city. The Union men slept in, finished their breakfasts, then mustered for their morning's work. Although there is some disagreement in respect to the timing, the squadron was formed up and prepared to sortie by about eight o'clock.[465] It was at this moment, while the Sanders men were lined up and waiting for the order to advance, that Captain Wyly's Georgia artillerymen marched in from the east, discovered their identity, and fled into the rebel lines.

Colonel Haynes ordered Wyly's battery to be held in reserve. As Haynes was making this assignment, sentries stationed atop Summit Hill observed blue-clad troops moving toward them. The enemy were at a distance estimated to be about 800 yards beyond the railroad workshops. When first sighted, the attackers were just emerging from their thicket and crossing an open field, while advancing toward the city. As a witness remembered: "We waited but a short while, when from the two hills could be seen a small body of the enemy's cavalry over on the face of the hill where Fifth Avenue is now located, moving among the trees. There were no houses there then, but some timber, which partially concealed the troops." The Yankees were approaching from the north along the Tazewell Road, which was the avenue that led north toward Cumberland Gap. At about a quarter past eight three rebel batteries opened fire with grape and canister. "The Summit battery made it hot for us as we were crossing the pine clearing to take position," a Yankee later conceded.[466]

Though Colonel Trigg stationed most of his men on the west side of the city, he also shifted some of his forces so as to protect the city's northern approach. Without consulting Haynes, Trigg withdrew an artillery battery from College Hill and moved it to a position further east, near the general hospital and closer to the city center. Haynes later expressed criticism of Trigg's order, which he said was warranted only because Trigg was the superior officer. Nonetheless, Trigg's decision proved to be wise. Moving the guns farther east strengthened the Confederate defensive positioning.

Sanders's men advanced until they found and occupied the brow of a hill which was located about 800 yards north of the enemy batteries stationed on Summit Hill. "The [rebels] worked their guns with frantic energy," remembered a Yankee, "but the shells and shots passed over our heads and pierced the upper stories of several houses in the vicinity." The low ridge shielded the Union men from the enemy's canister, but tragedy struck nonetheless. "The first shot the rebels fired passed over [us]," a veteran recalled. "We heard women scream, and afterward found that the house was filled with women and children; that the ball had killed a babe and torn off part of the dress off a woman."

The errant round that took the child's life struck a frame structure in a residential area located about a mile north of the railroad and which was home to a "very large majority" of Unionists. The trajectory indicated that it was fired by one of the guns in the Summit Hill battery which was under the command of Lt. John J. Burroughs, an East Tennesseean.[467]

The poor shooting was an embarrassment, but the killing of a baby was deplorable. One rebel spokesman, identified by the *Knoxville Register* only as "Volunteer," conceded that a gunner who missed his target by half a mile and killed an infant in the process might conceivably be deserving of "some censure." Nonetheless, he maintained that, under the circumstances, a wild shot was excusable. The gun crews were hastily assembled, were given no opportunity to practice, and in most cases were not even artillerymen.

The Summit Hill battery, which fired the fatal shot, was composed of convalescent soldiers and citizen-volunteers. One of the gun crews included William Sneed (a fifty-year-old former congressman known as a heavy drinker) and two lawyers. These "gray-headed sires," observed the "Volunteer," "had neither experience nor drill." The public should not be surprised if in the defense of their city "an occasional ball would strike the building, as a military necessity." "Volunteer" ventured that, in his opinion, a true patriot would salute the gunners' gallantry, not scold their aim.[468]

This unfortunate child proved to be one of two persons killed that day by rebel cannon. Most of the rebel grape and canister passed harmlessly over the raiders' heads, but one ball found its mark. Sanders ordered forty-two-year-old Captain Richard C. Rankin, who commanded a detachment of Ohio Cavalry, to take fifty men and form a picket line about 200 yards ahead of the Union guns. From this advanced but highly dangerous position, Rankin's men could shield the Union gunners with suppressing fire, in the event that the enemy attempted an infantry assault.[469]

Captain Rankin's assignment underscored the contrast between the opposing forces. The rebel press labeled the Sanders men "the Abolitionists," a highly pejorative term which did not apply to most of Sanders's troopers. In Captain Rankin's case, however, it was no mistake at all. Richard C. Rankin was indeed a lifelong abolitionist. Richard was a son of the Reverend John Rankin, an East Tennessee native who migrated to Ripley, Ohio, on the north bank of the Ohio River, where he led a Presbyterian congregation and spoke forcefully against slavery.

Reverend Rankin became one of the best-known abolitionists in the West because his home, perched 540 feet above the water, showed a lantern which served as a beacon for runaway slaves. The Rankin homestead was particularly notable because it allegedly inspired the most famous scene in Harriet Beecher Stowe's great novel, *Uncle Tom's Cabin*. In that riveting moment, the fictional slave "Eliza" makes her way to freedom by crossing the ice-clogged and highly treacherous river. Since, as a boy, Richard sometimes helped runaways climb the staircase which led to the family home, he became known as the man who saved Eliza.[470]

The enemies who faced each other along the Tazewell Road that morning included Captain Rankin, a lifelong Presbyterian, and the Reverend Joseph H. Martin, a slaveholder and the pastor of the Second Presbyterian congregation in Knoxville. Rankin and Martin were both committed Presbyterians, but they disagreed on a basic theological issue: may a faithful Christian, in good conscience, own a slave?[471]

When Captain Rankin's Ohioans took their exposed position above the Knoxville rail yards, most knew enough to "lay down with their faces to the ground." But twenty-three-year-old Private Orville N. Hosford of Company G, 2nd Ohio Cavalry, refused to take cover. "[Hosford] was standing within four feet of me," Rankin recalled, "when he was hit by a solid shot, breaking off three ribs and turning them back on the hinge of the backbone, where they hung. I looked right into the hollow of the man. He stooped down, half bent, and walked about three rods distant [fifty feet], and lay down behind a fallen tree." According to the official report, Hosford was wounded "on the right side and right arm and left at a private house near the city." He later succumbed from his wound.

In a near miss, 1st Lieutenant Charles D. Mitchell, the adjutant of the 7th Ohio Cavalry, was nearly struck while directing his unit's withdrawal from the field. "As I go along the line to tell the men to go back to their horses," Lieutenant Mitchell wrote in his diary, "I am knocked unconscious by the concussion of a shell which exploded just over my head." The addled lieutenant luckily managed to regain consciousness in time to move out with his men.[472]

Most of the rebel shots lodged in the upper stories of nearby buildings, such as the home where the baby died, but some fell short. A Union officer, finding himself at a loss to describe the scene, said he "could compare it to nothing better than that of a man taking up a handful of shelled corn or beans and throwing them around your feet." The artillery of the western Confederate army was plagued by poor ammunition, which may help to explain why some shot passed overhead, while the rest fell short.[473]

Unbeknownst to Sanders, the Confederates had no infantry nearby. Accordingly, Haynes had nothing with which to check the Union probe except cannon. He recalled from reserve Wyly's section of the 9th Georgia Artillery and ordered it to take a position near Temperance Hill, directly in front of the oncoming Yankees. As soon as Wyly's men reached the assigned location, the Georgia gunners opened fire with spherical case ammunition. The Confederate guns were 400 yards forward of their infantry support, and thus the gunners were dangerously exposed to Rankin's sharpshooters, who promptly advanced until they were within 200 yards of the Confederate battery.[474]

Without infantry support, Haynes could not answer the Yankee barrage. He recognized that the rapidly advancing sharpshooters posed the most immediate threat. "For a moment," he later admitted, "I supposed the day was lost." But he took personal charge of the situation, and (owing to his proficiency as a marksman) he believed that he saved the day for the South. "At this moment," Haynes averred, "the chief of the 12th Howitzer said to me, 'Colonel, I can't hit them fellows; please get down and try it yourself.' I dismounted, took my post as a gunner of the left, ordered canister and sighted the piece myself, and after two rounds the enemy was in full retreat and the day was won." Haynes's claim cannot be verified, but a Union veteran of the clash dismissed it as "very bombastic."[475]

Besides his forward battery, Haynes also had support from batteries stationed on Summit and Temperance Hills. Sanders correctly estimated that the Confederates' artillery strength totaled eight or nine pieces, some of which were protected by barricades made of cotton bales. His two guns were at a disadvantage in a duel against eight, particularly since the Confederates occupied the high ground. Sanders evidently misjudged the size of the Confederate infantry detachment (he reported that he was facing 3,000 men, though it was barely a third of that), but Trigg's men were not first-rate troops. All in all, the Union advantage in manpower, marksmanship, and small arms was great enough that, if Sanders had chosen to make a determined effort to take the city, he might have succeeded. But he did not. The artillery exchange lasted between sixty and ninety minutes, whereupon Sanders withdrew. As observers on both sides recognized, Sanders's "attack" was actually a demonstration intended to assure that the road leading to Strawberry Plains remained open and unimpeded.[476]

Losses were light. Sanders's casualties were just one enlisted man killed and two officers wounded, plus some missing. The Confederate claim that Sanders lost 45 men was exaggerated, but the Confederate report of losing only four men killed and four wounded was accurate.[477] Most of the Confederate dead resulted from a single cannon shot. The dead were twenty-nine-year-old 3rd Lieutenant James L. Snellgrove of Company F, 6th Florida Infantry, and two others. Snellgrove was sitting on a fence watching the fight from a position near the Asylum Hospital. A fellow soldier described the scene: "I was but a short distance when three fell, all killed by the same ball, it cut two of them nearly in two. It took off both the other man's legs."[478]

A Yankee fusillade also took the life of Captain Pleasant M. McClung, a great-grandson of Tennessee's territorial governor and founder of Knoxville. Pleasant McClung was an emphatic supporter of secession, and served as Chief of Ordnance of the Knoxville Arsenal.[479] In the artillery duel he commanded a battery atop Summit Hill, and when the Union guns began to take effect, he attempted to rally his men by exposing himself to the enemy fire. Reportedly, McClung cried out, "Don't be afraid–there's no danger!" Very shortly thereafter a Yankee shell passed between two cotton bales and struck McClung. Mortally wounded, with both legs severed below the knees, McClung remained conscious for two hours while he was comforted by Unionist minister Thomas Humes, an Episcopalian. Captain McClung expired while in the presence of his wife and children, and in his final moments he allegedly prayed for "forgiveness to those who killed me."[480]

McClung's death was a harsh blow for much of white Knoxville. He was one of Knoxville's own and was killed in action within the heart of the city. He received a hero's homage, but he was not uniformly admired. Scarcely grief-stricken, lawyer William G. McAdoo recorded in his diary that the young Captain was "a pig-headed little man, vain as a peacock, and worthless."[481] Nonetheless, the fallen soldier's memorial was a deeply touching, patriotic occasion, a state ceremony intended to unite as much as to mourn.[482]

The burial procession stretched the length of the town, with mourners lining the streets on both sides. Reverend David Sullins, who served the Methodist pulpit for a half-century, witnessed the terrible carnage at the battle of Shiloh and saw scores of young men perish in the prime of life. Yet, in spite of all the grief he observed, he was inspired to mention only the interment of Captain Pleasant McClung in his memoir. "All hearts were touched," praised Sullins, "when his riderless horse, carrying his holster and sword, passed by, led by a servant close behind the bier. All Knoxville was sad that day."[483] Or, to be more accurate, nearly all Knoxvillians who were both white and pro-Confederate grieved for the dead warrior.

Captain McClung was killed by one of the last rounds fired from Yankee cannon before the Sanders men left the field. The Yankees had shown their flag and bolstered the morale of loyal citizens. They had also caused the Confederates to concentrate their forces in defense of the city, leaving the more important rail connections east of Knoxville open to attack. Reverend Sullins understood the scheme: "Their feint was to keep the troops at Knoxville from following them or sending help to guard at the bridge. Our infantry remained in line till night . . . [when] good citizens went out carrying baskets and boxes, coffee-pots and pitchers filled with good things to eat and drink, good things and plenty of them for the boys still in line on the hill."[484]

Sullins was proud that the rebel soldiers behaved themselves with "gentlemanly recognition of the kind ladies who so gladly served them." Although they surely enjoyed good food and female companionship, they overstated the Yankee danger. Their estimate that Sanders vastly outnumbered them was doubtless a consideration behind their decision not to pursue the departing brigade.[485]

General Buckner's abrupt departure with many of his troops and most of his cannon implied that the Army might abandon the entire province without a fight. Confederate Treasury agent Dr. J. G. M. Ramsey was shaken. He had discussed defensive strategy with General Buckner and bluntly declared that failure to defend East Tennessee would spell the end of the Rebellion.[486]

Ramsey and others scoffed at the claim that Buckner's removal to Clinton as the enemy approached was simply a matter of "prudence." They noted that the general returned to the city shortly after the danger passed, which they construed as a sign of cowardice.[487] Lawyer William McAdoo went further yet. "Although I excise my heart to be as charitable as possible," he confided, "yet I cannot expel from my mind painful misgivings that Buckner is a traitor. His association has been exclusively with the Unionists in Knoxville."[488] When the Sanders men retired from the field, they left behind an uneasy community. Their damage to the rebel fighting capacity was minimal, but the effect on public trust was not.

CHAPTER THIRTEEN

Little Massachusetts

Day 12–13, Noon, Saturday, June 20 – 4:00 am, Sunday, June 21

AFTER LEAVING KNOXVILLE, the raiders trotted east, paralleling the East Tennessee & Virginia Rail Road. The rebel artillery continued to pound their vacated positions, but only a small cavalry detail pursued. Though wary of an ambush, the rebel cavalry kept in contact with the Sanders column. Major Tristram Dow of the 112th Illinois, in command of the rear guard, conceded that "our rear was considerably annoyed."[489]

At noon, when the northerners were twelve miles past Knoxville, the muffled rumble of guns shelling their empty positions was still audible. One raider chortled that the rebels were "firing with great vigor at imaginary Yankees." He was not the only one laughing. The booming in the distance came "greatly to the amusement of noncombatants, who knew that there was not a raider within five miles of the [target]."[490]

Secessionists received their best support in East Tennessee from communities lying along the railroad, but Strawberry Plains was an exception. Its citizens were so staunchly Unionist that rebel soldiers dubbed the town "Little Massachusetts." One northerner agreed. He described the locals as "strong—not milk-and-water—Union people." The area had erupted in violence twice in 1861, and during the summer of 1862 threats of sabotage became so serious that Confederate Secretary of War George W. Randolph felt compelled to inquire, "Is it safe to send arms through East Tennessee?"[491]

At no time, from the moment that the Sanders men crossed the Cumberland until they returned to safety in Kentucky, were they ever at a location where the civilians were hostile to their presence. The thirty-mile ride which took them eastward from Knoxville through Flat Creek, Strawberry Plains, and Mossy Creek was the most welcoming of all. The raiders remembered "Little Massachusetts" with great affection.

Several bridges in that section were attacked during the uprising of November, 1861, and as a result Confederate leaders stationed troops along the railroad to guard against further sabotage. These garrisons were large enough to discourage a band of saboteurs, but they could not fend off Sanders's men. The raiders stopped frequently to tear up ties and twist rails.

Small trestles at Woodson's Creek and Slate Creek went up in smoke, and the honor of striking the ceremonial match which incinerated the bridge at Slate Creek was awarded to a nineteen-year-old from Ohio, Corporal Samuel Cordell Fry.[492]

The first stop on the East Tennessee & Virginia was known as "McMillan's Station." According to one report, the garrison at McMillan's put up such slight resistance that the main body of the column rode by without even stopping to watch the depot and rail cars go up in flames. Another account said that the raiders took some time to strip the buildings before they incinerated them. McMillan's buildings may or may not have been combed before they were burned, but some stations did get ransacked.[493]

A small rebel detachment guarded the station at Flat Creek, three miles east of McMillan's and thirteen miles beyond Knoxville. Their assignment was to protect a covered railroad bridge and a county-owned wagon bridge, but they, too, fled without a fight. The Sanders men caught a few stragglers, then torched both trestles. The raiders released on parole some thirty-one prisoners before leaving Knoxville, and along the way to Strawberry Plains they bagged another twelve.[494]

Sanders's policy was to grant paroles to all prisoners. The northerners had no means of transporting prisoners, and in any case, the wisest course for a troop standing a good chance of being captured themselves is to treat prisoners well. At Flat Creek, one star-crossed rebel found that his freedom came at a price. Sanders chose him to carry a message back to his superiors in Knoxville.

The prisoner was 1st Lieutenant James C. Luttrell Jr. CSA, whose father, James Luttrell Sr., was both the mayor of Knoxville and also the most prominent Unionist still residing in East Tennessee.[495] Ignoring his father's views, James Jr. joined the Confederate army very early in the war, was wounded, and had returned home on convalescent leave. Having recovered well enough to ride, Lt. Luttrell mustered for the defense of Knoxville. But on the morning of June 19, he lost his horse while reconnoitering some twelve miles west of Knoxville. He managed to escape on that occasion, but on the next afternoon, he was captured (evidently after some hard riding) about ten miles *east* of the city.[496]

Since news of the capture of the mayor's son would embarrass the rebels, Sanders composed a personal message to be delivered to the enemy artillery commander (Lieutenant Colonel Haynes). "I send you my compliments," Sanders wrote (with tongue in cheek), "and say that but for the admirable manner with which you managed your artillery I would have taken Knoxville today." The Confederate side accepted Sanders's praise at face value, but his own men sensed that he was not being sincere. "Colonel Sanders, though a dignified gentleman, had a quiet vein of humor in his disposition," observed one of his admirers. "He was indulging in a little fun at the self-sufficient Lieutenant Colonel's expense."[497]

Flat Creek was just four miles from Strawberry Plains.[498] The Flat Creek bridges and their ruined trackage could be repaired without much trouble, but the bridge at Strawberry Plains was a quarter of a mile long. Strawberry Plains had been Sanders's primary objective ever since the failure to destroy the bridge at Loudon. The town's depot and warehouses bulged with grain, ammunition, small arms, and other supplies needed for the defense of Virginia. Its bridge and supply facilities required protection, and about 400 troops, supported by at least four howitzers, normally shielded the bridge. If that span could be destroyed, the mission would be successful, but if it remained standing the entire enterprise could be called into question.

Blockhouses stood at either end, and the span itself was a state-of-the-art "Howe truss."[499] This design combined threaded iron rods with heavy wooden timbers which were inflammable, but it had been strengthened. Plates of heavy sheet iron overlaid the framework, making it hard to break and slow to burn. The bridge was a land-based counterpart of the latest warship design—an ironclad bridge! These protections were sufficient to forestall saboteurs, but not a cavalry force. Most of the Strawberry Plains garrison had been called away to defend Knoxville, leaving no more than 200 men to safeguard the bridge, depot, and warehouses. Many of the men remaining were convalescents.

Shortly after noon, the Yankee column came upon a gravel bar about three miles below the town. Sanders led his men across the river at the shallow point with the intention of striking the rebel garrison from several directions at once. He first dismounted the 44th Ohio Mounted Infantry and ordered its men to march toward the bridge along the south side of the river. Their assignment was to distract the defenders' attention by threatening an assault. Sanders next directed Colonel Robert Byrd to take the rest of the raiding force, circle around the rebel positions, then attack from the east. Byrd's detachment included the two guns of the 1st Ohio Light Artillery.[500]

This maneuver reprised Sanders's Wartburg strategy, and it fooled the remaining bridge guards. As Sanders hoped, most of the Confederates shifted toward the west in hopes of repelling the 44th Ohio. Meanwhile, Byrd's main group took a position behind and to the east of the rebels. The Union cannon were sited upon high ground about three-quarters of a mile from the bridge. From this point the Union guns could rake enemy positions on both sides of the river, while remaining safely beyond the range of the rebels' smooth-bored cannon.[501]

When all units were ready, the troopers formed skirmish lines and charged. "The enemy had their guns planted," recalled a raider, "but when they saw us coming on the run they left their guns and took to the hills.... They broke some of their small-arms over rocks, and destroyed them as best they could." The engagement, which commenced about 4:00 PM and lasted only an hour, was "short but lively." A number of rebels fought from behind the four-foot stone wall which surrounds the Stringfield Cemetery on the east side of the Holston.

Evidently anticipating the outcome, the rebels kept up the steam in a locomotive, which allowed an unknown number to escape by train. Others scattered in every direction, or in the contemporary idiom, they "skeedaddled" [sic]. Before the Yankees' forward units came close to the enemy positions, the remaining defenders, who were now outnumbered by more than ten to one, raised a white flag. Colonel Byrd spent the night in the Stringfield residence, sleeping on Stringfield's feather bed. In the morning he had the bed moved into Stringfield's yard and from this place of comfort proceeded to receive the prisoners' paroles.[502]

This skirmish raised the total of captured guns to ten (three at Lenoir's Station, two at Knoxville, and five at Strawberry Plains). Also captured by Sanders at Strawberry Plains were 137 enlisted men, two officers, and a "vast amount" of small arms, ammunition, and provisions. The take included 600 sacks of salt, about seventy tents, and assorted camp equipment.[503]

The span stood on eleven piers and, including its approaches, stretched more than a quarter-mile. The Ohioans' cannon blasted its iron sheathing, and the fire was ignited at about 5:00 PM, probably with kerosene. The beams resisted ignition, merely smoldering for hours, and the deck did not become fully engulfed in flame until after darkness fell.[504]

The timbers reached their full heat at about 9:00 PM, and the conflagration was unforgettable. "It was a beautiful sight," remembered a raider. "Its whole length careened and plunged from its high piers to the river below." "It is dark when we fire it, and the spectacle is magnificent," another dazzled Yankee exulted. "The heavens glow as fire, and the river is a band of gold." The pro-Confederate *Knoxville Register* estimated that it would take "two or three months" to rebuild the bridge.[505]

Sanders ordered a rest for the night. His men were thoroughly exhausted, but despite their weariness some troopers remained awake to watch the bridge blazing. The fire, like the raid itself, was the experience of a lifetime. It was a larger conflagration than most of the men had ever seen, or ever would see.

The men cooked supper and savored their first decent meal in days. The hot food was particularly welcomed by the members of the rear guard who had been short of rations ever since they fell into the Clinch River two nights earlier. "Those of us who had got into the Clinch River . . . had been compelled to eat hardtack soaked with water and then soured in the hot sun. . . . Our sugar and salt had melted and mixed, and these mingled with our soaked and soured hardtack, with the mold and worms naturally belonging to the hardtack, made living upon it for any great length of time somewhat monotonous."[506]

CHAPTER FOURTEEN

Escape

Day 13, 4:00 am – 1:00 pm, June 21

THE NIGHT'S REST was badly needed. "We slept in line along the side of the road, our horses hitched to the fences by our side," remembered a raider. "We had neither bedding nor covering. My place in line brought me to a large rock, upon which I had the best night's sleep I ever enjoyed. We slept with our guns in our hands and our horses within reach, and could have been ready for a fight or a flight at a moment's warning. We were up and away with the morning light."[507]

The bugler blew "boots & saddles" at 4:00 AM, and the "greatly refreshed" troopers mounted up. But before they headed east, they had another task to perform: they confiscated and destroyed their prisoners' uniforms. They burned everything—all of the tents, blankets, jackets, shirts, pants, drawers, shoes, and socks worn by fifty-five members of Captain John T. Levi's company of Light Artillery, a unit of Thomas's Legion. The rebel gunners were free, but they were left without clothing as the villagers were preparing to attend Sunday services. There is no record of how or where the prisoners found garments to wear, but it was more than a week before new uniforms arrived.[508]

Mossy Creek

The raiders' next destination was the smaller but still very valuable rail bridge at Mossy Creek. This post was only about a two-hour ride beyond Strawberry Plains, but the men paused numerous times to pull spikes and twist rails. At the nine-mile point, Sanders sent a small detail to check the village of New Market, which then had a rail station. To their surprise, the raiders found ten rail cars parked there, all theirs for the taking. They burned the cars and ignited the depot as well.[509]

The cars should not have been left unprotected, since the threat was evident long before soldiers in blue uniforms could be seen. The rumble of guns dueling in Knoxville more than a day earlier was audible in New Market, and the cannonading on the previous afternoon in Strawberry Plains was much louder and nearer.[510] The timbers burning in Strawberry Plains produced a glow which could be seen in the sky for miles, and even if the noise and radiance were not enough to alert the residents, a steady stream of refugees trickled eastward. Some of the escapees were rebel sympathizers who were anxious to warn their compatriots of the coming Yankee visit. Sanders's route was in fact so easily guessed that an Atlanta newspaper forecast the strike on Strawberry Plains well before it took place.[511]

The warning spread faster than the column moved, and residents living along the road had ample time to prepare for the raiders' appearance. The morning was warm, the road was dusty, and the riders got thirsty. Though the young men from up north had neither bathed, shaved, nor changed their uniforms in more than a week, they were greeted by a bevy of comely young women dressed in their finest Sunday dresses. The visitors were offered a variety of refreshments which they washed down with buckets of cool water.

An Illinois trooper, clearly delighted by the surprise, remembered that "we found young ladies, well dressed and beautiful, standing at the gates of their residences, with platters loaded with pie and cake for each soldier.... Word had been conveyed that we would be there about a certain time, and they had cooked provisions and prepared purposely for us, but not a whisper was conveyed to the enemy." One of the many who were beguiled by the home cooking and pretty girls later gushed that "this part of our raid was more like a picnic than war."[512]

The East Tennessee & Virginia crewmen had received no official warning that raiders were approaching. Nine months earlier, General Joseph E. Johnston stripped the garrisons of their cavalry, hence they had no mounted lookouts to watch for raiders.[513] Colonel von Sheliha had wired Army headquarters in Richmond that raiders were headed east, but Richmond failed to alert the bridge garrisons of the danger. Von Sheliha did take the additional precaution of sending a rider to notify the stations, but the message failed to arrive. The courier rode "with all possible speed" but was too late. By the time he caught up to the Yankees, the garrison at Strawberry Plains was already surrounded. Realizing that the day was lost, he returned to Knoxville and made no further attempt to warn stations up the line.

Although the pleasant morning may have shown an outward similarity to a Sunday picnic, the expedition soon regained its military countenance. The president of the East Tennessee & Virginia, John R. Branner, had planned to spend a quiet Sunday at home, but his rest was rudely interrupted. Marauding Yankees arrived at ten o'clock and immediately set fire to his company's 300-foot-long railroad bridge. While they waited for the span to plunge into the Holston, they torched the E. T. & V. depot as well.[514]

Mossy Creek was a chance to unwind before the race back to home base began. The troopers were refreshed by a good night's sleep, proud of their success, and elated by the welcome extended by friendly young ladies. And after a long week in the saddle, it was Sunday. The riders were looking for a bit of diversion, and their commander, who had a fun-loving streak of his own, allowed the reins to go slack.

The frolic began just before noon. There were several scenes, and while the details were not reported in the official chronicle, some stories leaked out. Private Harvey Denney, then a nineteen-year-old from Ohio, told one of them. There was a small hotel near the depot, and Private Denney and several buddies decided to look inside. To their surprise, dinner was ready. A payroll train was expected soon, and the cooks had been ordered to have a hot meal ready for the paymaster and crew.

Denney and his friends were farm boys with healthy appetites, and had not eaten since a quick breakfast nearly eight hours earlier. The sight and smell of a hot dinner waiting on the rebel table proved difficult to resist. "About the time we got the dinner finished," Denney recalled, "the whistle blew and in she came." The train chugged right into town, loaded with currency to pay the rebel troops. The Yankees seized the locomotive, cars, crew, and some sixty soldiers. They then cracked the safe, confiscated the cash, and spread it among themselves. "Boys," Denney later reminded his comrades, "did you get your pockets filled with Confederate money?" With pockets bulging with currency, the visitors had no trouble paying their hosts generously. The paymaster and crewmen, however, faced empty plates.[515]

What was basically harmless mischief then took a darker turn. Mossy Creek, like all East Tennessee towns, was politically divided. Its population was largely Unionist, but included an enclave of wealthy secessionists, most of whom were business and professional men or landowners. Most if not all of the secessionist élite owned slaves. Their bondsmen, real property, and personal effects were secure only as long as Confederate bayonets protected them. Yet, for a few fleeting minutes that morning, Old Dixie was down and Old Glory was up. The Unionists had been waiting for just such a changing of the guard, and their hour had come.[516] They knew that the northerners must soon leave, but they would not miss a chance to settle old scores.

The first rebel household to feel their sting belonged to Henry H. Hubbard, a thirty-eight-year-old lawyer and farmer. Hubbard was a wealthy man, who owned eleven slaves and, in 1860, valued his property at $49,000. Hubbard was a bulwark of the Confederate revolution. He served the Confederate States Senate as its Recording Clerk, and the War Department as a contractor, having promised to provide it with 500,000 tons of iron. He and his wife were absent, reportedly visiting their son at school. Hubbard's house was spacious, and on the night before the raiders appeared, his slaves had removed a sizeable store of goods from the East Tennessee & Virginia depot and stashed them inside.[517]

As Hubbard recounted the story, the raiders "seemed to be preparing to leave, when some Unionists of the neighborhood enquired if they were not going to do something for Mr. Hubbard, 'one of the meanest Secesh in the country'? [*sic*]" Heeding their call, raiders poured into the house "by the hundreds, filling every room from garret to cellar."

Hubbard had left his three daughters in the care of his slaves, and all ran away when they saw blue uniforms. The Union men then had a field day, appropriating all of Hubbard's stores and household goods. The household inventory of this "meanest Secesh" provides a glimpse into the lifestyle of an upper-class East Tennessean at the midpoint of the Civil War. Hubbard claimed to have lost 170 boxes of tobacco "valued at least at $15,000"; 160 pounds of coffee "worth to me $800"; from 3,000 to 5,000 pounds of "bacon, mostly hams"; plus "all the preserves, wines, liquors, honey, butter, [and] two or three barrels of fine sugar." After emptying Hubbard's larder, the raiders allegedly seized "all the nice bed clothes that Mrs. H. had got from her mother and her grandmother's estate, besides what we had been accumulating for nearly twenty years, except a few old quilts and blankets." Hubbard contended that "we could not replace our bed clothes for $2500."[518]

Then the intruders changed course. "They broke up, destroyed, and *gave away to their good Union friends* [emphasis added] more than half of my large supply of tableware and cutlery, tablecloths, and silverware." Luxury goods were a sign of a family's social standing, and as the historian Fred Arthur Bailey has shown, Civil War Tennessee was a "land of social cleavages."[519]

Depending on one's point of view, confiscation of Hubbard's silver spoons and passing them out to less fortunate neighbors was either a well-deserved punishment, a form of class warfare, or a theft. In any case, the family wardrobe also fell victim to the intruders. The troopers took "all Mrs. H's, the children's and my own wearing apparel, not leaving us a change of garments," Hubbard grumbled. Significantly, "they tore up Mrs. H's silk dresses and fed their horses on them, on the ground." Silk dresses, tailored suits, and fine silverware symbolized the patrician status which the raiders resented. They also hacked Hubbard's fine furniture to pieces and absconded with the toys of his children.[520]

Many Tennesseans inherited a Jacksonian hatred of banks and bankers, and Hubbard held stock. "They also got about $100,000 of the old Central Bank," he reported, "which I have had in my possession since the bank failed . . . these they went to *putting off immediately in the neighborhood* [emphasis added]." Egged-on, and probably joined by local Unionists, the troopers (or looters), expropriated, confiscated, or stole the property of the hated "Secesh." They seized property in every form they could find, including at least ten slaves, livestock, currency, and merchandise.[521]

Hubbard's neighbors were not spared. The wrath of the Union revolutionaries spread to other households, like flames before the wind. The number of secessionist victims is uncertain, but those who have been identified were all wealthy slaveowners living in spacious houses. All but one were men, and all either had a financial interest in the East Tennessee & Virginia railroad or were closely dependent on it.

John R. Branner of the E.T. & V. was a prime example. Before the war, he estimated his net worth to be $35,000 in real estate and $180,000 in "personal property," most of which were slaves, of whom he owned thirty-eight. His house was trashed, as was the home of his younger brother, Benjamin M. Branner, likewise a stockholder in the E.T. & V. Though Benjamin Branner was just thirty years old, the value of his property was $20,000 in real estate and $30,000 in personal effects. He owned four slaves. The E.T. & V. station agent in Strawberry Plains, William W. Stringfield, was an avid defender of slavery and a Confederate provost marshal. He resided there with his widowed mother, brother, and sister. Though not as wealthy as the Branners or the Hubbards, the Stringfield family holdings totaled $19,500 in real estate and $10,600 in personal property, including six slaves. The Stringfield place was also trashed.[522]

All this property was taken, Hubbard complained bitterly, "from good Southern men," but Unionists were left unscathed. "Thus they reward our enemies and punish our friends," he growled.[523] The storehouses at Mossy Creek were bulging with contraband, and the men set to work with enthusiasm. Their inventory of ruined or confiscated items was rich: two hundred barrels of sugar and a large cache of corn, bacon, and other supplies being stored for the army. They also destroyed a locomotive and its train of cars.[524]

Some of the raiders loaded their horses with corn for the animals and their own use. Others preferred to stuff their saddlebags with tobacco, "believing," Major Tristram Dow of the 112th Illinois commented acidly, "this weed of more advantage to them than forage for their exhausted horses." Although Dow was sure that "there were none of this class in his regiment," he was mistaken. After the war, one of his men admitted that "the boys loaded themselves and horses with tobacco to carry back to their comrades in camp, but for several reasons very little of it was ever delivered to them."

The invaders also seized a considerable amount of Confederate States currency. As the bridges blazed and the plundering proceeded, a raider recounted that "the rebs are watching the bridge burners from the mountaintops, and swearing vengeance."[525]

With the Mossy Creek bridge engulfed in flames, Sanders turned his men toward the safety of their Kentucky refuge. They departed about noon, but not before making one more quick and destructive stop. About two and a half miles from Mossy Creek they wrecked a gun factory owned by Ratton Howell. A machine shop being used to manufacture guns received the same treatment—the men burned the building and smashed its machinery. They also demolished a saltpeter factory, along with its machinery and several hundred barrels of saltpeter.[526]

Sanders's plan was to head north at flank speed and cross over the mountains before they could be intercepted. "I knew every exertion was being made on the part of the enemy to capture my command," he mused. The party crossed the Holston at Hayworth's Bend and then dashed toward Powder Springs Gap of Clinch Mountain, seven miles north of the river.[527]

Powder Springs

The weary raiders reached Powder Springs Gap in the afternoon of Monday, June 22, after a twelve-mile ride. Two days earlier, just as Sanders and his men bid goodbye to Knoxville, the Confederates crafted a plan to block their escape. Colonel von Sheliha inferred that after leaving Strawberry Plains, Sanders would attempt to make his way back to Kentucky via the village of Rogersville and then escape through either Big Creek, Moccasin, or Mulberry Gap.[528]

He was mistaken. Sanders actually planned to stay thirty-five miles west of Rogersville and pass though Powder Springs Gap. When Sanders and his men arrived at Powder Springs Gap, they met a "large force" of cavalry blocking their escape. This unit, which was probably part of General Pegram's command, may have numbered as many as two thousand men. Meanwhile, another strong force caught up with the rear guard and began skirmishing with it. Trapped by enemy forces in front and at the rear, Sanders devised yet another ruse.

He pretended to attack, sending a strong line of skirmishers directly forward "in plain view" of the blocking force. Then, just as the forward ranks reached a convenient crossroad, they wheeled abruptly left, spurred their horses, and went "at break-neck speed in another direction." The rebels pursued, but after several sharp skirmishes with a rear-guard unit, darkness set in to mask the Yankee escape.[529]

In their flight, the northerners turned to back roads, where once again a loyal woman came forth as their guardian angel. "We had not gone far," remembered an Illinois trooper appreciatively, "until we saw a woman come out of a house, some distance from the road, waving her sunbonnet and calling for us to stop. She came to us and told us that a brigade of rebels was formed across the road just in front of us waiting for us to come up. We noticed a fork in the road not far in advance. The woman told us that the enemy were formed upon the left hand road, as that was the one leading towards the mountains. We took the right

The Sanders Raid
June 14 - 24, 1863

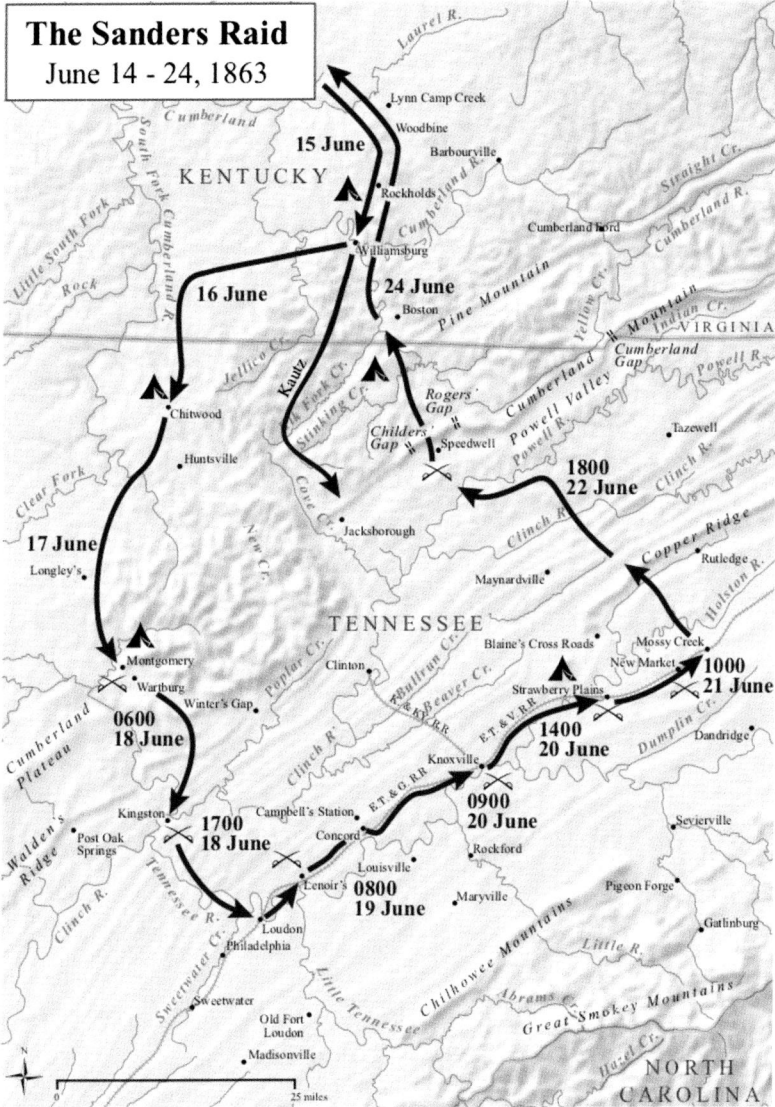

Map 1. The Sanders Raid.

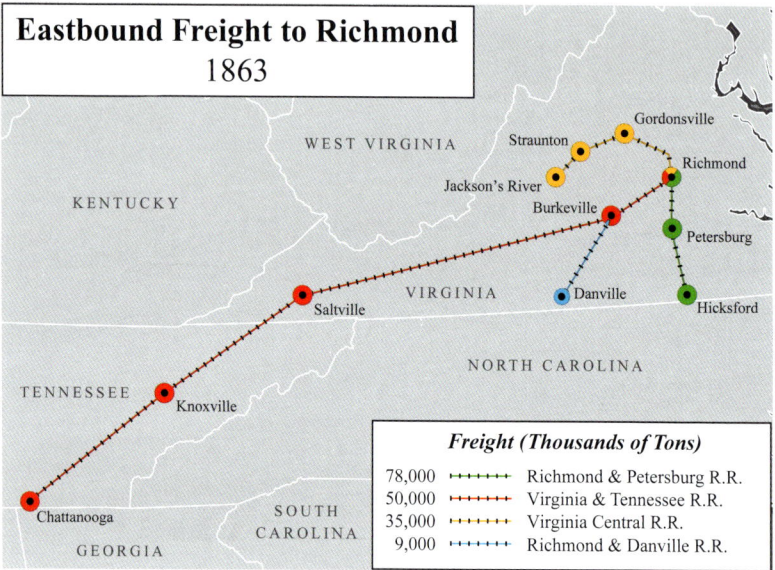

Map 2. Eastbound Freight to Richmond, 1863.

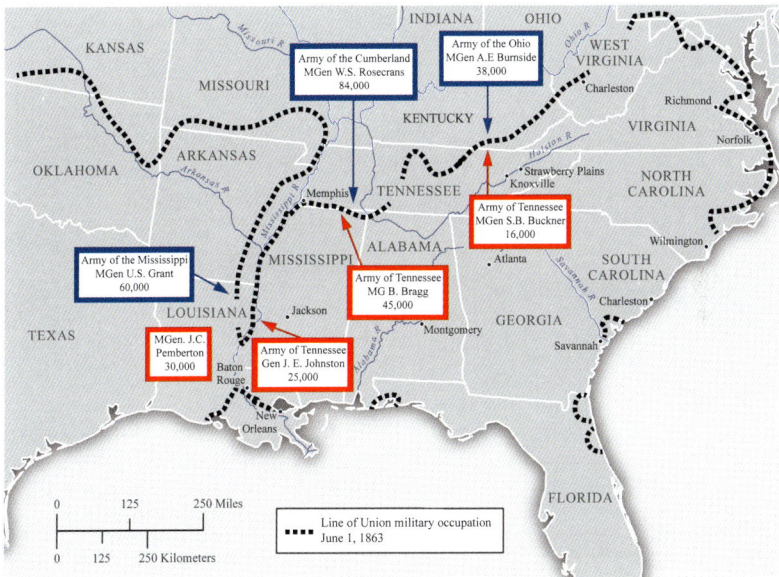

Map 3. Strength of the Armies, June 1, 1863.

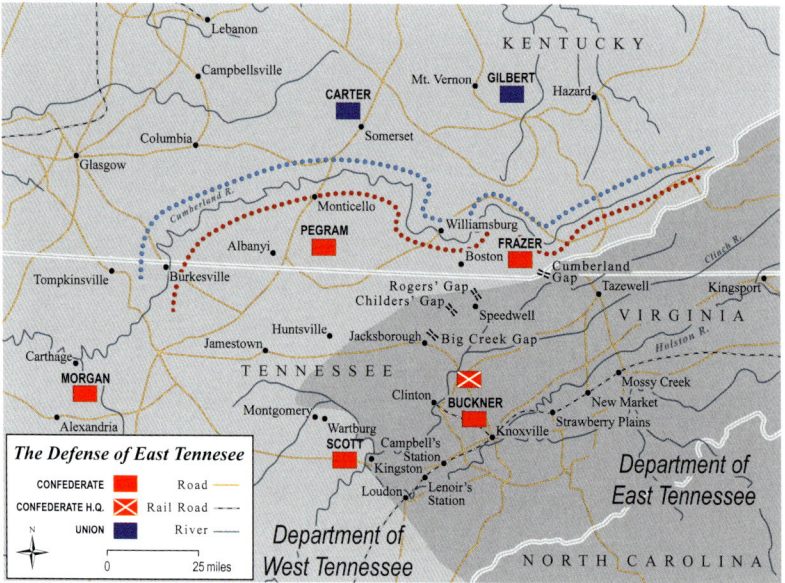

Map 4. The Defense of East Tennesee.

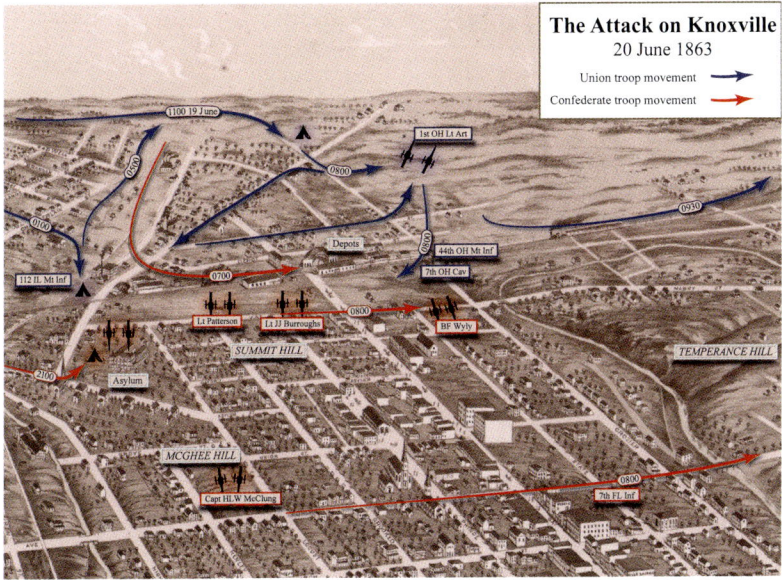

The Attack on Knoxville
20 June 1863

Union troop movement
Confederate troop movement

1100 19 June
0800
1st OH Lt Art
0950
Depots
44th OH Mt Inf
7th OH Cav
112 IL Mt Inf
0700
Lt Patterson
Lt JJ Burroughs
0800
BF Wyly
SUMMIT HILL
TEMPERANCE HILL
2100
Asylum
MCGHEE HILL
0800
Capt HLW McClung
7th FL Inf

Map 5. The Attack on Knoxville.

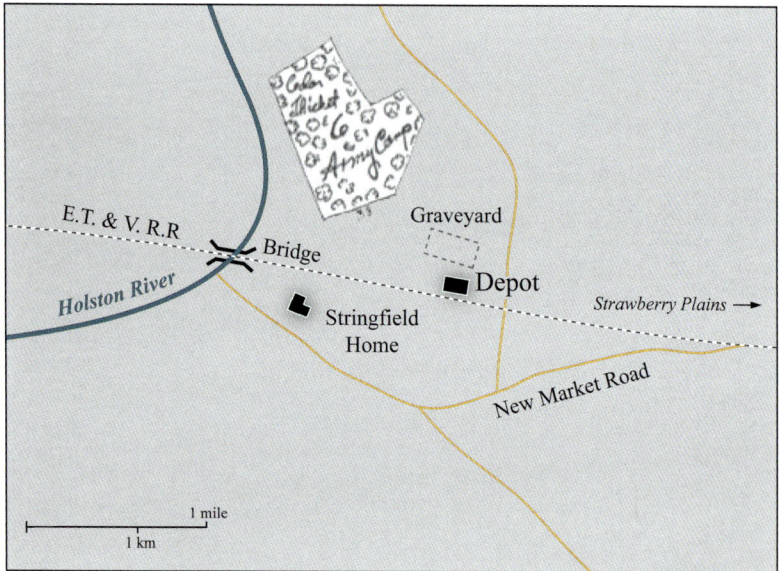

Map 6. Strawberry Plains. The Confederates knew that enemy cavalry were approaching from the west, following the East Tennessee and Virginia tracks. A locomotive kept up a head of steam, and when the Yankees appeared a few defenders managed to escape by rail. The remainder found cover behind the stone wall which surrounded the Stringfield cemetery or in the thicket where the Confederates camped. Since Sanders seldom attacked from the direction the enemy expected (west, in this case), he forded the Holston at a shallow point a couple of miles west of the bridge, then circled around and approached from the south. He divided his men into two units. The 44th Ohio remained close to the river, but the main body (including the 1st Ohio artillery) occupied a hill which overlooked the railroad from the south. Outnumbered by at least four to one, and facing well-positioned cannon, the Confederates exchanged fire briefly and then surrendered.

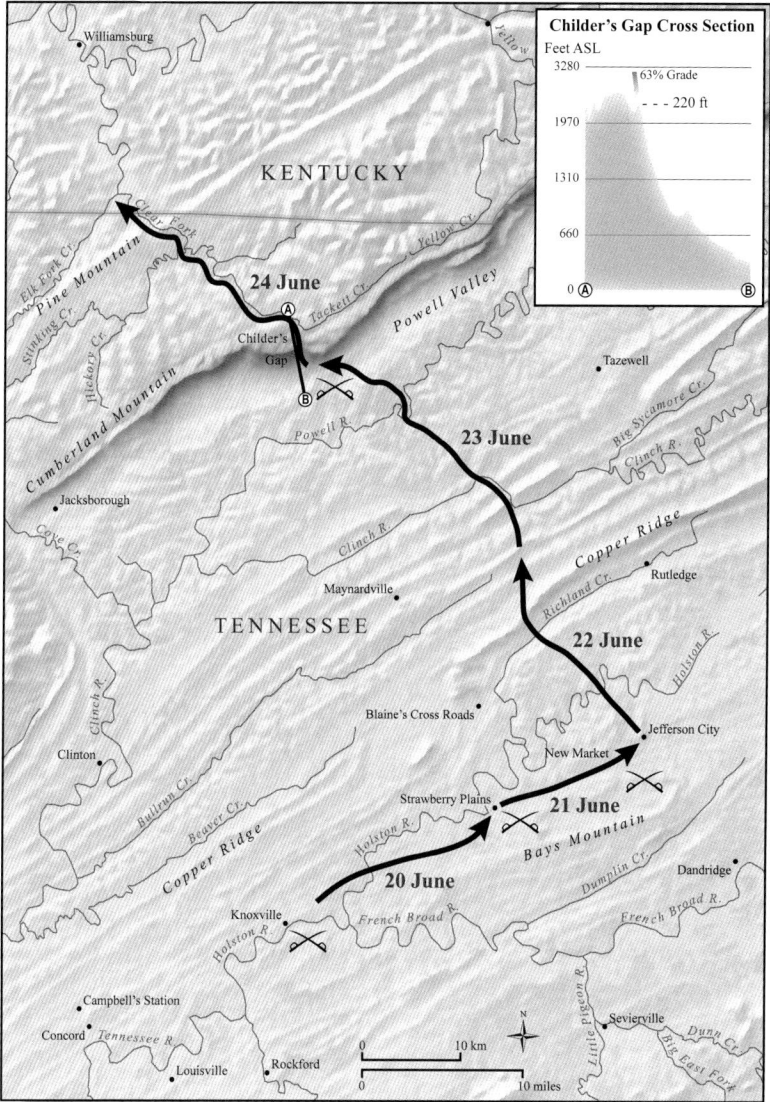

Map 7. Escape Route.

hand road [eastern], and riding quietly past the rebel line, struck across toward the other road and went on our way." One Yankee looking for a better horse was observed by Scott's cavalry, who chased him back to Sanders's main force. In that way the Confederates learned that the Yankees had dodged their trap.[530]

During the night of June 21 Sanders led his men toward the Clinch River, another seven miles north of Powder Springs. About ten o'clock they overtook a train of baggage wagons, the rear of a large enemy force ahead. They captured and paroled thirty wagoneers and then made a bonfire of their wagons. The wagons contained mainly flour, but the raiders also seized the luggage of one of the rebel generals, plus his unit's paymaster and treasury. The Yankees had some amusement with the Confederate cash. "We placed the paymaster in good shape to settle his accounts by borrowing his funds, so he could account for all he was out as having been captured by the enemy. The boys distributed a million or two of Confederate money, and I stuffed ninety-odd thousand dollars of it in my horse's empty nose sack," remembered a raider.[531]

Troopers of the 2nd Ohio were in the van, but some became so exhausted that they fell asleep in their saddles, snarling the entire march. When troopers in the middle of the column fell asleep, everyone behind them halted, and some of them fell asleep for an hour or two. Some troopers even dropped to the ground without waking up, remembered an astonished Ohioan, "and cry as children cry when disturbed." Somehow the men of the 7th Ohio lost their way and found themselves "in dense woods on a mere path." After groping about for two hours, they finally found the right track, but having fallen far behind the others they had to ride hard until dawn to catch up with their comrades.[532]

Early in the morning, after about ten more miles of hard riding, the Yankees found shallow water where they could ford the Clinch. In the process of crossing, they had yet another narrow escape. An Ohio boy described the crossing as "a trying ordeal"; there was more skirmishing and a captain was shot. After briefly stopping on the bank of the Clinch to feed their horses and to finish the last of their rations, the expedition headed toward the Powell River, about seven miles farther on. They forded the Powell at about noon, and then headed toward Rogers Gap. There was little fighting but much apprehension, when late in the afternoon they approached Rogers Gap.[533]

Rogers Gap was filled with rebels. With enemy forces of unknown strength both ahead and behind, they were in grave peril. The fate of the bridge burners of 1861 offered a frightening example of what might happen if they were captured. "We knew they had sworn vengeance upon us, and we believed that capture would be certain and speedy death. We doubted whether the acts we had done were authorized by the laws of civilized warfare, and therefore none of us intended to be taken prisoners."[534]

There was ample reason to be worried. The code of lawful warfare was both hotly contested and highly unsettled. The United States Army had adopted its General Order No. 100 ("the Lieber code") which would generally justify the actions of the Sanders raiders, but the Davis administration disagreed. On June 24, only three days after the raiders burned bridges at Strawberry Plains and Mossy Creek, Confederate Secretary of War James Seddon issued a sweeping repudiation. Seddon denounced the Lieber code as "barbarous" and declared it to be an excuse for "acts of atrocity and violence." Seddon also specifically accused the U.S. Army of committing the war crime of "incendiarism."[535] Just what he meant was uncertain, but since East Tennessee was littered by the ashes of bridges, depots, and rail ties, the raiders were justifiably wary of capture by soldiers who considered "incendiarism" to be a war crime.

Sanders and his men reached Rogers Gap at about 3 o'clock in the afternoon and found what they feared. Peering through the edge of the timber, they saw a mile-wide valley filled with enemy soldiers moving about in all directions. Sanders later reported that "on arriving within a mile and a half of Rogers Gap, I found that it was blockaded by fallen timber and strongly guarded by artillery and infantry, and that all the gaps practicable were obstructed and guarded in similar manner."[536] With no good choices, he diverted his force toward Smith's Gap, which was located four miles to the west. Before leaving for the alternate escape route, Sanders's men took axes and cut the spokes out of the wheels on their artillery trains. After the guns fell to the ground, they spiked them. They turned their extra horses and mules loose, saving some for mounts for the artillerymen.[537]

Sanders ordered a column of men to circle back through heavy timber and find a way to reach Smith's Gap. Sanders's chief scout, Sgt. William "Stud" Reynolds, of the 1st East Tennessee, marked a seven-mile trail to the gap, while a thirty-man contingent of the 7th Ohio was left behind as a rear guard. Their orders were that they must "hold the ford" of the Powell River for one hour. This was more easily said than done, and one frightened Buckeye told his diary that "Minutes seem like hours. It is the longest sixty minutes in the calendar of my life." The Ohioans were able to use large boulders as natural defenses, but the sentry saw "a long line of dust coming, and we know what that means. The suspense is fearful. We do a little sharp-shooting, and the watch is creeping forward." When a courier finally arrived with a message to "join the command as soon as possible," the Ohioans mounted up for a wild gallop to catch up to their friends.[538]

When the tired Ohioans arrived, they were told to hold the rear for yet another hour until the escape path was clear. Posting themselves on some high ground, they held for the allotted time, then threw away their baggage and spurred their mounts for another six-mile ride. They rejoined the main force while it still faced the enemy force blocking Rogers Gap.[539]

The scouts then piloted the entire force toward Smith's Gap. Fully mindful of the dangers ahead, but knowing there was no other option, a raider remarked dryly, "[we] tightened our belts around us, and formed in line." When the leading element reached the gap, they found it protected by only a single regiment, the 5th Georgia Cavalry. Major Tristram Dow, directing the raiders' forward units, ordered the 45th Ohio and the 112th Illinois to take the lead. Dow then commanded his men to clear the way for the main force.[540]"

"We rode down the ridge toward the valley quietly, in line of battle," remembered Captain James McCartney of the 112th. "We reached the foot of the ridge, and rode out into the plain at a walk toward a line of rebel infantry and cavalry a few hundred yards in front of us. When within a couple of hundred yards of them they seem to have discovered for the first time who we were. Driving the spurs into the sides of our horses, we charged, helter-skelter, upon and over them and struck straight for the side of the mountain in front. We started up its side, and the rebel forces by thousands closed in around its foot, and bringing their artillery, shelled us as we went up." The Georgians made their "hasty retreat" after receiving a volley from the 1st East Tennessee Mounted Infantry.[541]

An Ohioan in the rear guard who arrived just in time to join the "wild rush" across the valley, described a terrifying scene: "The artillery boys are spiking their guns and cutting harness to bits—crying and swearing the while. The conviction is that we are bagged." He remembered that the order (to move) "Forward!" was delivered in a tone of desperation and fright rather than as a calm and clear directive.

The raiders scrambled up the sheer side of the mountain, abandoning their horses out of necessity. They had found not even a footpath, and the base of the mountain was rugged and steep. But with enemy cannon behind them and their only chance of escape before them, they began to climb.[542]

Snake's Den

Their choices were grim: climb a steep mountain while being bombarded by artillery and musketry, or surrender and face prison, or even execution. Luckily, an Ohio boy remembered, "the rebels do not grasp the idea at first that we can escape this way, but when they do, they rush at us like madmen." Now it was the Yankees' turn to fight from the high ground. From a position halfway up the hill, they successfully fended off their pursuers until nightfall. The night was dark, the air was hot, and the only way out was up. Canteens were empty and hundreds of sweaty, parched, and haggard men searched for water. None was found until they cleared the first ridge and dropped into an adjacent valley, where they discovered a stagnant pool. After gulping deeply from this puddle, they fell asleep in "a confused mass." In the race to escape they had become so disorganized, that no ten men of any single unit slept near their comrades.[543]

Rushing up the mountain in the midst of the skirmish, a rear-guard unit composed of the 54th Ohio and 112th Illinois became separated from the main force, took a wrong path, and again lost their way. Meanwhile, most of the main body continued on and found a safe passageway. The main force climbed through Childers Gap, but it was slow going. The Cumberland escarpment in this region is very steep, rising from 500 to 1,200 feet above the floor of the Powell River valley. "The road through this pass is only a bridle-path and very rough," explained Sanders, and they did not get up the mountain until well after dark.[544]

Another group, under the command of Captain Richard Rankin of the 7th Ohio, also got lost. "The night being very dark and no road, not even a path to follow, nor any mounted guide left to guide them, they worked their way over rocks and timber in the direction they supposed the column had moved, and became scattered," Rankin recalled. He then commenced his personal adventure:

"After climbing around over the rocks, amid the darkness of the night, I found myself on the highest peak of the mountain, accompanied by one man. I wandered about for some time and heard no human voice save the tumult at the foot of the mountain"

"I struck out in what I supposed a northerly direction and after passing over several high ridges and coming to a cliff that had to be descended, and not thinking it safe to make the trial at night, we spread our blanket down, tied our horses, and went to sleep, being very much exhausted; and upon waking in the morning found the sun high up and no noise to be heard save the singing of the birds and the gnawing of my faithful horse on the trees. I at once arose, but finding no way to get my horse down this cliff other than southward, I was compelled to abandon him . . . I hated to part with so valuable [a] servant that had carried me safely through the campaign of '61, through Kentucky and Tennessee to Corinth, Mississippi, back to Ohio and through all the wanderings of the 7th Ohio Volunteer Cavalry, including this masterly 'raid,' being yet good in flesh and unbroken in spirit; to part with such a friend was no light affair. But with all the horrors of Libby Prison on one hand and life and liberty on the other, I was not long in making up my mind [on] which course to pursue"[545]

"I stripped my horse of everything and bid him adieu. Taking a strap from the saddle, I buckled my blankets together, ran my saber through, threw it over my shoulder and began my descent, and upon reaching the foot found myself in a deep dell, surrounded by high peaks of craggy rocks. The timber being overgrown with laurel through which ran a brook of clear water.

"After refreshing myself, I followed the stream for about two miles, which brought me to a stream known as Clear Fork, which I followed for a few miles, coming to a miserable old hut in which lived two old people, who had passed their four-score years, and in coming to this hovel I heard considerable talking"

"I sent my companion to eavesdrop, and when he returned he reported 'all right.' On entering the house I found ten or twelve of our own soldiers, among them a grandson of the occupants of the house. The old man was grinding corn on a hand mill, while the old lady was baking bread and cakes for the hungry soldiers. I ate a few morsels and explained to them where my horse had been left."

"The old gentleman gave me some encouragement by saying he thought he could get the horse. I told him he should have fifty dollars upon delivering the horse to me, and he at once started in search for him, while I spread my blanket and went to sleep"

"The old man returned in the evening without the horse. I procured a guide and set by footpath over the mountains, traveling all night, reaching London, Kentucky, twenty-four hours in advance of the command. [We reached] Lancaster on the 1st of July, being twenty days out. The men suffered greatly for want of sleep and from the swelling of their limbs, caused by constant riding"[546]

At the base of the mountain, the lost collection of Ohioans and Illinoisans were also scrambling up the rock field, while being chased by enemy soldiers in hot pursuit. The northerners, mostly farm boys from the prairies of Ohio and Illinois, were unaccustomed to climbing such steep slopes, and certainly never under fire. As Major Dow of the 112th observed with much understatement, "the men little knew what going up a mountain meant."[547] Since their lives and freedom were at stake, the flatlanders caught on quickly.

Captain James McCartney, who commanded Company G of the 112th Illinois, described their flight in a wartime letter to his wife. Using this letter to refresh his memory, and in collaboration with his companions, McCartney prepared the most complete, first-hand account of the escapade.[548] His story merits quotation at length:

"The mountain side was so rough and ragged that we could not ride, and dismounting, we hauled and lifted and pushed the horses over rocks, ravines and fallen timber, until it became dark. It was a very hot night, and our throats were parched with thirst and filled with dust.

Every man was acting for himself. Most of the 112th men kept together, however, and helped each other along, but it so happened that we got into the worst part of the mountain and our progress was slow. We did not reach the top until about midnight, and when we did reach it the remainder of the force had long before passed on, taking all the guides with them, and we knew not in what direction or where to go.

But the worst of all was, that we found that the rebels were amongst us. We heard men whispering and conferring together near us, and sometimes in the starlight we could see men with white rebel blankets around them, moving around among the trees. We here held a council as to what we should do.

We concluded that our only hope of safety was to wait until moonlight or daylight, and then try to find our way out. We did not dare follow anyone, for we might be following a rebel right into their lines. Many times persons would call to us to come that way or this way; but we did not dare follow them. We were suffering terribly from thirst, and concluded first to search for water. None had been seen since we came up the mountain side, and the only hope we had of getting any was by digging for it.

It was so dark that we could not see a favorable place to dig, so we tied our horses to trees and went along feeling with our feet for places in the ground where we would be most likely to find water. I had my naked sword in my hand and was using it to part the bushes and discover any obstacle in the dark. Presently I thought I felt a depression in the ground, and the dead leaves under my feet rustled as if they were somewhat damp.

As I was about to get down on my knees to dig with my hands, suddenly there sounded at my feet the loud rattle of a rattlesnake, and instantly it seemed as if a hundred snakes were rattling on every side of us. We knew at once we were in a rattlesnake den. We stood perfectly still and after a minute or two of continuous rattling it gradually ceased. I then took my sword, and after striking it around me in every direction, step by step walked out until we reached a fallen tree, and getting on that were safely out of the den.

But we got no water. We concluded then that we would lie down and rest until it became light enough to see where we were going. We, seven men of Co. G, lay down together, and the next thing I remember was feeling a pain in my side, and suddenly waking up I saw that it was daylight, and that it was [Sgt. Thomas] Townsend's elbow that was giving me pain. Tom whispered to me that two men in gray uniforms had come to where we were, looked at us, whispered together for a minute or two, pointed down the mountain to where the rebels were, and had just that moment gone away.

We woke up all the men at once, and fortunately finding our horses near us, started away to the north. We found that we were going down the north side of the mountain, and we soon heard the sound of water in front of us, and instantly men and horses, all together, made a rush in the direction of the sound. Lying down, some in and some on the bank of the small mountain rivulet, we enjoyed a drink of pure mountain water.

When we had satisfied our thirst we began to consider what was the best to do. About forty of us were together. We concluded that every outlet from the mountains must by this time be guarded, and that our best chance would be to abandon our horses and try to steal our way through the mountains. We concluded that it would be hopeless to try to fight, as that would only delay us and bring the whole rebel force upon our track. We therefore broke up and destroyed our guns, revolvers, and swords, cut up our saddles and bridles, threw away all surplus clothing and divested ourselves of everything that would delay or retard us.

I had to part with my little gray mare that had carried me over every obstacle, that had eaten hardtack out of my hand when I had nothing else to give her, and that I always found by my side when I wanted her. She had become a pet and was as dear to me as any friend I ever had. I was not the only one, however, of our party who shed tears when parting forever from our noble horses. I had about a quart of corn meal in a sack, which I divided, taking a pint in my pants pocket and gave the remainder to my horse.

We started from here toward the north in Indian file, three of the men with us keeping their guns and some ammunition. At about ten o'clock in the morning we came in sight of a clearing on the side of the mountain. By gathering a piece here and there from one and another, we finally secured a suit of citizen's clothing, and selecting one of the longest haired, lankiest and most awkward looking soldier[s] in the squad, we dressed him as a Tennessee mountaineer . . . and sent him to the house in the clearing.

In a few minutes he came out and motioned to us. A few of us went down to the house, and there we found Maj. Dow. We also found hidden in the house a genuine Tennessee mountaineer, whom we at once pressed into service as a guide. We doubted his loyalty to the Union, but we placed him in front, and two men with guns immediately behind him, and instructed the men in his hearing that at the first sign of danger to at once shoot the guide. We then told him to guide us by the most unfrequented paths to the Cumberland River.

But we found nothing whatever to eat, as the people in these mountains seemed to be poorer than the rocks themselves. We started on our long journey and marched all the first day, occasionally finding some of our men scattered along our route. [By] the evening of the first day we had two hundred men, but only nine guns among the whole number. We kept on all the first night [June 23]. At daylight we lay down in the woods and slept until about nine o'clock, when we got up and away again.

At about 11 o'clock we came to a little cabin in the mountains, occupied by a woman and two or three children, and searched it for something to eat, but found nothing. We finally saw a little fenced in lot near the house, and . . . found a bed of young cabbages with a few small leaves on. We made for them, and in less than two minutes the cabbag[e] lot was a bleak and desolate plain. I got one small plant for my share, and ate it root, branch, dirt, and all.

We traveled all day the 24th and about two o'clock in the afternoon we came to another mountain cabin occupied by two women and some children, but here they did not even have a few cabbage plants to eat. We finally convinced them that we were Union soldiers trying to escape, when they told us that their husbands had gone through to Kentucky and were then in the Union army. They then brought out from a bed-tick a peck of corn meal and offered it to us, but assured us that it was everything they had in the world to eat, and as we saw five or six children around the house, hungry as we were, we refused to touch their meal.

They told us that two separate companies of rebel cavalry had been at their house that day inquiring for "Yanks," and saying that a lot of them were lost in the mountains somewhere. They told the women they were going to catch and hang them as soon as found, for these "Yanks" had been murdering people and burning houses all through East Tennessee. The women cautioned us to be very careful, as the mountains were filled with rebels. They gave our guide full instructions... and wishing us all sorts of good fortune, sent us on.

Near sundown this day we suddenly came to a well-traveled highway, crossing our path at right angles. There was no way to avoid crossing it, but it was a dangerous point, and we believed that every place along this road must be guarded. We finally found a dense thicket of low bushes extending up the side of the road. We got into this thicket and arranged that one man at a time should cross the road as rapidly as possible, at the same time looking up and down the road and giving warning if anyone was seen, when all would scatter and do the best they could to save themselves. About sundown we were safely across, without discovery.

Going a couple of hundred yards into the woods we concluded to camp, as we were utterly worn out. A party was sent out to reconnoiter, and about nine o'clock that night came in with a side of bacon. We divided this up as well as we could, but it did not go far with two hundred men. I got a piece of pure fat an inch long and about as large around as my fore finger. We ate our meat raw, in the dark; and this was the first and only bite of food of any kind any of us had since four days before, except the handful of meal I had in my pocket, which I divided with some of my comrades. We lay down on the dry leaves and soon forgot our troubles and dangers in sweet and refreshing sleep. The night was so quiet and still that it seemed as if the stillness could almost be felt. It did not seem that the danger was from any living thing, but as if something ghostly or supernatural was near me.

Presently I heard a rustling in the dead leaves near me. I thought at once that some wild animals were among us. But in a moment I heard the leaves rustling in several directions.

I then thought that the enemy were among us at last, and that we would be captured just as we began to think there was some hope of our escape. Perhaps they were quietly numbering our men in their heavy sleep ... I was about to creep away and escape, when I thought I recognized Major Dow's whisper by my side. I reached my hand out and touched him and whispered very low, "Is this you, Major?" He replied, "Yes, but don't move or speak yet."

He took my hand and led me quietly off, where we found Captain [John] Dow and some other officers. The major then whispered, "Here is a little girl, fourteen years old, who lives at the house where we found the women this afternoon. She says that very soon after we left the house fifteen hundred rebel cavalry came to the house on our trail, swearing vengeance against us." They asked the women which way we had gone, how many there were of us, and swore they were going to hang us whenever they found us.

The women told them we had gone in a different direction from the one we really took, but the rebels did not believe them, and were then on our track. She also said the women, one of whom was her mother, got her out and told her to take through the mountains ahead of the rebels, and warn us of the danger.

The little girl had come on this dark night over seven miles through the rough wild mountains, filled with savage animals and poisonous serpents, to tell us of our danger. While she was whispering this to us we heard the clank of sabers on the road near us. It was the rebel cavalry passing along the road. We listened, but they passed by without discovering us. We asked the little girl, small of her age and but a child, what we could do for her. She told us that she wanted nothing, and now that she had found and told us, she would go back home. We offered to send a guard with her, but she said she was not afraid and wanted no guard.

The Major lighted a match and found that it was one o'clock in the morning. The Major asked if any of us had any money, and everyone contributed all the money he had, and we thus raised seven dollars and a few cents and gave it to the girl. It was all we could do. She refused the money, and seemed astonished that we thought she had done anything worthy of thanks even. But we finally forced the money upon her, and each one pressed her hand and thanked her for what she had done for us. We took up our lonely walk again, leaving her to make the best of her way home through the lonely mountains.

We never heard of her afterwards. I have no doubt the courage and loyalty of that little girl saved many, if not all, of our lives; She gave us her name, but I am sorry to say I have forgotten it. How I should like to see and thank again that brave loyal little mountain girl, for her brave act.

We marched all that night and the day following, and the next evening reached the settlements at the foot of the mountains, near the Cumberland River. We were still inside the enemy's lines, but felt comparatively safe, and as we were suffering from hunger separated to search for food. The men of Co. G remained together, and finding a farm house we got a good supper and a place to sleep. The next day we crossed the river and four days afterward joined our forces."

The wayward troopers reached safety shortly after they left Tennessee. Their destination was Boston, Kentucky, a hamlet nestled at the base of Pine Mountain, about one mile north of the Tennessee border. True to its namesake, Kentucky's Boston was a proudly Unionist settlement. A Florida Confederate passing through in 1862 found it disgusting. "Every person in it are Lincolnites," he complained. Yet, small as it was, Boston furnished a welcome haven for those who were fleeing the Confederate rifles.[549]

The main body of the brigade had been much more fortunate than the Ohio and Illinois men. It had proceeded unopposed after they passed through Childers Gap. The Ohioans and Illinoisans straggled into Boston two days after Sanders's arrival. Colonel Sanders and his men continued north without delay and reached Mount Vernon in mid-afternoon on Friday, June 26. Major Dow remained about twenty-five miles behind the leaders and stayed at London, Kentucky, that evening.[550]

When all elements finally united at Mount Vernon, they received a warm welcome. In his first report to Major General Henry W. Halleck, then the General-in-Chief in Washington, General Burnside commended the brigade warmly: "[Sanders] and his command deserve great credit for their patience, endurance, and gallantry." In a later report, Burnside hailed the expedition as "one of the boldest raids of the war." Unlike the short rations which had barely sustained the comrades in the darkest hours of their adventure, back in Kentucky there would plenty of glory for all to share.[551]

CHAPTER FIFTEEN

Assessment

TELEGRAPH LINES CRACKLED. Promptly upon Sanders's return to Kentucky, General Burnside spread the welcome news. On June 26 a bulletin bearing a Cincinnati dateline appeared in major East Coast newspapers. The *New York Herald* deemed Sanders's feat worthy of a front-page headline, and its story featured a map showing how the raiders had returned to their base safely and victoriously.

The news circulated throughout the South as well. On July 1, only six days after northern newspapers published Sanders's initial report, Confederate papers reprinted it. The *Richmond Dispatch* published his report verbatim, and four days later the *Knoxville Register* followed suit.[552] Civilian and military leaders, on both sides, proceeded to appraise the raid's effect. A first step was to estimate the amount of wreckage caused by the raiders, a matter about which neither side agreed. A corollary issue was the difficulty in repairing the damage, and again there was no agreement.

The investigation by Confederate military authorities was the most exhaustive, for sound reason. The raiders had passed through the Cumberland Wall, unobserved and unimpeded, and it was likely that the Army of the Ohio meant to strike again. The Confederates needed to identify the persons and/or procedures which were at fault and to make corrections without delay. They dared not leave the fissure open.

Besides the physical destruction, the raid had intangible effects. The Unionists in East Tennessee had been silenced for two years, but the raid gave them a moment of hope, however brief. There was a sizeable community of Tennessee expatriates in Ohio, and after two years in exile the news of the raid gave them good reason to celebrate. Conversely, the secessionist element in Knoxville was rattled. Two years of battlefield success had given them a sense of security, but blue uniforms within their sight tested their composure.

Both sides also addressed the question of *why* the raid succeeded. They agreed on almost nothing else, but in this case, they independently reached much the same conclusion. Both gave large measures of credit to East Tennessee Unionists for shaping the outcome of the event.

"Immense Destruction"

The *Baltimore American* proclaimed that the raid caused "Immense Destruction of Railroad Bridges and Other Property."[553] The *American* account was hyperbolic but not unreasonable. Though Sanders failed to raze the great bridge at Loudon, wreckage of the secondary targets was extensive. In his reports Sanders listed three bridges burned: Slate Creek (312 feet), Strawberry Plains (1600 feet), and Mossy Creek (325 feet).

His men also seized ten pieces of artillery, 200 boxes of artillery ammunition, and about 1,000 small arms. The list of prisoners contained 461 names. Stores destroyed included salt, sugar, flour, and saltpeter (plus one saltpeter works).

All this came with the loss of two killed, five drowned, five wounded, and twenty-seven missing. Sanders also acknowledged the loss of "a number of horses" plus two cannon. The tally was not trivial. According to a Union officer, the loss was about three hundred animals, though a Confederate placed the count at twice that number. The rebels may have captured between 600 and 700 mounts, and they were prime stock.[554]

General Burnside rated the destruction of the Strawberry Plains bridge as the raid's signal achievement. Along with the damage to the other bridges and trackage, the raid complicated the Confederacy's transportation problems, providing a boon to the Union. On June 23, only two days after the bridges burned, General Rosecrans and the Army of the Cumberland launched a long-delayed offensive against Tullahoma. Rosecrans may have gained his confidence in part because the severed rail artery safeguarded his left (eastern) flank. On July 1, the Confederates evacuated Tullahoma. The Union offensive succeeded as planned.[555]

For the Confederates, travel by rail from Richmond to Chattanooga was still possible, but only by crossing the Holston River by ferry. Passengers or freight requiring an all-rail route had to veer far to the south and pass through either Charlotte or Wilmington, North Carolina, then continue through Atlanta. These routes were considerably slower. The route which Sanders severed (Richmond to Chattanooga via Knoxville) stretched 552 miles, but going through Charlotte added 270 miles, while going by way of Wilmington added 340 miles. The Knoxville route included five railroad companies but did not involve a switch in track gauge. The two longer routes required as many as seven firms, and several different rail widths. The gaps in the Knoxville route did not bring east-west traffic to a halt, but the break did cause significant delay.[556]

What was not certain was how long the Knoxville connection would remain obstructed. Burnside spoke with a victor's assurance: "Intelligent men from that neighborhood assert that it will take months to rebuild it." Yet the losses could be minimized if the bridges could be patched more quickly, which was exactly what the southerners resolved to do.[557]

An "Affair of Lilliputian Dimensions"

In an effort to belittle its effects, a Floridian dismissed the raid as an "affair of Lilliputian dimensions." Similarly, a Tennessean characterized the damage as only "a trifling matter." Major General Simon Buckner, the senior officer in the field, was also eager to downgrade the harm. On June 24 Buckner wired Secretary of War James Seddon to assure him that he would have the track and small trestles repaired in just four days, and a new trestle bridge completed in just two weeks. "After that time there will be no delay or transfer of freight," Buckner promised. In the meantime, he vowed to send a steamer to Strawberry Plains to transport freight across the Holston.[558]

Secretary Seddon was not so quick to discount the seriousness of the damage and doubted whether repairs to such a massive structure could be completed so quickly. He forwarded a copy of Buckner's report to the Confederate Engineer Bureau with a query attached: "Do you understand how General Buckner can so speedily renew the bridges? It makes the damage to us less serious than supposed."[559]

Seddon's skepticism was warranted. Bridge repair is slow work in any age, but it was particularly sluggish in the South during the war, when cavalry attacks, bureaucratic wrangling, labor and equipment shortages, and deferred maintenance bedeviled the southern railroad network. Carpenters skilled in bridge repair were either serving on active duty or had found better-paying jobs in government munitions factories. The War Department kept responsibility for bridge reconstruction firmly in the hands of the Corps of Engineers. The Engineers showed imagination by prefabricating portable bridge frames which were held in readiness, in anticipation of bridge outages, but ingenuity and improvisation alone could not entirely prevent interruptions in service or keep rail beds from deteriorating.[560]

Burnside guessed that repairs would take "some months" while Buckner thought that rebel engineers could finish in two weeks. Unfortunately, surviving records do not entirely resolve the disparity. A July 5 article in the *Knoxville Register* admitted that the line had been cut but ridiculed the claim of extensive damage. The *Register* maintained that a trainload of Virginia troops had reached Knoxville within twenty-four hours of the raid. However, that train arrived in Knoxville from the *west*, by way of Chattanooga, not from the *east*, toward Richmond, where the bridges were down.[561]

The first credible evidence that the line east of Knoxville was open emerged after September 1. On that day a Union cavalry brigade under the command of Colonel John W. Foster dashed into Knoxville. Foster continued as the senior officer in the city until General Burnside took charge on September 2. A day or two later Burnside ordered Foster to survey the condition of the railway from Knoxville, east to the Virginia state line.

Foster commandeered a locomotive and ordered John R. Branner, the president of the East Tennessee & Virginia, to climb into the cab. Foster presumed that, if the captive's personal safety was at risk, he would give warning of any points of danger of which he was aware. Proceeding east, Foster's men had to stop to make some minor repairs, but with the help of their prisoner, they rode in safety to within twenty-five miles of the Virginia state line. At that point, an unseen saboteur threw a switch and caused a derailment.[562]

Although the road was passable by September, the rebel side had not completed the repairs. A brigade of Union troops arrived months later and found that the trestle at Strawberry Plains was too weak to transport all of the troops, animals, and supplies necessary for a major offensive. Union engineers rebuilt the deck, and the road remained in service until January 21, 1864, when the Yankees torched it again, before being driven away by Confederate forces.[563]

The resourcefulness of rebel engineers limited, but did not eliminate, the military advantage of the Sanders raid. Lee's troops needed provisions, and while the East Tennessee & Virginia was out of commission the great breadbasket of eastern Tennessee was closed to rebel quartermasters. Poor freight service led to inflated food prices in Richmond and hungry soldiers in the field, plus, poor passenger service and poor mail distribution gnawed at Southern morale. The Sanders raid did not alone create these conditions, but it worsened them for a period.[564]

General Buckner's investigation

The Tennessean who rated the destruction as only "a trifling matter" conceded that the raid "should be mortifying and humiliating to our pride." The rebel line had bowed under light pressure, and the Army of the Ohio might return in heavy force.

Corrections had to be made and tempers were short. A rattled correspondent declared that "the authorities" must "speedily awaken to the propriety and importance of sending more troops to this Department."[565]

General Buckner was furious. He knew that his conduct would be scrutinized by amateur tacticians throughout the South The raiders were barely out of sight when he began his inquiry. Buckner wanted to know how the raiders managed to sneak across the border without detection, why headquarters was not notified, and who failed to block their escape.

Embedded in these questions was the thorny matter of *who* should answer for the breakdowns. General Buckner asserted that his neighboring commander, Major General Braxton Bragg, bore responsibility. In a letter to President Davis, Buckner complained that Bragg withdrew several mounted units from the northern perimeter, leaving a fifty-mile stretch of the border unguarded. Bragg then allegedly compounded his mistake by failing to notify Buckner, who was taken by surprise.

Buckner also faulted the command structure of the Confederate armies in the West. Buckner maintained that "had the entire cavalry force been directed by a single commander the probability is that the recent cavalry raid into East Tennessee would have been intercepted at Wartburg."[566] By implication, the Confederate high command—which meant mainly President Davis—also deserved censure, because it denied Buckner the troops he needed to pursue invaders. Buckner's criticism underscored the position of Robert Garlick Kean, a rebel war clerk who, in an insightful diary, declared that "the radical vice of Mr. Davis's whole military system is the separate departmental organization, each reporting only to him. It ... deprives them of the mutual support and combination which might else be obtained. [*sic*]"[567]

Buckner's analysis was cogent, but he overlooked the context in which the senior staff made its deployments. Bragg's removal of the border guards was consistent with current strategy. The troops withdrawn were part of a brigade commanded by Brigadier General John Hunt Morgan, the cavalryman who wreaked havoc on Union supply lines in 1862. Since the senior staff expected more great things from

Morgan and his men during the summer of 1863, Bragg transferred the border guards so as to assemble the force which Morgan required for a northern expedition.

In a letter dated June 25, General Robert E. Lee endorsed the concept, adding that Morgan should cross into Ohio. Lee said that the absence of Burnside's Ninth Corps created an opportunity for "Buckner & Bragg to accomplish something in Ohio." Morgan's offensive commenced just seven days after Lee wrote and eventually became famous as the "Ohio Raid." Lee intended it to serve as a counterpart to his own invasion of Pennsylvania.[568]

Since Morgan's hope of success in Ohio depended upon secrecy, Bragg chose not to inform Buckner, seeking to conceal the movement for as long as possible. Buckner could reasonably feel slighted, but a basic military axiom teaches that the fewer who know about an operation, the greater is the likelihood that it will proceed in secrecy. Buckner's position implied that Sanders simply strolled down an empty corridor created by Morgan's absence. Yet, the actual route which Sanders followed—and Buckner was well aware of its location—ran about sixty miles east of Morgan's base at Sparta, Tennessee. Sanders's path actually came closer to Buckner's own outposts than to Bragg's.[569]

Pegram's command numbered about 1,800 men. The Sanders troop was hardly inconspicuous. Even riding two abreast—an impossibility on Tennessee roads—a squadron of its size would stretch out well over a mile, and when Sanders reached Knoxville, the rear guard was twelve miles behind. The squadron would require almost three hours to pass a specific point, and it would create noise and would leave numerous tracks. Morgan's base was sixty miles away, but Pegram's men were close enough to detect the intruders. Thus, even if Morgan's men had remained in their original positions, it is not clear that they would have detected Sanders. Bragg's men were simply too far away. Pegram was the dozing sentinel.[570]

Jefferson Davis approved of Buckner's recommendation, in part—the need to centralize the chain-of-command—but took no action against Bragg. If Davis had accepted Buckner's analysis, he might have reprimanded Bragg or relieved him from command. But Davis merely issued a directive which made it clear that Bragg was in full command of all Confederate operations in Tennessee, including cavalry maneuvers.[571] Buckner also contended that if he had held full authority, the Sanders squadron would not have escaped. This claim was also fragile. Morgan's men were far from Sanders's route, and the roads were muddy.

Sanders's men rode good horses and would have at least a full-day's head start. It would have been nearly impossible for Morgan to pursue and overtake Sanders. Buckner's effort to evade responsibility fizzled out. The transfer of Morgan's men was defensible, as was the lack of notification. Morgan's men were neither close enough nor fast enough to catch the raiding party, but Buckner's own men were bivouacked in a position, from which they might reasonably be expected to detect an enemy troop passing by. Fortunately for Buckner's reputation, neither President Davis nor Secretary Seddon examined his claims closely.

John Frazer's ordeal

Having failed to ensnare his superior, Buckner faced about and accused a subordinate. Davis refused to proceed against Bragg, but he did allow Buckner to prefer charges against Confederate Brigadier General John Wesley Frazer.[572] At Davis's direction, Buckner convened an official Court of Inquiry at Knoxville on July 28, five weeks after the raiders escaped. Brigadier General Archibald Gracie, Jr., who commanded the garrison at Cumberland Gap, served as President of the Court. His fellow judges were Colonel George Troupe Maxwell, the commander of the First Florida Cavalry, and Lieutenant Colonel Thomas Claiborne, the chief of cavalry of the Department of East Tennessee. All were experienced officers, and all were Buckner's subordinates. Gracie and Pegram were fellow members of the USMA Class of 1854, while Claiborne was a lawyer who fought in Mexico and served for fourteen years in the U.S. Army.[573]

The narrow question which the tribunal addressed was whether General Frazer had disobeyed a lawful order. The order under review was a verbal instruction relayed to Frazer by Lieutenant Colonel Victor von Sheliha, acting on General Buckner's behalf. Buckner's order directed Frazer to transfer the 65th Georgia Infantry from its station near Kingston, Tennessee, to a new position at Wartburg, twenty-four miles to the north.[574] While the testimony centered on a charge of simple insubordination, a deeper question underlay the debate. The salient issue was whether the weakness of the garrison at Wartburg allowed the enemy to breach their line. General Buckner contended that Frazer bore responsibility.

Buckner recalled that he had inspected his western positions a few days before the Sanders incursion, and had decided that Wartburg's garrison was too weak. To strengthen it, he directed General Frazer to move the 65th Georgia to that post. But ten days after he ordered the reinforcement, a messenger reported that Sanders had surprised and captured Wartburg. Wartburg's defenders, an irregular band of 109 men known as the "Wild Cats," had not been re-enforced at all. To add to their general's displeasure, the "Wild Cats" gave up after barely firing a shot. Buckner was convinced that if the 65th Georgia had been where he wanted it, Sanders's squadron would have been repulsed or delayed. Since a contingent of rebel troops led by General Pegram arrived in Wartburg shortly after the enemy departed, Buckner reasoned that if the Georgians had been in proper position, they would have crushed the invaders.

The questioning ranged far and wide, and the Court ultimately ruled that Frazer did in fact fail to carry out Buckner's order. Buckner seemed vindicated, but the Court's findings did not entirely flatter his performance. Frazer presented an able defense, and several deficiencies came to light. Taken as a whole, the testimony showed that General Frazer was not as culpable as Buckner contended, and Buckner was not as innocent as he maintained.

Colonel von Sheliha, Buckner's then acting chief of staff, was both a witness and the prosecutor. Von Sheliha related how he and Buckner, on or about June 9, left Knoxville on an inspection tour. They stopped at Clinton, Tennessee, where Pegram commanded. Frazer was present, and all three generals agreed upon a plan to reposition certain units in order to strengthen the defense of Knoxville. Buckner ordered Pegram to shift his base of operations to Wartburg, a movement of twenty-four miles, and promised that a regiment of infantry would be sent to augment his brigade.[575]

Buckner failed to keep that pledge. As a first step, he instructed Colonel von Sheliha to transmit an order to the 65th Georgia via General Frazer. As von Sheliha remembered the exchange, Buckner's order was clear and unambiguous. Von Scheliha enjoined Frazer to instruct the 65th Georgia "to march at once to Wartburg." Frazer was also told to inform the adjutant general of this movement.

The problem was that von Sheliha's message was confusing. First, the 65th Georgia was part of a brigade commanded by Colonel Robert Trigg. The Georgians were not part of Frazer's brigade, hence Frazer had no authority over them. Frazer was "uneasy" after being told to give direct orders to a regiment which was under another officer's command. Since the 65th Georgia belonged to Trigg, Frazer wondered why the commanding general would tell him, rather than Trigg, to move it. The procedure seemed irregular.

In a second confusing tangle, von Sheliha relayed Buckner's order orally. General Buckner, as the commander-in-chief, had the prerogative to transmit his orders however he pleased, but while every order was binding, all channels were not equally dependable. Orders delivered by a subordinate were more likely to be misunderstood, and an oral message relayed through Victor von Sheliha was particularly risky. Von Sheliha was a native of Poland. He had resided in the United States for twelve years but still spoke with an accent that many native-born Americans found difficult to understand.

In any event, Frazer misconstrued von Sheliha's message. But even if Frazer had no authority to give an order to Trigg, or even if von Sheliha's instruction was garbled, neither relieved Frazer of his duty to carry out his superior's lawful order. A subordinate's responsibility was to seek clarification of any directive which he did not understand. The testimony showed that Frazer had at least an hour to request clarification but failed to do so.

Frazer fought back. He protested that the weakness in the Confederate line was not his fault. He noted that the plan to strengthen Wartburg was originally *his* idea, not Buckner's. Frazer argued that it was he, not Buckner, who first noticed that the garrison at Wartburg was too small. Frazer had spoken on behalf of reinforcement on previous occasions and did so again during the war council at Clinton. Buckner conceded those points, yet continued to argue that Frazer's oversight spoiled the plan. Frazer contended, conversely, that without his *foresight* there would never have been a good plan to spoil.

Frazer also scolded Buckner for his confusion about the organization of the department. Buckner offered no explanation for failing to know that the regiment he wanted to transfer was not assigned to General Frazer. He simply assumed that because its station was physically close to Frazer's headquarters that it belonged to Frazer. Yet, as Frazer pointed out, on the day that Buckner misdirected his Wartburg order, he had been in command of the department of East Tennessee for six weeks. Frazer argued, convincingly, that Buckner had ample time to learn that the 65th Georgia belonged to Trigg, not to Frazer. The testimony embarrassed Buckner, who was made to admit that despite more than a month on the job he was still unfamiliar with the command structure of his own department.

Buckner's account of the exchange was a bit incomplete. Buckner was well aware that his chief of staff's accent made him difficult to understand. In an April letter to Secretary Seddon, Buckner described von Sheliha as an "intelligent officer," but then added the caveat that "his foreign accent is a considerable obstruction to those who are not much accustomed to hearing him."[576]

Nonetheless, Buckner issued his order to Frazer through Colonel von Sheliha, ignoring the possibility that it might be misinterpreted. Von Sheliha offered an excuse for Buckner's decision to transmit the order verbally rather than by setting pen to paper: "We were all day on the march inspecting troops etc." In other words, General Buckner was too weary to write out his orders. He omitted that step, and then after the damage was done, prosecuted the recipient—who was likewise fatigued—for failing to carry out a puzzling order delivered with a thick accent.

Colonel von Sheliha was also unaware at the time that the order should have been routed differently. Unlike his chief, however, he was willing to explain why he lacked knowledge of the extant troop disposition. He said that when he and Buckner arrived in May, they discovered that the organization of the Department of East Tennessee was in disarray. "At the time Major General Buckner took command of this department [May 1, 1863]," von Sheliha testified, "the organization of the troops, to use a mild term, was, at least, incomplete. An organization existed only nominally, not really. Not only regiments of one and the same Brigade, but some companies were scattered about."[577] As General Frazer observed, General Buckner had five weeks to straighten out the confusion but made no corrections.

Nonetheless, the testimony doomed Frazer's case. Buckner's directive was irregular and delivered in a confusing fashion, but Frazer had ample opportunity to seek clarification. Seven days after von Scheliha gave Frazer the order to move the 65th, the unit was still in Kingston. The Union men made short work of its garrison (the "Wild Cats"), and rode off in search of their next target. According to the Court, Frazer neglected his duty, and the losses were costly.

As procedure required, the Court of Inquiry referred the case to Secretary of War Seddon who reviewed its findings before passing the file to President Davis. Seddon ruled that Frazer was deserving of "serious blame." Frazer, declared Seddon, should have "explained the mis-apprehension existing" and should have "taken some steps to communicate [Buckner's] order to the Colonel of the Regiment and its Brigade Commander." Buckner and his Court had found Frazer at fault, but they were not so convincing, with respect to the importance of the infraction.

When it came to recommending whether to relieve a field commander for a "misapprehension," or simply to give him a dressing-down, Seddon waffled. He advised Davis that Frazer should receive a reprimand: "at least the censure of his Execution."[578]

The War Secretary's equivocation was justified, considering the flaws in the case. Seddon was not convinced that the infraction was sufficient to warrant Frazer's dismissal, so he did little more than register his disapproval. The Frazer case reached Davis's desk, but there the wheels of Confederate military justice ground to a halt. The case languished, unresolved. Meanwhile, its importance faded. The Confederates endeavored to hold East Tennessee, but by late August the Army of the Ohio outnumbered Buckner's men by about three to one. The Confederates elected not to fight for the province, so the need to correct the defects that led to Sanders's victory subsided.[579]

General Frazer's future also became moot, but for a different reason. Despite the charge pending against him, Frazer remained in command at Cumberland Gap. When General Buckner abandoned East Tennessee, he left Frazer behind. In two messages, both dated August 21, he gave Frazer parting instructions. The first went through Colonel von Sheliha, who was now officially Buckner's Chief of Staff. It advised Frazer that he was *"expected* to hold *your position* to the last" (emphasis added). But the verb "expected" is weaker than "ordered," and the term "your position" might allow for movement to a different location. To ensure that, this time, there would be no misunderstanding, Buckner penned a second dispatch which went out under his own signature. Its wording was unmistakable: "My orders to General Frazer are to defend Cumberland Gap to the last," Buckner wrote.

John Frazer's willingness to lay down his life for the commander who blamed him for the Sanders fiasco was soon tested. On September 9, General Burnside's troops surrounded Cumberland Gap, and through some deft sleight-of-hand, Burnside managed to convince Frazer that the Yankees outnumbered him by six to one. Since Frazer knew that no help would be forthcoming, he made a sensible, though perhaps not valorous, decision. He chose not to fight "to the last." In fact, he chose not to fight at all. He surrendered 2,026 men without firing a shot.[580]

Cries of cowardice and treason echoed across the South. A woman in Richmond wrote that "a feeling of intense disgust and indignation" had spread throughout the capital. Davis himself denounced the capitulation as "a shameful abandonment of duty."[581] Though Frazer's life was spared, his honor was lost. He sat out the final months of the war as a prisoner in Fort Warren, in Boston harbor. Finally, eighteen years later, Jefferson Davis acknowledged that he was wrong, but by then Frazer's reputation was beyond repair.[582] He lived out the remainder of his life as an outcast.

Unionist Spirits Buoyed

Abraham Lincoln had pressed for an invasion of East Tennessee, in part because he wished to sustain Tennessee loyalty. The Sanders raid was not the attack which he preferred, but it did nourish Unionist morale. While the wreckage of the rail system was clearly visible, the effect on the civilian spirit was not. Kate Livingston, a Union woman, confided to her diary on the day after the cannon exchange that there was "Great excitement about Knoxville in regard to the Yankees being at Knoxville," and on the next day she exulted that "'tis enough to make the most callous heart shudder."[583]

In 1861 the Confederate authorities arrested as many as 400 Unionists, including numerous public officials, many of whom fled to the north.[584] In 1863 a "host" of leading East Tennessee Unionists, including William G. Brownlow and Oliver P. Temple, clustered in Cincinnati, where they paid close attention to events at home. Far beyond the reach of Davis's jailers, these expatriates were not shy about expressing their delight when they heard that Yankee raiders had paid a visit to Knoxville.[585]

John M. Fleming, a former newspaper editor, entertained his fellow exiles with a satirical sketch titled *Chivalry in Knoxville*. This piece crowed over the hysteria which allegedly erupted when word spread that a detachment of Yankees was nearby. Knoxville's rebels were in such a rush to keep military supplies away from Yankee torches that they threw provisions down stairs and out windows, then packed them on trains and steamboats and hustled them out of town. Banks supposedly bundled cash and coins and rushed the money to safety.[586] Despite numerous boasts that "Yankees could only enter Knoxville over their dead bodies," Fleming maintained that when Sanders and his men got close, "the courage of the chivalrous knights began to ooze out at their fingers' ends, and . . . they fled in every direction." "Except," Fleming sneered, "toward Col. S."[587]

One such spooked rebel was bank president and former U.S. Congressman John H. Crozier, who had good reason for concern. Crozier was known as an "original secessionist" and lived up to his reputation in both word and deed. In February, 1862, the rebel-loving citizens of Knoxville organized a regiment for home defense. The proud volunteers proclaimed their readiness to fight by marching through the streets with the Stars-and-Bars flying and with the strains of "Dixie" played by fife and drum. Crozier and fellow former Member of Congress William H. Sneed headed the procession and addressed the crowd. Crozier had clearly marked himself as a leading rebel and was now allegedly terrified by the possibility of capture. Supposedly, Crozier fled in such great haste that, because he was afraid to wait for a boat to ferry him across the Holston, he straddled a pine log and paddled himself to safety.[588]

According to this tale, not just Crozier but the entire rebel leadership panicked. Jacob A. Sperry, the arch-rebel who edited the *Knoxville Register*, was supposedly so exercised that he "plunged frantically into the stream with his half emptied bottle in hand." Former Congressman Sneed was reputed to have hidden in his own cellar until two hours after the raiders were gone. Banker Dr. J. G. M. Ramsey was said to have withdrawn into his vault, moaning about how he did not want to meet his Maker. He "sat down in despair... Seizing a copy of 'Ramsey's Annals' and clasping it to his bosom he fell back into his chair crying 'Bury me thus!'"[589]

Although these yarns were dreamed up by angry expatriates, they were not entirely baseless. An aggrieved Floridian published an account of the rebel defense in an Atlanta journal which he intended to serve as a corrective to the inflated claims of gallantry that permeated Sperry's *Knoxville Register*. "It is true," he wrote, that "a *few* citizens [*sic*] did arm themselves and assist in defense of the city, but by far the greater portion of the 'militia' remained in the streets, far more solicitous for their personal safety, than for the defense of their homes. As they were not allowed to cross the ferry, numbers of them inquired anxiously about a *ford* in the vicinity. [*sic*]"[590]

Under the circumstances, a hasty exit was hardly unwise. Some Unionists, Parson Brownlow in particular, demanded the execution of key rebels. The Knoxville gallows remained in good working order, and outspoken secessionists had ample reason to fear its function. If the Yankees took the city and resolved to hang secessionists, Knoxville's élite were candidates for the noose. The reports of panic spreading through the rebel ranks, whatever their truth, served to revive the spirits of the loyal community.

"I Felt that Disaster was the Future of Our History"

As Unionists rejoiced, rebels flinched. As one official noted, "the tone of our papers [is] rather depressed & the people somewhat apathetic—so long a series of victories has left them unprepared for any reverse." Another observer wrote that, owing to the several defeats, the spirits of people were "deeply bowed down." Eliza Fain, a deeply religious, pro-Confederate housewife, feared that a major invasion would be next. This melancholy prospect, she said, was evidence of divine wrath imposed upon a sinful people who had violated the "commands of God." "O we do tremble at times lest our Father in Heaven should make us feel the horrors of an invasion," she moaned.[591]

Like the Unionists who chortled when the Confederate glitterati departed, rebel sympathizers also monitored the conduct of their leaders. The short-fused rebel lawyer William G. McAdoo reported that, as the Yankees approached, five leading rebels, including "the old scoundrel William Horner" and Mayor James C. Luttrell, "went to *plotting*, [and] kept it up till the Yankee repulse was consummated." McAdoo added scornfully, "They did not take up arms for defence [*sic*]." Five days later he was still disdainful of Knoxville's warm-weather patriots. When Yankee cannon barked, they stood aside, as McAdoo put it, *"without arms,"* doing nothing more than "talking in a *conspiratory* manner under . . . shelter. [*sic*]"[592]

McAdoo's disdain extended to General Buckner, whom McAdoo suspected of being a traitor to the Cause. According to a rumor circulating among rank-and-file rebels, Buckner evacuated Knoxville when he heard that the Yankees were coming and followed the fighting from afar. In McAdoo's caustic version, "when the Yankees approached Knoxville, Gen[eral] Buckner and staff prudently mounted their horses and rode away; and the day after the Yankees were repulsed, they prudently mounted and rode back."[593] Buckner now stood accused of cowardice, as well as being suspected of betrayal.

Before Unionists could tire of gloating over their victory or rebels could persuade themselves that the Yankee visit was little more than a passing nuisance, greater events snatched the raid from the public eye. The raid exercised East Tennessee rebeldom, but it was possible to write it off as a brief aggravation, if one was willing to believe the "pretty tales" which the press "invented to keep the courage of the people up."[594]

"Treasonous Pilots"

The findings of the various inquiries made possible a deeper understanding of the raid than was achievable in those dark days. As Secretary Seddon sensed, the Frazer court found part of the truth. Its report showed that cooperation between Generals Bragg and Buckner was minimal and that General Buckner's Department of East Tennessee was poorly coordinated—his men were out of position when the enemy appeared. As one civilian observed, the commanding officer of the Department was "too often changed." Citing six different commanders in a four-month period, he averred that such turnover "must surely be deleterious."[595]

Colonel George Baird Hodge, Buckner's Inspector General at Cumberland Gap, was particularly scornful. Hodge, a graduate of the United States Naval Academy, served as a member of the Confederate States Congress while remaining on active duty. In preparing a report on the raid, the congressman-colonel's pen dripped with acid. "The most extraordinary feature of the whole affair," Hodge seethed, "is that although [the squadron] passed within twenty miles of Clinton, the headquarters of Brigadier General Frazer, along a road crowded with pickets and couriers of that Brigade, information of the capture of Wartburg reached General Buckner twelve hours before it was heard by General Frazer at Clinton."[596]

Yet, while the tactical and organizational errors which the investigations uncovered were serious and doubtless contributed to the Union success, missteps do not fully explain the defeat. The probes attributed the failure to routine decisions made by General Buckner and his fellow officers but did not touch upon the deeper, more systemic problems which afflicted the Confederate enterprise. The former were detectable in 1863; the latter were not.

As Sanders exploited brilliantly, a few scattered strong points separated by stretches of fragility formed the Confederates' northern defensive perimeter. General Buckner's situation mirrored that which bedeviled President Davis. Both had vast areas of land to protect and fewer troops than they needed. Confederate armies managed to keep the Yankees at bay for long periods, but they could not hold off the invaders indefinitely.

Like Davis, Buckner coped with shortages by shuffling troops as circumstances warranted. When Sanders threatened Knoxville, Buckner called out a band of civilians, invalids, and clerks. While this helped, the rebel defense was stretched to its limit, and there was little room for error. A small mistake—such as when Colonel von Sheliha garbled an order or when Buckner accepted the ruse that a major invasion was underway—could have large consequences. On both occasions, Buckner's troops ended up far out of position.

Buckner was further encumbered by stale intelligence. In May, reports indicated that Burnside's Army of the Ohio was about to march on Knoxville in heavy force. At the time it was made, this forecast was accurate, but after June 1 it was out-of-date. Once Burnside transferred half of his men, invasion became impossible. Burnside was tethered, but Buckner could not confirm this until he saw a story published in a Cincinnati newspaper.

When Sanders's force approached Knoxville from the west, Buckner realized he had guessed wrongly. Buckner had stationed his men along a ridge north of the city and was reluctant to send a significant portion of them chasing after Sanders. He dared not thin out his northern perimeter in case Burnside's attack came as predicted. Buckner suspected that the Sanders unit was bait and refused to rise to it. By the time he discovered the truth, it was too late.

Sanders had an overall view of the operation but could not see the rebel problems. He did not denigrate the enemy performance, but he was eager to give credit to his own men. Civil War commanders customarily commended key subordinates in after-action reports.

Sanders mentioned the contributions of his second-in-command, Colonel Robert K. Byrd, and the commanders of his rear guard, Majors Tristram Dow of the 112th Illinois and Alpheus S. Moore of the 44th Ohio.[597]

Commendations of this kind were normal, but Sanders's differed. He awarded primary credit for the success of the expedition to seven enlisted men. Sanders wrote that he was "chiefly indebted for the main success" to Sergeant William S. "Stud" Reynolds of the First East Tennessee Volunteers and his team of guides. "His knowledge of the country," praised Sanders, "was invaluable."[598]

Ironically, the "northern invaders" knew the land better than the rebels, though the rebels ruled it for two years. Reynolds and his comrades were lifelong residents. Captain James McCartney of the 112th Illinois echoed Sanders: "We had with us seven of the best guides in the army, who were thoroughly acquainted with the mountains and the country beyond." Although Buckner attempted to seal the gaps in the Cumberland escarpment, Sanders's scouts found unguarded openings. Sanders's men could and did cut paths through the forest when necessary, but the guides' experience meant that this was seldom necessary; nor was it imperative that the Yankees cross the mountains through one of the main thoroughfares. "We made a gap of our own through the mountains," McCartney recalled.[599]

The rebels shrewdly refused to believe that enemy troops could have made their way through the rugged escarpment on their own. Its roads were neither marked nor mapped. The Confederates did not know Sergeant Reynolds by name, but they were certain that they had been betrayed. "It is manifest," fumed the *Knoxville Register*, "that [the Yankees] were piloted round the town during the darkness by some person or persons who were very familiar with all our roads and localities." Another commentator echoed the *Register's* disgust: "It seems to be a fact," he mused, "that at least the greatest portion of the raiders would have been captured but for the piloting of a tory."[600] Both Sanders and the rebels were correct. Without Reynolds and his scouts, the raiders would surely have become lost, as did their rear guard on three occasions.

Rebel civilians also concluded that spies must have helped the Union squadron. Believing that the invaders had the benefit of inside knowledge, rebel leaders demanded a crackdown on all persons who might have given information to the enemy. "No movement of our troops can take place in all this country, from the salt works in Virginia to Cumberland Gap or Jonesburgh," thundered a writer in Richmond, "accurate information of which is not at once conveyed to the enemy by these people. [*sic*]" In Knoxville, meanwhile, a writer complained that "the late raiders who galloped through our country were manifestly informed of the numbers and position of our troops from the time they left Kentucky to the time they recrossed the mountain on their return."[601]

They were right—active assistance rendered by Tennesseans was invaluable. On at least two occasions, Unionist women, at grave risk, warned the Sanders men that enemy troops were operating nearby or would soon be arriving. On both occasions the Yankees were able to escape. In the raid's final phase, moreover, a brave mountain girl led them through miles of forest until they could find their own way to safety.[602] Yet, while local knowledge saved the operation several times, there was a dark side. The Sanders troop actually lost more lives due to the treachery of two rebel civilians (who misled them about where to ford the Clinch River), than due to enemy gunfire.

The two enemies concluded their assessments of the Sanders raid with little agreement. Yankees attributed their victory to a careful plan, skillfully executed, while rebels faulted their loss to poor cooperation and poor communication. Yet in one respect, the two sides found common ground. Colonel William Sanders lavished credit on Sergeant "Stud" Reynolds and his intrepid scouts, while rebels heaped blame on the treachery of unknown and unseen "Treasonous Pilots."

Sanders's gallant scouts and the rebels' "Treasonous Pilots" were, of course, one and the same: Sergeant "Stud" Reynolds and his brothers-in-arms. Like the majority of the Sanders troopers and hundreds of thousands of others, black and white, Reynolds and his scouts were examples of the "anti-Confederate Southerners" whom the historian William W. Freehling credits with having "shaped the course of the Civil War." The Sanders troopers were only a tiny facet of the Grand Army, but they exemplified the edge the Union gained, owing to the support and service of thousands of southern Unionists.

CHAPTER SIXTEEN

A Soldier's Death

I have done my duty, and served my country as well as I could.
—*Brigadier General William Price Sanders, on his death bed*

THE FIGHTING IN THE WEST raged on throughout the autumn of 1863. Bloody clashes at Chickamauga and Chattanooga dominated the nation's attention, but Sanders and his men fought elsewhere. Sanders was in the saddle almost constantly from July through November, earning new laurels.

Following his return to Kentucky, Sanders paused only briefly before mounting up to pursue his rebel counterpart, Brigadier General John Hunt Morgan. Morgan had embarked on his most audacious venture, the "Ohio Raid." His plan was to push north through Kentucky, cross the Ohio River, and despoil southern Indiana and southern Ohio. Once his men were on Union soil, Yankee cavalry would have to give chase. His thrust would delay forthcoming Union invasions and might also influence the fall elections in Indiana and Ohio.[603] The advance of Sanders and his squadron into Tennessee compelled Morgan to postpone the venture for two weeks, but on July 2 he marched north with 2,000 men.

Morgan passed through Kentucky as planned and reached the south bank of the Ohio. His orders dictated that he remain in Kentucky, but he crossed into Indiana on July 8. General Burnside, having no other choice, responded by ordering his entire cavalry force to join in pursuit of Morgan.

Sanders organized a brigade of 1,800 and headed toward Ohio. Sanders and his troopers travelled by steamer to Cincinnati and gave chase. Morgan had a head start and kept his men in the saddle for twenty-one hours per day, cutting a swath through the Ohio Valley, but the Yankees were numerous and fast. A squadron led by Sanders's old comrade, Colonel August Kautz, marched ninety miles in a single day, and on July 19 Union forces cornered Morgan's men at Buffington Island, only seventy-five miles south of Lake Erie. Surrounded, exhausted, and short of ammunition, about 900 rebels surrendered.[604] Many of the prisoners were Kentuckians whom Sanders recognized from boyhood. He greeted several by first name: "Jim, John, Joe, Frank," etc.[605]

Morgan, along with a few hundred stragglers, evaded capture for a few days but eventually surrendered. With most of Morgan and his men safely confined, Sanders and his troopers returned to Kentucky. General Burnside then led the Army of the Ohio forward. Advancing in five columns, Burnside's men converged on Williamsburg, Kentucky, passed through Montgomery and Wartburg, Tennessee, and seized Knoxville.[606] When the celebration of September 2 subsided, Sanders prepared his command for the defense of the city. It was to be his last fight.

On the eve of the Sanders raid, an Ohio lieutenant assured his parents that his officers were the best men for "rough weather." His description was apt, for Sanders weathered many storms. Sanders embraced the soldier's life and accepted its hazards, but he faced the gale once too often.

Union troops wrested much of Tennessee from Davis's grasp, but it was by no means certain that they could hold it. Chattanooga was the rebels' main objective, but when that effort failed, they attempted to recapture East Tennessee. In early November, word reached Knoxville that the enemy was advancing in heavy force. Lieutenant General James Longstreet commanded the Confederate column, which numbered 17,000 men. It included 5,000 cavalry and thirty-four cannons.

Burnside had placed a string of outposts in the valley of East Tennessee extending from Knoxville toward Chattanooga. He assigned

Colonel William Sanders to command all cavalry elements which were stationed near Loudon, about thirty miles southwest of Knoxville. These troops were no match for Longstreet's powerful army, so Burnside ordered his forces to retire to the safety of the earthworks then under construction on the west side of Knoxville.

Burnside paused while directing the countermarch to inform Colonel William Sanders, his protégé, of some welcome news: "Doc" Sanders had been promoted to the rank of brigadier general of volunteers. It was an impressive achievement. When the war began, Sanders, at twenty-seven, was a second lieutenant in the Regular Army. Yet in the space of just twenty-nine months, he rose six grades. He received his star when he was just three months past his thirtieth birthday.[607]

There was no time for celebration, for Longstreet was coming. Burnside's men fought a running battle as they withdrew toward Knoxville. After a successful holding action at Campbell's Station, the Union infantry fled for the safety of the city. General Sanders and a cavalry division assumed their customary position as the rear guard.

Sanders's troop fell back toward Knoxville, skirmishing and covering the retreat. The bone-tired Union infantry reached the outskirts of the city at daybreak on November 17, only to discover that the fortifications they needed were unfinished. The troopers rested briefly, then worked all day digging trenches and building parapets. Spades were in short supply, so some men moved dirt with their dinner plates.

A mile to the west of the city, Sanders and an eclectic band of 700 dismounted cavalrymen endeavored to keep the enemy at bay. Though these men were not used to operating together as a unit, they "kept a fierce and gallant contest with Longstreet's infantry," an admiring veteran remembered. Yet while gallantry could stave off the enemy temporarily, Sanders's unit was too weak to hold the line, for long.[608]

The officer supervising construction of the fortifications was Sanders's West Point classmate, Captain Orlando M. Poe, the Chief Engineer of the Twenty-Third Corps.[609] At eleven o'clock on the night of the 17th, Sanders, Poe, and Burnside held a council of war. Poe stated that he needed until noon on the 18th to finish the earthworks. Sanders knew that his own situation was precarious, but he promised to keep the enemy away as long as he could. The two old friends then retired to Poe's quarters and talked until midnight. When Poe arose at dawn, Sanders had left to rejoin his men.[610]

Throughout the morning of the 18th, the rebels pounded Sanders's position. Their only protection was a row of piled-up fence rails, but hour after hour, the little band stood their ground. Occasionally, Poe remembered, a few men would begin to fall back, but "at such critical times Sanders would walk up to the rail piles and stand there erect, with fully half his height exposed to a terrific fire at short range, until every retreating man, as if ashamed of himself, would return to his proper place." Sanders and his force held fast—one admiring witness said that Sanders "had not given back an inch" and "his life seemed to be charmed."[611]

But in early afternoon the stymied rebels brought up two Napoleons. Colonel E. Porter "Alec" Alexander CSA, Sanders's old friend from West Point, commanded Longstreet's cannon. Neither Sanders nor Alexander had seen each other since April, 1861, when they whiled away a last few peaceful days playing billiards in San Francisco. They pledged to keep in touch, but their paths did not cross again until the afternoon of November 18, 1863, when Alexander opened fire on Sanders's position. Alexander was close enough to discern which officer was in command, but he was too far away to identify his face. He remembered the barrage vividly, though: "We could see rails flying in the air."[612]

The Union line buckled. Some of the men began to bolt, but again Sanders showed his mettle. "Sanders and his officers rallied their men and brought most of them back to the line, where they poured a heavy fire," remembered Alexander. Some of the Union troopers, who were armed with repeating carbines, held their position until two South Carolina regiments were brought up to drive them off. The Carolinians advanced to within thirty yards of the rail pile, then dropped to the ground. After taking a few moments to collect themselves, they rose with a yell, sprinted forward, and carried the Union position. They killed or captured many of Sanders's men, while the remainder retreated to the rear. The 112th Illinois suffered ninety-four casualties, or a third of its total number.[613]

"Doc" Sanders had fought many fights since he last saw Alec. He survived the Peninsula, Antietam, Dutton's Mill, the Sanders raid, Buffington Island, and countless other skirmishes. But on Wednesday, November 18, at about 4:00 PM, an enemy ball finally found its mark.[614] Sanders was struck in the abdomen—a mortal wound. His men carried their young general from the field, alive but bleeding. They took him to a temporary hospital, and set him up in the finest suite, in the finest hotel in the city, to await his solemn hour.

Meanwhile, as General Sanders arrived in Knoxville on a stretcher, the President of the United States was *en route* by train to Gettysburg, Pennsylvania. Abraham Lincoln had agreed to speak at the dedication of the Soldiers' National Cemetery, on the following day. As he polished his speech, Lincoln was unaware that four hundred miles to the west a brave young officer lay stricken on his deathbed.

At about eleven o'clock on the following morning, November 19, 1863, the president mounted his horse for the ride to the cemetery. At nearly that very moment, Sanders's wound claimed his life. Sanders's mentor, friend and commanding officer, General Ambrose Burnside, knelt at his bedside when he breathed his last. At the stricken soldier's request, he was baptized into the Methodist Episcopal faith, though he expired before he could receive communion.[615] He joined the ranks of the stouthearted men whom, Lincoln extolled that day, "gave the last full measure of devotion."[616]

In an elegiac General Field Order No. 31, issued to formally notify the Army of the Ohio of the passing of General Sanders, Ambrose Burnside captured the essence of his character: "Distinguished always for his self-possession and daring in the field, and in his private life eminent for his genial and unselfish nature . . ., he has left both as a man and as a soldier an untarnished name." His comrades understood. When Sanders's physicians advised him that his wound was mortal, he replied, "I have done my duty, and served my country as well as I could." It was a fitting epitaph for a hero's life.

APPENDIX ONE

Important Persons and Locations

Corporal Abner Baker CSA, 2d Tennessee Cavalry, the only son of Dr. Harvey Baker, shot and killed Will Hall, a Union veteran and the deputy clerk of the circuit court for Knox County, in the county courthouse on September 4, 1865. That night, he was removed from the county jail and hanged by a group of Union veterans.

Colonel Robert King Byrd USA ran for a seat in the U.S. House of Representatives in 1865, finishing fourth. He was later elected to the Tennessee State Senate as a conservative Democrat.

Brigadier General Samuel P. Carter USA, a graduate of the United States Naval Academy, returned to sea duty. In 1877 he married Martha Custis Williams, a descendant of Martha Washington. He retired as a Rear Admiral of the United States Navy.

Reverend William Blount Carter served as emissary of the Knoxville East Tennessee Relief Association. He toured northern states (as far as Maine) in a successful campaign to solicit funds to relieve suffering of Unionists. After the war, he engaged in farming.

Major H. Crumbliss USA, adjutant, 1st Tennessee Cavalry, became Sheriff of Roane County, Tennessee, and served as Postmaster of Kingston, Tennessee. He and his wife raised eight children.

Colonel John W. Foster USA created a diplomatic dynasty. Foster himself won appointment as U.S. Secretary of State under President Benjamin Harrison (1892-93). He was also the father-in-law of President Woodrow Wilson's Secretary of State, Robert Lansing, as well as the grandfather of both President Dwight Eisenhower's first Secretary of State, John Foster Dulles, and his Director of Central Intelligence, Allen Dulles.

Colonel Archibald Gracie Jr. CSA, who served as a judge in the court martial of General John Frazer, fought at Chickamauga, then transferred to the Army of Northern Virginia. He was killed in the trenches before Petersburg on December 2, 1864.

Colonel Thomas J. Henderson USA, 112th Illinois Mounted Infantry, chose the men of his regiment to ride with Sanders, then subsequently was severely wounded at Resaca, May 14, 1864. After "suffering much from the wound and from diarrhea, [he] had considerable fever and sweat freely in the Evening, began to feel weak." Nonetheless, he recovered from his wound, survived the war, returned to Illinois, and served ten terms as a U.S. Congressman. He died in 1911.

Loudon Bridge survived until the Confederates evacuated East Tennessee in September 1863 when they burned it. Union troops rebuilt the bridge in March 1864.

First Sergeant Eli K. Mauck USA, 112th Illinois Mounted Infantry, who nearly drowned in the Clinch River, was later captured and paroled. Commissioned a first lieutenant, he survived the war and resided in Boonesboro, Iowa.

Captain James McCartney USA, 112th Illinois Mounted Infantry, was promoted to company commander and survived to become a resident of Springfield, Illinois. He wrote a lengthy chronicle of the raid.

Brigadier General John Pegram CSA transferred to the Army of Northern Virginia. Wounded in The Wilderness in May 1864 he recovered only to be killed at Hatcher's Run in 1865.

Captain Richard C. Rankin USA returned to Ripley, Ohio, where he penned a history of the 7th Ohio Cavalry.

Strawberry Plains Bridge was rebuilt by Confederates after the Sanders raid but was burned when they withdrew. U.S. troops rebuilt it in February 1864.

Major General Orlando B. Willcox USA commanded a division of the IX Corps for the rest of the war. Mustered out in 1866, he resumed his military career as colonel of regulars and served in several posts before retiring as a Brigadier General in 1887.

Captain Benjamin F. Wyly CSA moved to Stephenville, Texas, where he lived to age eighty and sired ten sons.

APPENDIX TWO

The Legal Issues in the Baker Case

Baker's status as a soldier or civilian was problematic for those who contended that his death was simple murder. "Murder" does not normally apply to a combat mortality, and while both sides would agree that Baker's status was defined by military law, there was no consensus about which statute applied in this case. The rules that governed American military practice prior to the Civil War originated in Europe and were framed to regulate contests between sovereign nations. These statutes pursued a noble goal—to protect ordinary citizens from the vicissitudes of war—but the Civil War blurred the distinction between civilians and soldiers.[617]

European rules designed to regulate international conflicts were unsuited to a belligerency in which bushwhacking and other forms of irregular warfare were commonplace. The European conventions posited a sharply defined separation between civilians and soldiers, but as Harvey Baker's case demonstrates, in the American Civil War a clear differentiation in these roles frequently did not exist.

Nevertheless, since Harvey Baker fitted the European definition of a guerrilla fighter—he wore no uniform, was not acting under the orders of a superior officer, and was not carried on the roll of any unit in the Confederate Army—he could legally be killed, even if he threw down his rifle and attempted to surrender.[618]

The commanding general of the U.S. Army, Major General Henry W. Halleck, recognized this enigma and arranged for a German-born legal scholar, Dr. Francis Lieber, to revise United States military law. The "Lieber code" became the U.S. Army's General Order No. 100 and went into effect just a few weeks before Sanders's men departed for Tennessee. Its 157 articles addressed nearly every conceivable situation which soldiers might encounter.

Lieber's broad purpose was to adapt military regulations to current conditions, but he placed special emphasis on controlling irregular warfare. The code's basic thrust granted sweeping authority to a conventional army (such as the Sanders raiders) to employ almost any means it deemed necessary to crush irregular fighters (such as Confederate partisans).[619]

Order No. 100 failed to eliminate all ambiguity from the regulations, and its rules were too complex to be absorbed quickly by troops in the field, but it defined the law of land warfare with more clarity and greater specificity than had ever been known before.[620] It was a milestone in legal history.

According to the Lieber code, the killing of Harvey Baker was a lawful act. When the action commenced, Baker fit Lieber's definition of a noncombatant, because he was not enrolled in a regularly authorized unit of the Confederate army. (Enrollment in a regular unit was the determining factor.)[621] Baker imperiled whatever protection military law afforded him (under either the Lieber code or the older "Westphalian" rules) when he openly carried arms during an active engagement. When he aimed and fired at a Union soldier, he extinguished his noncombatant standing irreversibly. Once he became a belligerent, under either form of military law, his life could be taken with impunity. Article 157 of the Lieber code spoke directly to the point: "Armed or unarmed resistance by citizens of the United States against the lawful movement of their troops, is levying war against the United States, and is therefore treason."[622]

The Confederates flatly rejected the Lieber code. A leading Atlanta journal, the *Southern Confederacy*, denounced the statute as a devious attempt by the Yankees to "cover the flagitiousness of their [own] violations" of accepted military law. Though the Confederate interpretation of the law of war was vague in comparison to the Lieber code,[623] the rebels still claimed that the letter of the law established beyond question that an innocent noncombatant had been brutally murdered.

On the very page that it presented its censure of the Lieber code, the *Southern Confederacy* published an account of Baker's death which described the encounter as simple murder. The article dismissed such pertinent factors as the actions of Wiggs's cavalry, Baker's Confederate partiality, the exchange of gunfire, and his display and discharge of weapons.[624]

APPENDIX THREE

Confederate Provisional Infantry Detachment,
Knoxville, Tennessee, June 20, 1863

Captain P. B. Thompson CSA, commanding

Volunteer	Age	Occupation (1860)	Net Worth (1860)	Slaves Owned (1860)
J. P. Akers				
R. W. Anderson				
A. Armour	37	farmer		
J. H. Barker	23	farm laborer		
H. Bentley	n/a	n/a		
Charles Berry	19	farmer		
William A. Blair	19	farm laborer		
E[mmanuel?] Bowle [Bolli?]	22	machinist [b. Brazil]		
R. H. Brown	39	merchant	$1,500	
T. V. Brown				
J. A. Burrier				
James G. Campbell	64		$8,600	17 slaves
Rev. Charles W. Charlton*	38	postmaster, editor (Methodist)	$26,000	6 slaves
Auten Charney	38	butcher [b. France]		
A[drain] Chavanne	36	[b. Switzerland]	$12,000	
A. B. Crozier	20			
Dr. Carrick W. Crozier*	56	physician	$6,500	2 slaves
A[lexander] S. Douk [Doak?]	18			
S[F?]. M. Drake	28	cooper	$300	
Charles Ducloux [b. Switzerland]				
B. C. Edwards				
O. N. Fanning				
George A. Gammon	21			

P. Gilroy

Sen. Landon C. Haynes*	47	lawyer, editor	$11,145	3 slaves
John E. Helms	28	dentist		
A. R. Humes	57	farmer	$1,200	
J. H. J[arnigan?]				
W. W. Johnson				
James S. Kennedy	27	farmer		
E. Long				
George Litta				
Rev. Joseph H. Martin*	41	clergy (Presbyterian)		
W. T. Miles				
W. Owings				
D. B. Palmer				
George B. Parker	23	merchant	$200	
J. O. Patton	39	professor	$22,500	
R. Power				
John Ray[al?]	37	bookseller[?]	$2,000	
J. H. Renshaw	37	cabinet maker	$6,500	3 slaves
A. N. Rinz				
Charles Ristine				
A. O. Roberts	42	carpenter	$3,000	
W. W. Shields	39	physician	$10,400	4 slaves
[John?] H[oward] Smith	39	clergy [Episcopal]		
William Henry Sneed*	47	lawyer	$172,000	
Charles Verry	17	farmer (b. Switzerland)		
John Vincent	34	machinist	$50	
William W. Wallace*	48	lawyer, r.r. president		14 slaves
J. H. Walker	38	farmer	$2,250	1 slave
[W?] W[ilburn?] Walker*	39	dry-goods merchant		

B. S. Willis			
J. R. Worrall Dan Wood 52	farmer	$4,000	
Rev. Lucien B. Woolfolk 34	clergy (Baptist)	$6,500	early advocate of secession*

Sources: The number of private citizens who mustered to defend Knoxville on June 20, 1863, is uncertain. Some concealed their involvement, and some records are imprecise or illegible. Most of the names listed above appeared in the *Holston Journal* [Knoxville] on July 9, 1863, while others were found in the *OR*. Data on occupation and net worth are from the *Eighth Census of the United States, 1860* (National Archives Microfilm Publication M653). The estimated net worth is the sum of the value of real estate and other property as reported in the 1860 census return. Data on slave ownership are taken from slave schedules included in the 1860 return. Secondary sources, such as Robert Tracy McKenzie, *Lincolnites and Rebels* (New York: Oxford Univ. Press, 2006) and W. Todd Groce, *Mountain Rebels* (Knoxville: Univ. of Tennessee Press, 1999), confirmed the identity of some participants.

NOTES

Introduction

1. Maj. Gen. H. W. Halleck, Telegram to Major-General Burnside, June 3, 1863, quoted in U.S. War Department, *The War of the Rebellion: A Compilation of the Official Records of the Union and Confederate Armies*, 1889: ser. 1, vol. 23, pt. 2 (Washington: Government Printing Office, 1880–1901), 384. Cited hereinafter as *OR*. For other abbreviations, see Bibliography.

2. The Lost Cause position asserted that Southerners were united in support of secession, but their government collapsed only because their armies could not withstand the overwhelming number of troops which the Union Army fielded against them. William C. Davis, *The Cause Lost* (Lawrence: Univ. Press of Kansas, 1996), *passim*; Robert T. McKenzie, *Lincolnites and Rebels* (New York: Oxford Univ. Press, 2006), 80; Richard N. Current, *Lincoln's Loyalists* (Boston: Northeastern Univ. Press, 1992), 215; Robert T. McKenzie, "'An unconditional, straight-out Union man,'" in *Sister States, Enemy States: The Civil War in Kentucky and Tennessee*, eds. Kent T. Dollar, Larry H. Whiteaker, and W. Calvin Dickinson (Lexington: Univ. Press of Kentucky, 2009), 90; Edward H. Bonekemper III, *The Myth of the Lost Cause: Why the South Fought the Civil War and Why the North Won* (Washington: Regnery History, 2015), 97–98; Dwight Pitcaithley, "When Tennessee Turned South," *New York Times*, June 1, 2011.

3. Matthew E. Stanley, "The Original 'Forgotten Americans,'" *Civil War History* 65 (Dec. 2019): 390.

4. Digby G. Seymour, *Divided Loyalties* (Knoxville: Univ. of Tennessee Press, 2002), 74–79; McKenzie, *Lincolnites and Rebels*, 146–47 (see note 2); Earl J. Hess, *The Knoxville Campaign* (Knoxville: Univ. of Tennessee Press, 2012), 5–9.

5. William P. Sanders, "Reports of Col. William P. Sanders . . . Commanding Expedition," *OR*, 1889, ser. 1, vol. 23, pt. 1: 386–89. Cited hereinafter as Sanders Report.

Chapter 1

6. John C. Inscoe, "Mountain Unionism, Secession, and Regional Self-Image," in *Looking South*, eds. W. B. Moore Jr. and J. F. Tripp (Westport: Greenwood Press, 1989), 115; James S. Cowdon and James D. Holman, eds., *Statistical Map of the United States of America (1865)*, map, 49 x 78 cm., LC Civil War Maps 2 ed., U.S. Library of Congress Geography and Map Division (Washington: M. Joyce, Eng., 1888), 62.6. Accessed at: www.fold3.com, image #260557673.

7. The population of Tennessee in 1860 was 1,109,801. The population of the thirty-one counties generally defined as "East Tennessee" comprised 32 percent of the total, or about 355,000. W. Todd Groce, "The Social Origins of East Tennessee's Confederate Leadership," in *The Civil War in Appalachia*, eds. K. W. Noe and S. H. Wilson (Knoxville: Univ. of Tennessee Press, 1997), 6; "1860 United States Census Results," table, *Civil War Wiki, The American Civil War Home Page*, Civilwarhome.com [part of the *Civil War Talk Network*, CivilWarTalk.com. and Civil War Wiki.net]. Accessed at: https://civilwarwiki.net/w/index.php?title=1860 _United_States_Census_Results.

8. The American Civil War Home Page, "1860 United States Census Results" (see prev. note).

9. McKenzie, *Lincolnites and Rebels*, 16, 21–22; Robert T. McKenzie, "Contesting Secession, 1860–1861," *Civil War History* 48 (Dec. 2002): 298; Robert T. McKenzie, *One South or Many?* (New York: Cambridge Univ. Press, 1994), 4.

10. Walter D. Kamphoefner and Wolfgang Helbich, eds., *Germans in the Civil War* (Chapel Hill: Univ. of North Carolina Press, 2006), 374–76, 378.

11. Melba L. Murray, *Bradley Divided* (Collegedale: College Press, 1992), 19–20, 104–5; Leroy P. Graf and Ralph W. Haskins, eds. *The Papers of Andrew Johnson: Vol. 6. 1862–1864* (Knoxville: Univ. of Tennessee Press, 1983), fn 95; Mayme P. Wood, *Hitch Hiking Along the Holston River from 1792–1962* (Nashville: Richland Press, 1964), 24.

12. Brian D. McKnight, *Contested Borderland* (Lexington: Univ. Press of Kentucky, 2006), 190.

13. Ella Lonn, *Salt as a Factor in the Confederacy* (Tuscaloosa: Univ. of

Alabama Press, 1965), 13, 59, 138; Herman Hattaway and Richard E. Beringer, *Jefferson Davis* (Lawrence: Univ. Press of Kansas, 2002), 193–94; Richard E. Beringer, et al., *Why the South Lost the Civil War* (Athens: Univ. of Georgia Press, 1986), 229; Mary E. Massey, *Ersatz in the Confederacy: Shortages and Substitutes on the Southern Homefront* (Columbia: Univ. of South Carolina Press, 1993), 16, 64, 125–26; *OR*, ser. 4, vol. 1, pt. : 487.

14. David L. Bright, comp., *Confederate Railroads* (2002–6), csa-railroads.com. Accessed at: www.csa-railroads.com; Wood, *Hitch Hiking*, 34.

15. Herman Hattaway and Archer Jones, *How the North Won: A Military History of the Civil War* (Urbana: Univ. of Illinois Press, 1983), 351.

16. *Knoxville Register*, March 20, 1863.

17. Robert C. Black III, *The Railroads of the Confederacy* (Chapel Hill: Univ. of North Carolina Press, 1952), 65; Julius White, Brevet Major-General, U.S.V., "Burnside's Occupation of East Tennessee," in *Military Essays and Recollections, Vol. 4* (Chicago: Illinois Commandery, Military Order of the Loyal Legion of the U.S. [MOLLUS]; Cozzens & Benton Co., 1907), 305; Inscoe, "Mountain Unionism," 116 (see note 6); Charles F. Bryan, Jr., "'Tories' Amidst Rebels," *East Tennessee Historical Society's Publications* 60 (1988): 4.

18. Charles G. Moffatt, "East Tennessee, the Railroad and the Bridge Burners," *Confederate Chronicles of Tennessee* 1 (1986):17–19; David D. Madden, "Unionist Resistance to Confederate Occupation," *East Tennessee Historical Society, Publications* 52 (1980): 23.

19. Thurman Sensing, *Champ Ferguson, Confederate Guerrilla* (Nashville: Vanderbilt Univ. Press, 1970), vii.

20. McKenzie, *Lincolnites and Rebels*, 32; "The Tennessee Manumission Society," at *Jefferson County, Tennessee, Genealogy & History* (July 6, 2008), jefferson.tngenealogy.net. Accessed at: https://jefferson .tngenealogy.net/research-aids/36-records/456-the-tennessee -manumission-society; Donna B. Jacobson, *Borderland of Light* (Uncasville: 2011); Alice D. Adams, *The Neglected Period of Anti-Slavery in America* (Boston: Atheneum, 1908), 61; Joseph P. Smith, "Captain Richard Calvin Rankin, 1821–1899," in *History of the Republican Party in Ohio* (Chicago: Lewis Publishing, 1898), 782.

21. Noel C. Fisher, *War at Every Door* (Chapel Hill: Univ. of North Carolina Press, 1997), 20.

22. On February 9, 1861, just days after representatives of the lower South formed the Confederate government, ninety-four percent of Johnson County voters rejected an invitation to hold a state convention to consider whether Tennessee should join the rebellion. Sensing, *Champ Ferguson, Confederate Guerrilla*, vii; Martin Crawford, *Ashe County's Civil War* (Charlottesville: University Press of Virginia, 2001), 73.

23. Hermann Bokum, pamphlet, *The Testimony of a Refugee from East Tennessee* (Philadelphia: privately printed, 1863), 5; McKenzie, *Lincolnites and Rebels*, 86–89.

24. Mark E. Neely, Jr., *Southern Rights* (Charlottesville: Univ. Press of Virginia, 1999), 107; Robert T. McKenzie, "Prudent Silence and Strict Neutrality," in *Enemies of the Country*, eds. John C. Inscoe and Robert R. Kenzer (Athens: Univ. of Georgia Press, 2001), 82; Murray, *Bradley Divided*, 42 (see note 11).

25. According to Confederate constitutional theory, a state legislature could withdraw from the Union whenever it wished. A bloc of counties, however, could not secede from a state without permission. Article IV, §3 of the United States Constitution prohibits portions of existing states from becoming parts of a new state without the consent of the U.S. Congress and the existing state legislature. John E. Stealey III, "West Virginia's Constitutional Critique of Virginia," *Civil War History* 57, no. 1 (March 2011): 13.

26. McKenzie, *Lincolnites and Rebels*, 85.

27. Felix K. Zollicoffer, Brig. Gen. CSA, "To the People of East Tennessee!" Aug. 7, 1861, broadside handbill, in *Their Eyes Have Seen the Glory: East Tennessee Unionists in the Civil War*, comp. Donahue Bible (Mohawk: Dodson Creek Publishers, 1997).

28. Crawford, *Ashe County*, 108 (see note 22).

29. McKenzie, *Lincolnites and Rebels*, 93, 253 fn 29; Neely, *Southern Rights*, 171 (see note 24).

30. McKenzie, *Lincolnites and Rebels*, 93, 101; Gen. Simon B. Buckner to Samuel Cooper, May 21, 1863, *OR*, ser. 4, vol. 2, pt. 2: 563.

31. General Simon Buckner reported in August, 1863, that "some of the

parties are pursued; some are overtaken and killed or captured, but lawless violence is on the increase." Buckner to Samuel Cooper, August 4, 1863, *OR*, ser. 1, vol. 23, pt. 2: 950.

32. James M. McPherson, *Tried by War* (New York: Penguin, 2008), 61.

33. *OR*, ser. 1, vol. 4, ch. 12: 343, 348.

34. The similarity of Little Switzerland to its namesake was not entirely due to its terrain; a substantial number of Swiss immigrants resided there. Current, *Lincoln's Loyalists*, 37 (see note 2); Thomas L. Connelly, *Army of the Heartland* (Baton Rouge: Louisiana State Univ. Press, 1967), 6–8, 13; White, "Burnside," 305 (see note 17); Moffatt, "Railroad," 17 (see note 18); James L. McDonough, *War in Kentucky* (Knoxville: Univ. of Tennessee Press, 1994), 39; Murray, *Bradley Divided*, 156.

35. Oliver P. Temple, *East Tennessee and the Civil War* (Cincinnati: Robert Clarke,1899), 444; Graf and Haskins, *Papers of Andrew Johnson*, 29, 32 fn, 163 (see note 11); John G. Nicolay and John Hay, *Abraham Lincoln* (New York: Century, 1890), 60–65.

36. Temple, *East Tennessee*, 444 (see note 35); Current, *Lincoln's Loyalists*, 36–37; Fisher, *War at Every Door*, 122–23 (see note 21); McDonough, *War in Kentucky*, 34 (see note 34); Peter Wallenstein, "Helping to Save the Union," in *The Civil War in Appalachia*, eds. K. W. Noe and S. H. Wilson, 1–3; Graf and Haskins, *Papers of Andrew Johnson*, 44, 94–95, 114, fn 198, 219, fn 232, 233, 275, 294, fn 315, 323, 720; Black, *Railroads*, 58 (see note 17); Murray, *Bradley Divided*, 68–69.

37. The family also included at least nine members who joined the Confederate army.

38. William G. Piston, *Carter's Raid* (Johnson City: Overmountain Press, 1989), 9.

39. Graf and Haskins, *Papers of Andrew Johnson: Vol. 5, 1861–1862*, xlvii, 517–19; Harry S. Stout, *Upon the Altar of the Nation* (New York: Viking, 2006), 42–43, 123–24.

40. Bokum, *Testimony of a Refugee*, 13 (see note 23).

41. Temple, *East Tennessee*, 379; Madden, "Unionist Resistance," 22, 24–27 (see note 18); Current, *Lincoln's Loyalists*, 35–36; Fisher, *War at Every Door*, 52.

42. The officers were Capt. David Fry, of the 2nd Tennessee Infantry

(U.S.), a prominent Unionist from Greene County, and William Cross, of Scott County. Fry subsequently served as a guerrilla chieftain in East Tennessee and then as a participant in the ill-fated Andrews raid. Charles S. McCammon, ed. and comp., *Loyal Mountain Troopers: The Second and Third Tennessee Volunteer Cavalry in the Civil War* (Maryville: Blount County Genealogical and Historical Society, 1992), 4; Marvin Byrd, *A Unionist in East Tennessee* (Charleston: History Press, 2011), 123; Donahue Bible, "Further Insight Into the Life and Military Service of Captain David Fry," *Tennessee Ancestors* 22, no. 2 (2006): 121; Jonathan Morgan, "Letter Written by 'Pottertown' Potter... Concerning the 'Bridge-burning,'" in Bible, *Their Eyes Have Seen the Glory: East Tennessee Unionists in the Civil War* (Mohawk: Dodson Creek Publishers, 1997), 1-4.

43. He saved the bridge at Strawberry Plains, which remained intact until the Sanders raiders burned it two years later. Two heavily-protected spans escaped destruction.

44. Current, *Lincoln's Loyalists*, 32-38; Madden, "Unionist Resistance," 30-33; Samuel W. Scott and Samuel P. Angel, *History of the Thirteenth Regiment, Tennessee Volunteer Cavalry, U.S.A.* (Philadelphia: P. W. Ziegler, 1903), 80-97; Fisher, *War at Every Door*, 55-56; Abraham Jobe, "Autobiography of Dr. Abraham Jobe of Elizabethton, Tennessee," MS-1552, UTK, 50; Dorothy E. Kelly, "The Bridge Burnings and Union Uprising of 1861," *Tennessee Ancestors* 21, no. 2 (Aug. 2005): 131-32.

45. Felix Kirk, letter to Father, Nov. 24, 1861, MS-2152, UTK; Graf and Haskins, *Papers of Andrew Johnson: Vol. 5*, fn42, 49-50, 73-74; Black, *Railroads*, 69-70; David C. Smith, *Campaign to Nowhere* (Strawberry Plains: Strawberry Plains Press, 1999), 3; William C. Davis, *Look Away!* (New York: Free Press, 2002), 174; McKenzie, "Prudent Silence," 83 (see note 24); Neely, *Southern Rights*, 2-5; James B. Jones, Jr., comp., *Tennessee in the Civil War* (Jefferson: McFarland, 2011), 54-55; U.S. National Archives and Records Administration (NARA), "Southern Claims Commission Approved Claims, 1871-1880: Tennessee, Knox County" (Washington: NARA, n.d.), 217. *Fold3.com* (2008), accessed at: www.fold3.com/image/#258084206.

46. W. B. Wood to Felix Zollicoffer, telegram, Nov. 10, 1861, *OR*, ser. 1, vol. 7,

ch. 17, 233; Fisher, *War at Every Door*, 57–58; Temple, *East Tennessee*, 378–88, 395; Thomas W. Humes, *The Loyal Mountaineers of Tennessee* (Knoxville: Ogden Bros., 1888), 131–49; Scott and Angel, *Thirteenth Regiment*, 93 (see note 44); Bryan, "Tories," 8–9 (see note 17).

47. Edward Younger, ed., *Inside the Confederate Government: The Diary of Robert Garlick Hill Kean, Head of the Bureau of War* (New York: Oxford Univ. Press, 1957), 17–18.

48. Margaret E. Wagner, Gary W. Gallagher, and Paul Finkelman, eds., *The Library of Congress Civil War Desk Reference* (New York: Simon & Schuster, 2002), 182; William J. Cooper, Jr., *Jefferson Davis* (New York: Knopf, 2000), 426–27; Hattaway and Beringer, *Davis*, 270, 302 (see note 13); William H. Russell, *My Diary, North and South* (New York: Harper & Bros., 1863), 70.

49. Daniel E. Sutherland, *A Savage Conflict* (Chapel Hill: Univ. of North Carolina Press, 2009), 42–54.

50. Davis assumed for himself full authority to suspend the writ of *habeas corpus* at will, or in other words, whenever he alone determined that emergency circumstances warranted such action. In this respect, he and Lincoln agreed. But unlike Lincoln, Davis did not have a Supreme Court to object to his policy. See Jonathan W. White, *Abraham Lincoln and Treason in the Civil War* (Baton Rouge: Louisiana State Univ. Press, 2011), 88–89; Cooper, *Jefferson Davis*, 371 (see note 48); Linda L. Crist, Mary Seaton Dix, and Kenneth H. Williams, eds., *The Papers of Jefferson Davis, Vol. 9: January–September 1863* (Baton Rouge: Louisiana State Univ. Press, 1997), 110–11, 229, 375.

51. Jane Singer, *The Confederate Dirty War* (Jefferson: McFarland, 2005), 24, 85; Brian R. Dirck, *Lincoln and Davis* (Lawrence: Univ. Press of Kansas, 2001), 235; Sutherland, *Savage Conflict*, 99–100 (see note 49); Wagner, et al., *Library of Congress Desk Reference*, 179–80 (see note 48); James M. McPherson, *Battle Cry of Freedom* (New York: Oxford Univ. Press, 1988), 429.

52. Fisher, *War at Every Door*, 106; McKenzie, *Lincolnites and Rebels*, 94–95.

53. Two months earlier, President Lincoln forbade the Union commander in Missouri, General John C. Frémont, to execute prisoners who had been apprehended for burning bridges. But only a few days after Benjamin

issued his "hang the bridge burners" directive, Union Major General Henry Halleck issued orders that effectively reversed Lincoln's leniency. Halleck's sterner policy permitted the shooting of bridge burners who were convicted after a hearing before a military commission. Halleck's policy could not have been promulgated without Lincoln's permission; Lincoln had sacked Frémont, in part because of Frémont's insubordinate treatment of prisoners.

Over the course of the war, Union army courts-martial convicted six bridge burners of treason, five of whom were Missourians. Another was imprisoned for an undefined violation. None of the offenders were executed, however. Sutherland, *Savage Conflict*, 23–25, 59–61; William A. Blair, *With Malice toward Some* (Chapel Hill: Univ. North Carolina Press, 2014), 234, 311-12, 322.

54. Davis evidently regarded bridge burning a particularly unspeakable offense. A bridge burner could be (and some were) put to death, even though no enemy lives were lost as a result of the attack for which they were prosecuted. Benjamin to Wood, Benjamin to John Crozier Ramsey, telegrams, Nov. 25, 1861, *OR*, ser. 1, vol. 7, ch. 17, 701; Graf and Haskins, *Papers of Andrew Johnson: Vol. 5*, 88; Fisher, *War at Every Door*, 58–59; Richard S. Brownlee, *Gray Ghosts of the Confederacy* (Baton Rouge: Louisiana State Univ. Press, 1958), 77; Temple, *East Tennessee*, 389–93; Robert R. Mackey, *The Uncivil War* (Norman: Univ. of Oklahoma Press, 2004), 123; William C. Davis, *An Honorable Defeat* (New York: Harcourt, 2001), 136; Cooper, *Jefferson Davis*, 426–27; Dirck, *Lincoln and Davis*, 101-2 (see note 51); Brian R. Dirck, "Posterity's Blush," *Civil War History* 48, no. 3 (September 2002): 256; Elizabeth D. Leonard, *Lincoln's Avengers* (New York: W. W. Norton, 2004), 44; Phillip S. Paludan, *Victims* (Knoxville: Univ. of Tennessee Press, 1981), 113.

55. Tariq Kochi, "The Partisan: Carl Schmitt and Terrorism," *Law Critique* 17, no. 3 (2006): 271–75.

56. Paludan, *Victims*, 87–88, 113 (see note 54).

57. Carroll to Benjamin and Benjamin to Carroll, Dec. 10, 1861, *OR*, ser. 1, vol. 7, ch. 17, 754.

58. Kelly, "Bridge Burnings," 137 (see note 44); Donahue Bible, "The Hangings of the Greene County Bridge Burners," *Tennessee Ancestors*

21, no. 2 (August 2005): 137; Madden, "Unionist Resistance," 38; Mark E. Neely, Jr., *Confederate Bastille* (Milwaukee: Marquette Univ. Press, 1993), 12–14.

59. Davis, *Honorable Defeat*, 10 (see note 54); Cooper, *Jefferson Davis*; David J. Eicher, *Dixie Betrayed: How the South Really Lost the Civil War* (New York: Little, Brown, 2006), 49–50, 148; Younger, *Inside the Confederate Government*, 29–30 (see note 47).

60. Clemant A. Evans, ed., *Confederate Military History* (Wilmington: Broadfoot, 1987), 133; Temple, *East Tennessee*, 392; Bertram Wyatt-Brown, *The Shaping of Southern Culture* (Chapel Hill: Univ. of North Carolina Press, 2001), 52, 284, 286; Crist, Dix and Williams, *Davis Papers, Vol. 9*, 375 (see note 50).

61. Temple, *East Tennessee*, 392–93, 397–99; Madden, "Unionist Resistance," 37; Moffatt, "Railroad," 22.

62. *Richmond Dispatch*, Jan. 10, 1862.

63. Jobe, *Autobiography*, 51 (see note 44); Moffatt, "Railroad," 22.

64. Bible, "Captain David Fry," 121 (see note 42); Bible, "Hangings," 131–32 (see note 58); Fisher, *War at Every Door*, 64; "Robert King BYRD." Accessed at: www.roanetnheritage.com/research/assembley/17.htm.

65. Temple, *East Tennessee*, 399; John W. Foster, *War Stories for My Grandchildren* (Washington: privately printed, 1918); William G. Brownlow, *Brownlow's Knoxville Whig and Rebel Ventilator*, Jan. 9, 1864.

66. Madden, "Unionist Resistance," 24–25; William C. Davis and Meredith Swentor, eds., *Bluegrass Confederate: The Headquarters Diary of Edward O. Guerrant* (Baton Rouge: Louisiana State Univ. Press, 1999), 244, 320; "Yankee Trick with the Telegraph," *Southern Confederacy* [Atlanta, GA], July 6, 1863: 1; Black, *Railroads*, 58.

67. These units were still in place when the Sanders raiders arrived. Fisher, *War at Every Door*, 107–8.

68. William W. Stringfield, "Memoirs of the Civil War," n.d., unpublished manuscript, Stringfield Papers, Special Collections, Hunter Library, Western Carolina University, Cullowhee, NC; E. Porter Alexander, *Fighting for the Confederacy: The Personal Recollections of General Edward Porter Alexander*, ed. Gary W. Gallagher (Chapel Hill: Univ. of North Carolina Press, 1989), 124.

69. McKenzie, *Lincolnites and Rebels*, 118; William Marvel, *A Place Called Appomattox*, (Chapel Hill: Univ. of North Carolina Press, 2000), 110; John C. Inscoe and Gordon B. McKinney, *The Heart of Confederate Appalachia* (Chapel Hill: Univ. of North Carolina Press, 2000), 111.

70. Fisher, *War at Every Door*, 68, 108–9; Inscoe and McKinney, *Heart of Confederate Appalachia*, 111 (see prev. note); Marvel, *Appomattox*, 110 (prev. note); Thomas J. Henderson, letter, to Gov. Richard Yates, Aug. 18, 1863, Henderson Papers, Illinois State Library, Springfield, Missouri; McKenzie, *Lincolnites and Rebels*, 118, 120; Bryan, "Tories," 8–9, 12–13.

71. U.S. Census, "1860 Federal Census, Roane, TN," trans. Don K. Robbins, *U.S. GenWeb Project*, U.S.-Census.org. (2004), Mf. 653, reel 1269. Accessed at: ftp://ftp.us-census.org/pub/usgenweb/census/xtn /roane/1860/; NARA, "Compiled Service Records of Volunteer Soldiers Who Served During the Mexican War in Organizations from the State of Tennessee" [Company C, 1–7: Robert K. Byrd, 1847], R.G. 94, M638.

72. Fisher, *War at Every Door*, 64; William R. Carter, *History of the First Regiment of Tennessee Volunteer Cavalry in the Great War of the Rebellion . . . 1862–1865*, reprint (Johnson City: Overmountain Press, 1992), 19; NARA, "Southern Claims Commission Approved Claims, 1871–1880," *Fold 3.com* (2008), 217. Accessed at: www.fold3.com /image/#258084225; J. A. Brents, *The Patriots and Guerrillas of East Tennessee and Kentucky*, Pamphlet, 1863, reprint (Danville: Kentucky Jayhawker Press, 2005), 12, 22.

73. "The Raiders Not Gone Yet," *Knoxville Register*, July 4, 1863: 2.

74. Fisher, *War at Every Door*, 103–20; William M. Churchwell, letter, to Mrs. Robert K. Byrd, May 14, 1862, *OR*, ser. 2, vol.1: 892.

75. Marvin Byrd, *A Unionist in East Tennessee* (Charleston: History Press, 2011), 58–60.

76. Humes, *Loyal Mountaineers*, 403 (see note 46); Temple, *East Tennessee*, 152; Moffatt, "Railroad," 22; Steven V. Ash, ed., *Secessionists and Other Scoundrels* (Baton Rouge: Louisiana State Univ. Press, 1999), 293.

77. James McCartney, "Saunders Raid Into East Tennessee," in *History of the 112th Regiment of Illinois Volunteer Infantry in the Great War of the Rebellion, 1862–1865*, ed. B. F. Thompson (Toulon: Stark County News, 1885), 438–39; Brents, *Patriots and Guerrillas*, 13 (see note 72).

78. John Will Dyer, *Reminiscences; or, Four Years in the Confederate Army* [1861–1865] (Evansville: Amelia W. Dyer, Keller Printing and Publishing Co., 1898), 104; W. Todd Groce, *Mountain Rebels* (Knoxville: Univ. of Tennessee Press, 1999), 111.

79. Carter, *Tennessee Volunteer Cavalry*, 17 (see note 72); Stringfield, "Memoirs" (see note 68); Paul A. Thomsen, *Rebel Chief* (New York: Tom Doherty, 2004), 193; Jefferson County, Tennessee Genealogy & History, *The Tennessee Manumission Society*, n.d. (see note 20).

80. Jennifer C. Bohrnstedt, ed., *While Father Is Away: The Civil War Letters of William H. Bradbury* (Lexington: Univ. Press of Kentucky, 2003), 152.

81. Thomsen, *Rebel Chief*, 193, 199, 200 (see note 79); Katherine Newman, et al., "History of Strawberry Plains," unpublished essay (Strawberry Plains: Rush Strong High School, 1936). http://jefferson.tngenealogy .net/about-jeff/20-history/23-history-strawberry-plains; E. Stanley Godbold, Jr., and Mattie U. Russell, *Confederate Colonel and Cherokee Chief* (Knoxville: Univ. of Tennessee Press, 1990), 105–11.

Chapter 2

82. The Confederate armies numbered 291,000 men. Leonard J. Fullencamp, ed. and comp., *An Overview of the Gettysburg Campaign* (Carlisle Barracks: Army War College, 2006), 12

83. This concept is now termed *concentration in time*. Richard Carwardine, *Lincoln: A Life of Purpose and Power* (New York: Alfred A. Knopf, 2003), 252; McPherson, *Tried by War*, 70–71, 268–69.

84. These estimates of troop strength are for June 1, 1863, when the Sanders raid was in its planning stage.

85. Jacob D. Cox, *Military Reminiscences of the Civil War* 1 (New York: Scribner, 1900), 475.

86. Noel C. Fisher, "Definitions of Victory," in Daniel E. Sutherland, ed., *Guerrillas, Unionists, and Violence on the Confederate Home Front* (Fayetteville: Univ. of Arkansas Press, 1999), 100; McKenzie, *Lincolnites and Rebels*, 60–63; Fisher, *War at Every Door*, 35, 71; Georgia L. Tatum, *Disloyalty in the Confederacy* (Chapel Hill: Univ. of North Carolina Press, 1934), 13–21, 195; James B. Campbell, "East Tennessee During the Federal Occupation, 1863–1865," *Journal of East Tennessee History* 19

(1947): 65; James I. Robertson, Jr., ed., *Soldier of Southwestern Virginia* (Baton Rouge: Louisiana State Univ. Press, 2004), 93–94; George W. Morgan, "Cumberland Gap," in *Battles and Leaders of the Civil War, Vol. 3: The Tide Shifts*, eds. R. U. Johnson and C. C. Buel (Secaucus: Castle, 1887), 62; Alexander, *Fighting for the Confederacy*, 313 (see note 68); A. C. Myers, "Trouble in Knoxville," telegram, to Felix Zollicoffer (1861) in *Confederate Railroads*, David L. Bright, comp., csa-railroads.com. Accessed at: www.csa-railroads.com/Essays/Original; David Williams, Teresa T. Williams, and David Carlson, *Plain Folk in a Rich Man's War* (Gainesville: Univ. Press of Florida, 2002), 2, 157.

87. Madden, "Unionist Resistance," 23; Crawford, *Ashe County*, 127; Thomas L. Livermore, *Numbers and Losses in the Civil War* (Bloomington: Indiana Univ. Press, 1957), 24.

88. Cox, *Reminiscences of the Civil War* 1, 475. Also: Cox, Reminiscences 2, 36 (see note 85).

89. William Marvel, *Burnside* (Chapel Hill: Univ. of North Carolina Press, 1991), 248.

90. Michael Burlingame, ed., *Lincoln Observed* (Baltimore: Johns Hopkins Univ. Press, 1998), 32–33, 226–27; McKenzie, *One South or Many?* 4 (see note 9); A. R. Lawton, "Corn for Lee's Army" (1863) in *Confederate Railroads*, David L. Bright, comp., www.csa-railroads.com: Walter S. Griggs, Jr., *General John Pegram C.S.A.* (Lynchburg, VA: H. E. Howard, 1993), 70–72.

91. *OR*, ser. 1, vol. 23, pt. 2: 365.

92. James Longstreet, "Lee's Invasion of Pennsylvania," in *Battles and Leaders of the Civil War* 3, eds. R. U. Johnson and C. C. Buel (New York: Century Magazine, 1884–88), 244–46.

93. Jeffery D. Wert, "James Longstreet and the Lost Cause," in *The Myth of the Lost Cause and Civil War History*, ed. G. W. Gallagher and A. T. Nolan (Bloomington: Indiana Univ. Press, 2000), 243–47; Hattaway and Jones, *How the North Won*, 362 (see note 15).

94. Buckner to Cooper, June 24, 1863. *OR*, 315–16, 337, 355, 383–84.

95. William Marvel, *The Battles for Saltville* (Lynchburg: H. E. Howard, 1992), 46.

96. Marvel, *Burnside*, 244–45, 264 (see note 89).

97. Crawford was a 43-year-old lawyer from Greeneville, Tennessee. His rank in 1863 is unknown, but he served for three months in 1864 as colonel of the 3rd Tennessee Mounted Infantry USA. His unit saw no combat action. See: 1860 U.S. Federal Census, Population Schedule, Greene County, Tennessee, District 10, 90, and also: Civil War Centennial Commission of Tennessee, "Federal Cavalry Units: 3rd Tennessee Mounted Infantry Regiment, U.S.A.," in *Tennesseans in the Civil War, vol. 1* (1964); *OR*, ser. 1, vol. 23, pt. 2: 371.

98. The distance from Loudon to Bristol was 158 miles; Lee's line of defense was 125 miles. In Thomas L. Connelly, *Army of the Heartland* (Baton Rouge: Louisiana State Univ. Press, 1967), ix; Murray, *Bradley Divided*, 116.

99. Thomas L. Connelly, *Autumn of Glory* (Baton Rouge: Louisiana State Univ. Press, 1971), 107–8.

100. Orlando B. Willcox to Burnside, May 31, 1863, *OR*, ser. 1, vol. 23, pt. 2: 375. The original document is in the Willcox papers at the Army War College, Carlisle, PA.

101. Ibid.

102. Marvel, *Burnside*, 88.

103. Willcox fought on after being wounded. For this gallantry, he was awarded the Congressional Medal of Honor in 1895.

104. Neutrality in the context of the Civil War constituted support for the rebels. Robert N. Scott, comp. "Instructions for the Government of the Armies of the United States in the Field (April 24, 1863)," in *An Analytical Digest of the Military Laws of the United States* (Philadelphia: Lippincott, 1873), 306; Allan Nevins, *The War for the Union, Vol. 1: The Improvised War, 1861-1862* (New York: Charles Scribner's Sons, 1959), 134–35; Arndt M. Stickles, *Simon Bolivar Buckner* (Chapel Hill: Univ. of North Carolina Press, 1940), 88-9; Leonard, *Lincoln's Avengers*, 25–27 (see note 54).

105. John H. Eicher and David J. Eicher, *Civil War High Commands* (Stanford: Stanford Univ. Press, 2001), 4, 152; Mark M. Boatner III, Allen C. Northrup, and Lowell I. Miller, eds., *Civil War Dictionary* (New York: David McKay Company, Inc., 1959), 455.

106. Kentucky's duly elected legislature remained loyal to the Union, but the

Confederate congress recognized a council known as the "Provisional Government of Kentucky." On November 20, 1861, two months after Buckner joined the rebel army, this extra-legal body approved an ordinance of secession. In Lowell H. Harrison, *The Civil War in Kentucky* (Lexington: Univ. Press of Kentucky, 1975), 13, 16–17, 20–21; Stickles, *Buckner*, 51–99, passim (see prev. note).

107. Twenty years later, Abraham Lincoln's private secretary, John G. Nicolay, denounced Buckner as the state's "most active lieutenant in contemplated treason." Lincoln had offered Buckner a commission as a general officer, but he rejected it. Kentucky's duly elected legislature remained loyal to the Union, but the Confederate congress recognized a council known as the "Provisional Government of Kentucky." On November 20, 1861, two months after Buckner joined the rebel army, this extra-legal body approved an ordinance of secession. Stickles, *Buckner*, 105–7; Nevins, *War for the Union 1*, 134–35 (see note 104); John G. Nicolay, *The Outbreak of Rebellion* (New York: Thomas Yoseloff, 1963), 130; Robert G. Scott, ed., *Forgotten Valor* (Kent: Kent State Univ. Press, 1999), 464.

108. *OR*, ser. 1, vol. 23, pt. 2: 375.

109. Fisher, *War at Every Door*, 133.

110. Amy M. Taylor, *The Divided Family in Civil War America* (Chapel Hill: Univ. of North Carolina Press, 2005), 91.

111. *OR*, ser. 1, vol. 23, pt. 2: 126; William A. Strasser, "A Terrible Calamity Has Befallen Us," *Journal of East Tennessee History* 71 (1999): 73–74; Graf and Haskins, *Papers of Andrew Johnson, Vol. 6*, 246 fn, 333; John C. Inscoe and Gordon B. McKinney, "Highland Households Divided," in *Enemies of the Country*, eds. J. C. Inscoe and R. C. Kenzer (Athens: University of Georgia Press, 2001), 65–67.

112. Neither Mrs. Lee nor her husband have been identified.

113. *OR*, ser. 1, vol. 23, pt. 2: 229, 351, 371, 440.

114. Stephen Z. Starr, *The Union Cavalry in the Civil War: The War in the West, 1861–1865* 3 (Baton Rouge: Louisiana State Univ. Press, 1985), 20–22.

115. Gary R. Mathews, *Basil Wilson Duke* (Lexington: Univ. Press of Kentucky, 2005), 163; *OR*, ser. 1, vol. 10, ch. 22, pt. 2: 183.

116. Piston, *Carter's Raid*, 63.

117. Allan Nevins, *The War for the Union, Vol. 2: The Organized War, 1863–1864* (New York: Scribner and Sons, 1971).

118. Carter found that a quarter of his men were almost completely untrained and were incapable of carrying out the maneuvers which he had designed. He also discovered that the troops which mustered at the assembly point were only a fraction of the force which he had been originally promised. Piston, *Carter's Raid*, 36–37 (see note 38); Boatner, Northrup and Miller, *Civil War Dictionary*, 671– 72 (see note 105).

119. McKnight, *Contested Borderland*, 125–28 (see note 12); Davis and Swentor, *Bluegrass Confederate*, 195 (see note 66).

120. McKnight, *Contested Borderland*, 125–29; Scott and Angel, *Thirteenth Regiment*, 107; Robert C. Burns, "General and Admiral Too," *East Tennessee Historical Society's Publications* 48 (1976): 29; Marvel, *Battles for Saltville*, 35–38 (see note 95); Boatner, *Civil War Dictionary*, 130.

121. Piston, *Carter's Raid*, 64–66.

122. Nevins, *War for the Union 2* (see note 117); McKnight, *Contested Borderland*, 126–28.

123. Colonel Samuel Carter was assigned to lead a separate raid which failed owing to flooded river conditions. He compiled a distinguished combat record. In Scott, *Forgotten Valor*, 447 (see note 107).

124. Davis and Swentor, *Bluegrass Confederate*, 16, 19; Bohrnstedt, *While Father Is Away*, 115 (see note 80).

125. Bohrnstedt, *While Father Is Away*, 114.

126. Thompson, *112th Regiment*, 102 (see note 77).

127. Graf and Haskins, *Papers of Andrew Johnson, Vol. 6*, 243–45.

128. Simon B. Buckner, "Abstract from field return Department of East Tennessee . . ." May 31, 1863, *OR*, ser. 1, vol. 23, pt. 2: 855; Inscoe and McKinney, *Heart of Confederate Appalachia*, 129.

129. The Sanders men actually encountered fewer than 1,000 Confederate soldiers guarding the railroad east of Knoxville, but some men had been recalled to Knoxville in anticipation of Sanders's strike on June 20. In Graf and Haskins, *Papers of Andrew Johnson, Vol. 6*, 243.

130. Ibid., 243, 245fn; Crawford, *Ashe County*, 108.

131. Graf and Haskins, *Papers of Andrew Johnson, Vol. 6*, 245.

132. *OR*, ser. 1, vol. 23, pt. 2, 375.

133. Burnside also invested heavily (and lost) in an ill-fated attempt to manufacture breech-loading carbines. In Marvel, *Burnside*, 6, 11–14, 81.

134. William B. Hesseltine, ed., *Dr. J. G. M. Ramsey* (Nashville: Tennessee Historical Commission, 1954), 118.

135. W. H. Bristol, "Diagrams for rebuilding Loudon Bridge," Loudon Bridge Civil War Collection, 1862–65, manuscript MS-2686, University of Tennessee, Knoxville, TN.

136. It cost more than two million dollars to build, an unprecedented sum. in Groce, *Mountain Rebels*, 9–16; Bohrnstedt, *While Father Is Away*, 173; Donald C. Maness and H. Jason Combs, eds. *Do They Miss Me At Home?: The Civil War Letters of William McKnight, Seventh Ohio Volunteer Cavalry* (Athens: Ohio Univ. Press, 2010), 126.

137. A. C. Myers, "Wallace to Run East Tennessee & Virginia," telegram, to C. Wallace (Sept. 18, 1861), in *Confederate Railroads*, comp. D. L. Bright., www.csa-railroads. com; Myers, "Trouble in Knoxville" (see note 88).

138. Groce, *Mountain Rebels*, 39.

139. Edward G. Longacre, *Lincoln's Cavalrymen* (Mechanicsburg: Stackpole, 2000), 76.

140. Horace Porter, *Campaigning with Grant* (New York: Bantam, 1991), 147.

141. Isaac Gause, *Four Years with Five Armies* (New York: Neale Publishing, 1908), 122, 169.

142. D. W. Edmiston, "Fighting at Philadelphia," *National Tribune* 14 (Feb. 7, 1895): 2; George B. Davis, Leslie J. Perry, and Joseph W. Kirkley, *Atlas to Accompany the Official Records of the Union and Confederate Armies* (Washington: Government Printing Office, 1891–95), plate 111, sketch 6.

143. *OR*, ser. 1, vol. 23, pt. 2: 375.

144. Inscoe and McKinney, *Heart of Confederate Appalachia*, 129.

145. James D. Brewer, *The Raiders of 1862* (Westport: Praeger, 1997), 136, 180–86.

146. General Ambrose Burnside had been wounded by an Indian arrow in New Mexico. In modern terms the principle of surprise dictates: "Accomplish your purpose before the enemy can effectively react." Quoted from Boatner, *Civil War Dictionary*, 672.

148. Eastham Tarrant, *The Wild Riders of the First Kentucky Cavalry* (Lexington: Henry Clay Press, 1969), 159, 165–66; *OR,* ser. 1, vol. 23, pt. 2: 229, 344–46, 370–71, 375, 389.

149. *OR,* ser. 1, vol. 23, pt. 2: 316; Whitelaw Reid, *Ohio in the War, 1861-1865* 2 (Cincinnati: Moore, Wilstach & Baldwin, 1868), 799; Ezra J. Weaver, "George Lucas Hartsuff," in *Generals in Blue: Lives of the Union Commanders* (Baton Rouge: Louisiana State Univ. Press, 1964), 213; John D. Smith and William J. Cooper, eds., *A Union Woman in Civil War Kentucky* (Lexington: Univ. Press of Kentucky, 2000), 131; George W. Cullum, "George L. Hartsuff," in *Biographical Register of the Officers and Graduates of the U.S. Military Academy* (Boston: Houghton Mifflin and Company, 1891), 682.

Chapter 3

150. Hattaway and Jones, *How the North Won,* 216–17.

151. Lewis Sanders, "A List of Articles Purchased by Lewis Sanders 1810," and "private letters," both in Sanders Family Papers, Filson Historical Society, Louisville, KY; Lewis Sanders, "History of Kentucky Cattle," *The Cultivator,* March, 1849.

152. Despite the confusing implication conveyed by their names, Lewis Sanders Jr. was not the son of Lewis Sanders Sr. He was his nephew. Lewis Sr. adopted a son of his brother Nathaniel and christened him "Lewis Jr." While Lewis Sr. served as the surrogate grandfather of Lewis Jr.'s children, including young William, he was actually their great-uncle. The Sanders family was also evidently linked to George Nicholas, a Revolutionary leader in Virginia and an early settler of Kentucky. Clyde N. Wilson, ed., *The Papers of John C. Calhoun, Vol. 17, 1843-1844* (Charleston: Univ. of South Carolina Press, 1986), 719n; Evelyn Welch, "Carroll County's Sanders Left Legacy as a Cattle Breeder," *RoundAbout Entertainment Guide,* www.roundaboutmadison.com (Madison: Kentuckiana Publishing, 2001); Anna V. Parker, *The Sanders Family of Grass Hills* (Madison: Coleman Printing, 1966), 3, 5–6, 9–10, 15–16, 19, 32–34, 114–15; Charlotte R. Conover, *The Patterson Log Cabin* (Dayton: Press of the National Cash Register Co., 1906); Bernie Spencer, "Sanders

& the Sanders Family," *Northern Kentucky Views* (2008), www.nkyviews
.com/carroll/text/carroll_sanders_2.htm; George N. Sanders obituary,
New York Times, Aug. 13, 1873.

153. Dorothy Kelly, *GENERAL WHO? William P. Sanders* (Knox-
ville: Knoxville Civil War Roundtable, 1999). Knoxville Civil War
Roundtable.org., post, June 18, 2016, in *Remembering the Civil War in East
Tennessee*. Accessed at: https://kcwrtorg.wordpress.com/ 2016/06/18
/dorothy-e-kelly-general-who-william-p-sanders/; William P. Sanders
["Doc"], letter to Cousin May [Sanders?], Nov. 7, 1863, Sanders Family
Papers (see note 151); Eicher and Eicher, *Civil War High Commands*,
609–10 (see note 105).

154. Sanders obituary, *New York Times* (see note 152).

155. Whitelaw Reid, *After the War* (New York: Harper & Row, 1866), 480–81;
Michael Wayne, *The Reshaping of Plantation Society* (Baton Rouge:
Louisiana State Univ. Press, 1983), 1, 9– 10; "Lewis Sanders, Jr.," *The
Political Graveyard* (2009), www.politicalgraveyard.com.

156. NARA, *Population Schedules of the Seventh Census of the United States,
1850*, Mississippi [Adams County, City of Natchez, July 16, 1850],
Microcopy No. 432, roll 368 [1963], 4; also see: *Population Schedules
of the Seventh Census of the United States, 1850*, Mississippi [Slave
Schedules: Adams County, City of Natchez, July 13, 1850], Microcopy
No. 432, roll 363 [1963], 351. Both in: (Washington: National Archives
Microfilm Publications, 1963).

157. Record-keeping in frontier Kentucky was imperfect, and the exact
nature of the probable familial relationship between Davis and Sanders
remains obscure.

158. James T. McIntosh, ed., *The Papers of Jefferson Davis, Vol. 2: June 1841–
July 1846* (Baton Rouge: Louisiana State Univ. Press, 1974), 71, 80, 117.

159. James H. Hawkins to John Sanders, March 2, 1823, and Edmund St. J.
Hawkins to George N. Sanders, June 20, 1823, letters, both in Sanders
Family Papers, FHS.

160. John Sanders was breveted a major "for Gallant and Meritorious
Conduct in the Several Conflicts at Monterey." In Parker, *Sanders
Family*, 3, 5–6, 95, 97–98 (see note 152).

161. Sanders was accepted for admission on March 1, 1852. Brown won

election to the U.S. House of Representatives as an at-large member from Mississippi, as did Jefferson Davis. Sanders is listed in the records of the Military Academy as representing Adams County of the 4th District of Mississippi. Brown served as governor during the Mexican War and later served in both the United States and Confederate States Senates. NARA, *Register of Cadet Applications, 1819–1867*, No. 24: 1851–52. M2037, Roll 3, R.G. 94. (Washington: NARA Microfilm Publications). Ancestry.com., *U.S., Military and Naval Academies, Cadet Records and Applications, 1800-1908* (Lehi: Ancestry.com Operations, Inc., 2008). Accessed at: https://www.ancestry.com/search/collections/1299/; Ancestry.com, *U.S., Military and Naval Academies, Cadet Records and Applications, 1805-1908* [Record for William P. Sanders] (Lehi: Ancestry. com Operations, Inc., 2008), 51, 88. Accessed at: https://www.ancestry .com/search/ collections/1299/; NARA, *Register of Cadet Applications, 1819–1867*, No. 26: 1853–54. M2037, Roll 3, R.G. 94. Ancestry.com., *U.S., Military and Naval Academies, Cadet Records and Applications, 1805– 1908* [Record for William P. Sanders] (Lehi: Ancestry.com Operations, Inc., 2008), 52. Accessed at: https://www.ancestry.com/search /collections/1299/.

162. Basil W. Duke, *Reminiscences of General Basil W. Duke* (West Jefferson: Genesis Publishing, 1998), 87.

163. Parker, *Sanders Family*, 35–42; Dorris C. James, "Antebellum Natchez" (PhD diss., Univ. of Texas, Austin, 1964), 274.

164. Joseph W. Wilshire, 1993. "A Reminiscence of Burnside's Knoxville Campaign," in *Sketches of War History, 1861–1865, Vol. 9*, ed. and comp. Ohio Commandery, MOLLUS, War Papers Index, accessed at: https:// suvcw.org/mollus/war/warpapers.htm. Reprint, www.broadfoot publishing.com. (Wilmington: Broadfoot Publishing, 1993), 6; William P. Sanders ["Doc"], letter to Cousin May [Sanders?], Nov. 7, 1863 (see note 153).

165. Nina Silber, "When Charles Francis Adams Met Robert E. Lee," in *Inside the Confederate Nation*, eds. Lesley J. Gordon and John C. Inscoe (Baton Rouge: Louisiana State Univ. Press, 2005), 350.

166. Charles R. Bowery, Jr., and Brian D. Hankinson, eds., letter of Jefferson Davis to Totten, Jan. 24, 1853, in *United States Military Academy*

Superintendent's Letter Book No. 2 and No. 3, The Daily Correspondence of Brevet Colonel Robert E. Lee, Superintendent, United States Military Academy Sept. 1, 1852 to Mar. 24, 1855 (West Point: U.S. Military Academy Press, 2003), Occasional Papers #5, Special Collections and Archives, United States Military Academy Library, West Point, NY; John F. Witt, *Lincoln's Code* (New York: Free Press, 2012), 84.

167. Bowery and Hankinson, letter of Davis to Totten, Jan. 24, 1853 (see prev. note).

168. Jennifer R. Green and Patrick Kirkwood, "Reframing the Antebellum Democratic Mainstream," *Civil War History* 61 (September 2015): 234.

169. Cooper, *Jefferson Davis*, 30–38; Hattaway and Beringer, *Davis*, 302.

170. Davis's upbraiding made no mention of his own comportment at the Academy, which, though not quite as wobbly as was Sanders's, was so poor that he barely escaped expulsion on three occasions. Linda L. Crist and Mary Seaton Dix, eds., *Papers of Jefferson Davis, Vol. 5: 1853–1855* (Baton Rouge: Louisiana State Univ. Press, 1985), 417; Cooper, *Jefferson Davis*, 33.

171. Eliza was well-positioned to ask for a favor because, besides probably being related to Davis herself, she was married to James B. Haggin, a California Gold Rush millionaire who was a friend of Davis.

172. U.S. Military Academy, *Roll of the Cadets, According to Merit in Conduct, for the Year Ending, June 15th, 1853* (Washington: Government Printing Office, 1853), 21.

173. U.S. Military Academy, *Official Register of the Officers and Cadets of the U.S. Military Academy, West Point, New York* (Washington: Government Printing Office, 1853–56); Donald C. Caughey and Jimmy J. Jones, *The Sixth United States Cavalry in the Civil War* (Jefferson: McFarland, 2013), 11.

174. Leonard L, Richards, *The California Gold Rush and the Coming of the Civil War* (New York: Knopf, 2007), 117–20.

175. Crist and Dix, *Davis Papers, Vol. 5*, 131–32 (see Note 170).

176. Steven E. Woodworth, *Jefferson Davis and His Generals* (Lawrence: Univ. Press of Kansas, 1990), 48, 113, 126, 266, 283.

177. Serving with Sanders on his frontier posts, the rosters list future Union

Generals John Buford, Jr., William P. Carlin, Nathan A. M. Dudley, George H. Gordon, John G. Kelton, William S. Ketchum, Wesley Merritt, Charles H. Morgan, Alfred Pleasanton, Charles Henry Smith, and William R. Terrill. NARA, *Returns from U.S. Military Posts, 1800–1916*, National Archives Publication M617, in Records of the Adjutant General's Office, 1780s–1917, Records Group 94 (1857): 228; Also see: NARA, *Returns from U.S. Military Posts, 1800–1916*, Nat'l. Archs. Publ. M617, in Records of the Adjutant General's Office, 1780s–1917, Records Group 94 (1857–61): [Camp Floyd] 110, 118. Both at: National Archives, Washington, D.C., and accessed at *U.S., Returns from Military Posts, 1806–1969* (Provo: Ancestry.com Operations, Inc., 2009), *Ancestry.com*, https://www.ancestry.com/search/collections/1571/ .

178. Alfred E. Bates, "The Second Regiment of Cavalry 1 (1836–65)," in *The Army of the United States*, comp. T. F. Rodenbough (New York: Maynard, Merrill, 1896), 173; William P. Sanders ["Doc"], letter to Cousin May [Sanders?].

179. August V. Kautz, "Reminiscences of the Civil War," August V. Kautz Papers, box 4, LOC. Also: Typescript copy, Andrew Wallace, The August Valentine Kautz Papers, 1828–1895, LC control no. ocm50598522, Kautz Papers collection, LOC, Washington, D.C.

180. Augustus Woodbury, *Major General Ambrose E. Burnside and the Ninth Army Corps* (Providence: Sidney S. Rider, 1867), 291–92; Gilbert C. Kniffin, "General Wm. P. Sanders," *Daily National Intelligencer*, May 6, 1882: 1.

181. Wayne, *Plantation Society*, 9–10 (see note 155); William K. Scarborough, "Lords or Capitalists?" *Journal of Mississippi History* 54, no. 3 (August 1992): 240–49, 254; James, "Antebellum Natchez," 333–34 (see note 163); NARA, *1850 Census: Mississippi [Adams County, City of Natchez]*, 4 (see note 156, first entry). Evidently some of these slaves worked on plantations; their residence is uncertain.

182. If Sanders's conscience had dictated that he not fight against the people of Mississippi, there were ways to avoid it. Few career soldiers elected to sit out the war, but that course was open. Sanders could have resigned his commission or obtained a posting which would keep him away from

the fray. Most who stayed out of the fighting were beyond military age. In Wayne W. Hsieh, *West Pointers and the Civil War* (Chapel Hill: Univ. of North Carolina Press, 2009), 92, 102.

183. Hsieh, *West Pointers*, 92, 102 (prev. note).

184. Hsieh, West Pointers, 92, 110.

185. Lewis Sanders, "Petition to Thomas P. Metcalfe, member elect of the House of Representatives, 1828," and Sanders to Gov. Beriah Magoffin, 1860, both in Sanders Family Papers, FHS, Louisville, KY.

186. Alexander, *Fighting for the Confederacy*, 28; Hsieh, *West Pointers*, 110; Seymour, *Divided Loyalties*, 124 (see note 4).

187. Johnston had been the colonel of the Second Dragoons during Sanders's service, and Lee was the regiment's second-in-command. Both men became full generals in the Confederate army. In Cooper, *Jefferson Davis*, 363.

188. Bates, "Second Regiment of Cavalry 1" (see note 178); Edward M. Coffman, *The Old Army* (New York: Oxford Univ. Press, 1986), 60; Starr, *Union Cavalry* 3, 337 (see note 114).

189. While stationed at Camp Floyd, Utah, Sanders and a sergeant were ordered to retrieve deserters. After a ride of 1600 miles in 59 days, they located their quarry in Los Angeles. Sanders then stopped at San Francisco to visit his sisters and their families before returning to duty. In George T. Ness, Jr., *The Regular Army on the Eve of The Civil War* (Baltimore: Toomey Press, 1990), 235; NARA, "Returns from U.S. Military Posts, 1800–1916," 110, 118 (see note 177, 2nd entry).

190. Alexander, *Fighting for the Confederacy*, 27–28; Hsieh, *West Pointers*, 96, 110–11; NARA, "Returns from U.S. Military Posts, 1800–1916,"118.

191. Southerners of all ranks who were West Point graduates divided almost evenly between the two armies. Fifty-one percent joined the Confederate forces, while forty-nine percent remained loyal to the Union. There were also 130 Southern officers in the Regular Army who were appointed from civilian life. Of these, all but one joined the Confederate Army. In Boatner, *Civil War Dictionary*, 495.

192. Haggin moved to Sacramento in October, 1850, at age 25. He listed the value of his real property at $8000. In 1870 Haggin and Tevis estimated their net worth at $1,500,000 each. In *California State Census of 1852,*

microfilm M/F 144 (6 rolls), California State Library, Sacramento, CA. Accessed at: *California, U.S., State Census,* 1852 (Provo: Ancestry .com Operations, Inc., 2010), *Ancestry.com,* https://www.ancestry.com /search/collections/1767/; McPherson, *For Cause and Comrades,* 108–10.

193. William P. Sanders ["Doc"], letter to Cousin May [Sanders?], Nov. 7, 1863.

194. Sanders was a highly trained, seasoned professional soldier. West Point graduates were in short supply, and senior officers of the U.S. Army must have realized that the Confederates might very well offer this Southern-born officer a tempting appointment. The northerners acted swiftly, and they may have done so in order to ensure that Captain Sanders did not join the Rebellion.

195. Captain William H. Carter, "Sixth Regiment of Cavalry," in *The Army of the US Historical Sketches of Staff and Line with Portraits of Generals-in-Chief,* eds. Theo F. Rodenbough and William L. Haskin (New York: Maynard, Merrill & Co., 1896)233. See also: *U.S. Army Center of Military History,* Ft. McNair, D.C., digital reprint, n.d., accessed at: https:// history.army.mil/books/r&h/R&H-6CV.htm; Lawrence G. Kautz, *August Valentine Kautz, USA: Biography of a Civil War General* (Jefferson: McFarland, 2016), 71.

196. Carter, "Sixth Regiment of Cavalry," 233 (see prev. note); Sanders Report, *OR,* 439; Alfred Pleasanton, "The Peninsular Campaign," *OR,* ser. 1, vol. 11, pt. 2: 966.

197. William B. Franklin, "Reply to S. Williams," *OR,* ser. 1, vol. 19, pt. 1: 378; Alfred Pleasanton, "The Maryland Campaign," *OR,* ser. 1, vol. 19, pt. 1: 212–13.

198. Alfred Pleasanton, "Operations in Loudon County [Virginia], etc. (1862)," *OR,* ser. 1, vol. 19, pt. 2: 127–28; David M. Gregg, "Operations in Loudon County [Virginia], etc. (1862)," *OR,* ser. 1, vol. 19, pt. 2: 131.

199. Donald C. Caughey and Jimmy J. Jones, *The Sixth United States Cavalry in the Civil War: A History and Roster* (Jefferson: Mc Farland & Co., 2013), 47, 52, 124, 256–57.

200. Kautz, "Reminiscences" Kautz Papers, LOC (see note 179); Ezra J. Warner, ed., "William Price Sanders," in *Generals in Blue: Lives of the Union Commanders* (Baton Rouge: Louisiana Univ. Press, 1964), 419–20.

201. William P. Sanders ["Doc"], letter to Cousin May [Sanders?], Nov. 7,

1863; Fred Brown, "Sanders Found Romance in Knoxville Amid Civil War," *News Sentinel* (Knoxville), April 10, 2011. Accessed at: https://www.knoxnews.com/news/local/sanders-found-romance-in-knoxville-amid-civil-war-ep-405089286-357932691.html.

202. *OR*, ser. 1, vol. 10, ch. 22, pt. 2: 183.

203. William P. Sanders, "U.S. Army Service Record, OFF352063, Mar. 13-Nov. 19, 1863, Records of William P. Sanders," War Department, Record and Pension Office, RG 94 (1863), NARA.

204. He assumed this position formally in September, 1863.

205. Tarrant, *Wild Riders*, 147–48 (see note 148); Marvel, *Burnside*, 226; Charles D. Mitchell, "The Sanders Raid Into East Tennessee, June 1863," in *Sketches of War History, 1861–1865, Vol. 6*, eds. Theodore F. Allen, Edward S. McKee, and J. Gordon Taylor (Cincinnati: MOLLUS, Commandery of Ohio, Monfort & Co., 1908), 238, 240. Accessed at: *Sons of Union Veterans of the Civil War*, MOLLUS/Website Index/ Historical MOLLUS Information/ MOLLUS War Papers, Ohio Commandery, Sketches of War History, Vol. 6. Accessed at: https://suvcw.org/mollus /warpapers/warpapers.htm; Reid, *Ohio in the War*, 798 (see note 149).

206. Starr, *Union Cavalry 3*, 336.

207. William P. Sanders, letter to the Secretary of War, Dec. 22, 1851. Records of the Adjutant General's Office, Record Group 94.2.6: Records relating to the U.S. Military Academy, U.S. Military Academy Library, West Point, NY; William P. Sanders ["Doc"], Letter to Cousin May [Sanders?], Nov. 7, 1863; Brown, "Sanders found romance" (see note 201).

208. Tarrant, *Wild Riders*, 166, 172; Horace H. Thomas, "Personal Reminiscences of the East Tennessee Campaign," in *Military Collections and Recollections Vol. 4*, ed. and comp., IL Commandery, MOLLUS, War Papers Index, https://suvcw.org/mollus/war/warpapers.htm. Reprint, https://broadfootpublishing.com (Wilmington: Broadfoot, 1992), 286–87.

209. Wilshire, "Reminiscence," 6 (see note 164).

210. Mitchell, "Sanders Raid," 240 (see note 205).

211. Thomas, "Personal Reminiscences," 293, 300 (see note 208).

Chapter 4

212. Samuel P. Carter to S. D. Sturgis, June 10, 1863, *OR*, ser. 1, vol. 23, pt. 1: 371.

213. Don K. Robbins, comp., 1860 Federal Census: Roane, TN. Accessed at: ftp://ftp.us- census.org/pub/usgenweb/census/xtn/roane/1860; NARA, Compiled Service Records of Volunteer Soldiers Who Served During the Mexican War in Organizations from the State of Tennessee, National Archives Microfilm Publication M863, Record Group 94, TN 4th Infantry, Company C – Robert K. Byrd (1847), 1–7. Accessed at: https://catalog.archives.gov/id/59992943.

214. Graf and Haskins, *Papers of Andrew Johnson, Vol. 5*, fn27.

215. William M. Churchwell to Mrs. R. K. Byrd, May 14, 1862, *OR*, ser. 2, vol. 1, 888; Fisher, *War at Every Door*, 74.

216. Yet, like many others of his generation, Byrd tempered his desire for revenge with an attempt to maintain at least a thread of comity with past friends. Corresponding with an old friend who now commanded a regiment in the enemy army, Byrd lamented that "'tis the common lot of nearly all now to be sorely troubled." Robert K. Byrd to Henry J. Welcker, Oct. 24, 1862, in Roane County, TN, Records; Fisher, *War at Every Door*, 64, 74; Murray, *Bradley Divided*, 121–22; *OR*, ser. 2, vol. 1, 888.

217. Scott and Angel, *Thirteenth Regiment*, 76–79, 85–86, 95, 321–62 *passim*; Madden, "Unionist Resistance," 35–36.

218. William P. Sanders, "Sanders Report," OR, 386.

219. Richard C. Rankin, "The 2nd and 7th Ohio Cavalry," *National Tribune*, Sept. 22, 1887: 3.

220. James R. James, *To See the Elephant* (Leawood: Leathers Publishing, 1998), 71.

221. Patented in 1861, the Schenkl projectile featured a self-igniting fuse that could be set to detonate after a time of flight selected by the gunner as marked on each shell. It employed a papier-maché sabot which expanded to maintain contact with the rifling and prevented premature ignition. The Schenkl was susceptible to the effects of humidity and had other flaws which caused many duds.

222. Andrew J. Konkle, "Report to Col. James Barnett, June 29th, 1863," in *A Military Record of Battery D, First Ohio Veteran Volunteers, Light Artillery,* eds. S. C. Frey, A. Perry and P. G. Clark (Oil City: Derrick Publishing, 1908), 94–95; Samuel Kelso, "The Saunders Raid: Sketch of the Part Taken by Two Guns of Battery D, 1st Ohio L.A.," *National Herald,* May 22. 1893: 3.

223. Mitchell, "Sanders Raid," 239.

224. Burnside to William S. Rosecrans, June 8, 1863, *OR,* ser. 1, vol. 23, pt. 2: 386–87; Nicholas Bowen to Samuel P. Carter, April 29, 1863, *OR,* ser. 1, vol. 23, pt. 1: 294; Reid, *Ohio in the War,* 799, 896; McCartney, "Saunders Raid," 434 (see note 77); Tarrant, *Wild Riders,* 166.

225. Tarrant, *Wild Riders,* 64.

226. John W. Henderson, "Life of John Wimberly Henderson," unpublished memoir, Thomas Jefferson Henderson Papers, Part 1 (1902), Illinois State Library, Springfield, IL. Hereinafter as ISL.

227. Thomas J. Henderson, "Consolidated List of Officers Below the Rank of Colonel of the 2d Brigade, 3d Division, 23d Army Corps [1865]," Henderson Papers, Part 2, 5, 7–8; also: Henderson, note, n.d. [1865?], Henderson Papers, Part 2. Both in ISL.

228. Thomas J. Henderson, "General Order No. 10, Aug. 22, 1863," Henderson Papers, ISL; Duke, *Reminiscences,* 210 (see note 162).

229. Two months after the raiders returned to their base, the Tennesseans had not yet returned the borrowed pistols to the Illinoisans. Henderson to E. G. Bond, June 12, 1863, Henderson Papers, ISL; Reid, *Ohio in the War,* 798; Henry W. Chester, *Recollections of the War of the Rebellion,* ed. A. R. Adamson (Wheaton: Wheaton History Center, 1996), 44–45; Samuel C. Fry to Robert K. Byrd, Aug. 13, 1863, Henderson Papers, Part 2, ISL.

230. Marvel, *Burnside,* 10–12; Sean McLachlan, *American Civil War Guerrilla Tactics* (New York: Osprey Publishing, 2009), 32; Maness and Combs, *Do They Miss Me At Home?* 143 (see note 136); Earl J. Hess, *The Rifle Musket in Civil War Combat* (Lawrence: Univ. Press of Kansas, 2008), 54–55.

231. Fry to Byrd, Henderson Papers (see note 229); Henderson to Lewis (?) [Sept. 1863], Henderson Papers, pt. 2, ISL; Gause, *Four Years,* 120 (see note 141).

232. Emory S. Bond, letter to Thomas J. Henderson, June 12, 1863, Henderson Papers, pt. 2, ISL.

233. Mitchell, "Sanders Raid," 239–40.

234. Ibid., 239–40.

235. McCartney, "Saunders Raid," 433–34; Mitchell, "Sanders Raid," 238; Tarrant, *Wild Riders*, 166; Gause, *Four Years*, 130; Burnside to Rosecrans, June 8, 1863, *OR*, ser. 1, vol. 23, pt. 2: 400.

236. Halleck to Burnside, June 3, 1863, *OR*, ser. 1, vol. 23, pt. 2: 163; Rosecrans to Burnside, June 9, 1863, *OR*, ser. 1, vol. 23, pt. 2: 417; Rosecrans to Burnside, April 8, 1863, *OR*, ser. 1, vol. 23, pt. 2: 222.

237. Burnside to Julius White, June 15, 19, 24, 1863, *OR*, ser. 1, vol. 23, pt. 2: 431, 439, 454; White to Burnside, June 7, 16, 21, 1863, *OR*, ser. 1, vol. 23, pt. 2: 393, 433, 441; White, "Burnside's Occupation," 301, 315–17; Marvel, *Burnside*, 248–50.

238. Buckner, "Abstract from field return of the Department of East Tennessee . . . ," May 31, 1863, *OR*, ser. 1, vol. 23, pt. 2: 855; Buckner, "Abstract from field return of the Department of East Tennessee . . . ," July 31, 1863, *OR*, ser. 1, vol. 23, pt. 2: 945.

Chapter 5

239. Mitchell, "Sanders Raid," 239.

240. Michael R. Bradley, *Tullahoma* (Shippensburg: Burd Street Press, 2000), 94; Mitchell, "Sanders Raid," 239; John A. Widney, Diary (1863), Reference Division, ISL; Glen V. Longacre and John E. Haas, eds., *To Battle for God and the Right* (Urbana: Univ. of Illinois Press, 2003), 81–82; Gilbert C. Kniffin, "Manoevering Bragg Out of Tennessee," in *Battles and Leaders of the Civil War*, 3, eds. R. U. Johnson and C. C. Buel (Secaucus: Castle, 1887), 635, 637; James D. Barnett, letter to wife, July 6, 1863, Barnett Papers, container 1, folder 1 (Cleveland: Western Reserve Historical Society); Thomas W. Fisher, letter to parents, March 23, 1863, in "Civil War Letters of Pvt. Thomas Winton Fisher, CSA," comp. Diane McGinley Gardner. Accessed at: www.ted.gardner.org/630323tf.html.

241. Andrew H. Morris, letter to Jane [Mrs. A. H. Morris], July 11, 1863, Records of the 65th Georgia Volunteer Infantry. http://www.izzy.net /~michaelg/65ga-vi.htm; David J. Burt, letter to wife, July 11, 1863,

Francis Burt Barrett Papers, Archives of the Park Historian, Chickamauga National Military Park, Fort Oglethorpe, GA. www.izzy.net
/-michaelg/65ga- vi.htm; Richard F. Patman, "46 Years Ago," *Calhoun*
[GA] *Times*, Apr. 7, 1910.

242. London, Kentucky, is not to be confused with *Loudon*, Tennessee, which
is about ninety miles farther south. Laurel Creek is now the "Laurel
River."

243. Mitchell, "Sanders Raid," 240.

244. Ibid., 245; Ibid.

246. Ibid.; McCartney, "Saunders Raid," 433–34; D. S. Stanley to J. B. Turchin,
June 4, 1863, *OR*, ser. 1, vol. 23, pt. 2: 386; Mitchell, "Sanders Raid," 240.

247. Tarrant, *Wild Riders*, 159; Basil W. Duke, Orlando Willcox, and Thomas
H. Hines, "A Romance of Morgan's Rough Riders," *Battles and Leaders of
the Civil War*, 6, ed. Paul Cozzens (Urbana: Univ. of Illinois Press, 2004),
317.

248. McCartney, "Saunders Raid," 434; Mitchell, "Sanders Raid," 240.

Chapter 6

249. Gause, *Four Years*, 123–29.

250. Kautz, "Daily Journal," entry of June 4, 1863, Kautz Papers, LOC; Maness
and Combs, *Do They Miss Me At Home?* 94.

251. Kautz, "Daily Journal," June 4, 1863 (see prev. note).

252. Victor S. Sheliha to Samuel Jones, W. W. Mackall, Archibald Gracie, and
John Pegram, June 5, 1863, *OR*, ser. 1, vol. 23, pt. 2: 864.

253. Paludan, *Victims*, 53.

254. Two were political generals, one was an old army pal of Davis, and the
others served only brief or intermittent terms. Felix K. Zollicoffer mistook a group of Union officers for his own men and was shot and killed.
George B. Crittenden had once been cashiered from the U.S. Army for
drunkenness. He had another bout with the bottle and after just five
weeks in office was arrested for intoxication and compelled to resign.
Vernon H. Crow, *Storm in the Mountains: Thomas' Confederate Legion
of Cherokee Indians and Mountaineers* (Press of the Museum of the
Cherokee Indian, 1982), 40; Woodworth, *Davis and His Generals*, 61–69

(see note 176); Graf and Haskins, *Papers of Andrew Johnson, Vol. 5,* fn 352, 357; Bryan, 'Tories,' 8–14.

255. Allan Nevins, *The War for the Union Vol. 4: The Organized War to Victory, 1864–1865* (New York: Charles Scribner's Sons, 1959); Bryan, "Tories," 15–18; Crow, *Storm in the Mountains,* 40 (see prev. note).

256. Confederate States Army, Adjutant and Inspector General's Office, Special Order No. 136, Paragraph 21 (1863), *OR,* ser. 1, vol. 23, pt. 2: 871.

257. *OR,* ser. 1, vol. 23, pt. 2: 945.

258. Hesseltine, *Ramsey,* 113 (see note 134).

259. Archer Jones, "Tennessee and Mississippi, Joe Johnston's Strategic Problem," *Tennessee Historical Quarterly* 18, no. 2 (1959): 141–43.

260. Victor von Sheliha to Samuel Cooper, June 20, 1863, *OR,* ser. 1, vol. 23, pt. 2: 868.

261. Ibid., 864; John Pegram to Basil Duke, May 30, 1863, *OR,* ser. 1, vol. 23, pt. 2: 854–55; Samuel Jones to Simon Buckner, June 7, 1863, *OR,* ser. 1, vol. 23, pt. 2: 870.

262. *OR,* ser. 1, vol. 23, pt. 2: 384.

263. Kautz, "Daily Journal," June 4, 1863.

264. Buckner to Samuel Cooper, Samuel Jones, W. W. Mackall, and John S. Williams, June 6–7; and: Charles S. Stringfellow to John S. Williams, June 7, 1863. Both in: *OR,* ser. 1, vol. 23, pt. 2: 868-69.

265. Buckner to Samuel Jones, June 10, 1863, *OR* ser. 1, vol. 23, pt. 2: 872.

266. Marvel states that Buckner learned of the detachment of the Ninth Corps on June 16 from Maj. Gen. Samuel Jones, who notified him that the movement had been reported in the June 10 edition of the *Cincinnati Commercial.* Jones's warning was not entirely unquestionable, however. In: Jones to Buckner, June 16, 1863, *OR,* ser. 1, vol. 23, pt. 2: 875; Crist, Dix and Williams, *Davis Papers, Vol. 9,* 243–45; Marvel, *Burnside,* 248.

267. James A. Seddon to Buckner, June 10, 1863, *OR,* ser. 1, vol. 23, pt. 2: 872.

268. *OR,* ser. 4, vol. 2, pt. 2: 563; J. N. Galleher to A. E. Jackson, June 17, 1863, *OR,* ser. 1, vol. 23, pt. 2: 876; Stickles, *Buckner,* 217, 224; Jones, *Tennessee in the Civil War,* 139.

269. *OR,* ser. 1, vol. 23, pt. 2: 872.

270. *OR,* ser. 4, vol. 2, pt. 2: 563–64.

271. E. Porter Alexander, "Longstreet at Knoxville," in *Battles and Leaders of the Civil War: The Tide Shifts* 3, eds. R. U. Johnson and C. C. Buel (New York: Thomas Yoseloff, reprint, 1956), 751; Mrs. Alexander E. Smith, letter, to husband, May 26, 1863, Civil War Letters from Mrs. A. E. Smith to her husband, Special Collections, University of Tennessee, Knoxville, TN. Accessed at: www.utk.edu/spcoll.

272. Stickles, *Buckner*, 217, 224; *OR*, ser. 1, vol. 23, pt. 2: 563.

273. Maness and Combs, *Do They Miss Me At Home?* 96.

274. Kautz, "Reminiscences," vol. 1, 42–43; Kautz, "Daily Journal," entries of June 8, and June 9, 1863, Kautz Papers, box 4, LOC.

275. Janet B. Hewett, et al., eds., *Supplement to the Official Records of the Union and Confederate Armies* (Wilmington: Broadfoot Publishing Co., 1994-2001), vol. 50, pt. 2: 62, 626; Andrew Wallace, *General August V. Kautz and the Southwestern Frontier* (Tucson: privately printed, 1967), 39; Gause, *Four Years*, 125; Henry W. Chester, letter, to brother [Charles Chester], June 21, 1863, Chester Papers, Center for History, Wheaton, IL.; Maness and Combs, *Do They Miss Me At Home?* 96.

276. Gause, *Four Years*, 382.

277. C. Vann Woodward, ed., *Mary Chesnut's Civil War* 1 (New Haven: Yale Univ. Press, 1981), 476.

278. Kautz Papers, entry of June 10, 1863; Chester, *Recollections*, 48–49 (see note 229); Burnside, "Abstract from return of the Army of the Ohio ...," June, 1863, 489, 491.

279. Marvel, *Burnside*, 4–6; Stickles, *Buckner*, 13–15, 19.

280. Buckner's wife was an heiress to the "Kingsbury estate," an enormous fortune worth more than a half-million dollars. Her father had purchased thirty-six acres which became part of Chicago's Loop.

281. By a strange twist of fate, war entangled their destinies even further. Buckner's brother-in-law, Lieutenant Henry W. Kingsbury of the Union army, was killed in action shortly after naming his commanding officer, Ambrose Burnside, as the executor of his estate. Lt. Kingsbury's estate included a share of the Chicago land, hence when Burnside was chosen to be his executor, he temporarily obtained direction of Mrs. Buckner's fortune. At the time of the Sanders raid, Lt. Kingsbury's estate was still open and the will was contested in the courts of Illinois. The estate was

not settled until five years after the war ended, when the Illinois supreme court ruled in favor of Mrs. Buckner. In Stickles, *Buckner*, 13, 24, 36–38, 77–78; Marvel, *Burnside*, 15, 24–42, 432n.

Chapter 7

282. McCartney, "Saunders Raid," 434.

283. The poll was 521 to 19. In 1986 the county voted to "rejoin" Tennessee. In Bali Buttram, Tennessee secession election returns from Scott County, June 10, 1861, Record Group 87, box 64, Tennessee State Library and Archives, Nashville, TN; Mary E. Campbell, *The Attitude of Tennesseans Toward the Union, 1847–1861* (New York: Vantage Press, 1961), 291; Bert Walker (Huntsville, TN), letter to the author, April 14, 2012. Author's collection; *IH* Staff, "Remembering Scott's Defiant Independence," *Independent Herald* (Oneida, TN), July 3, 2018. Accessed at: http://www .ihoneida.com/2018/07/03/remembering-scotts-defiant-independence/

284. Jeremiah H. Boynton, "Army Correspondence," *Union Post* (Athens, TN), Sept. 2, 1863, reprint, in *History of the 112th Regiment of Illinois Volunteer Infantry in the Great War of the Rebellion, 1862–1865*, ed. B. F. Thompson (Toulon: Stark County News, 1885), 87–88.

285. This settlement was originally called "James Chitwood," or occasionally, "Camp Chitwood," after a hero of the Revolution. The city is now named "Winfield," after General Winfield Scott. In 2016 its population was 960. See also Hewett, et al., eds., *Supplement to the Official Records*, vol. 65, ser. no. 77, pt. 2: 647 (see note 275); Reid, *Ohio in the War*, 96; McCartney, "Saunders Raid," 435; Mitchell, "Sanders Raid," 241.

286. Sperry, Frey, and Clark, *Battery D*, 84 (see note 222, Konkle).

287. McCartney, "Saunders Raid," 434.

288. William D. Hamilton, *Recollections of a Cavalryman of the Civil War After Fifty Years* (Columbus: F. J. Heer, 1915), 55–59.

289. Ibid., 57.

290. Ibid., 56–58.

291. Ibid., 54–59.

292. The meadow was near Emory Creek. Their route was later followed by the Cincinnati Southern Railway and today by US highway 27. In: McCartney, "Saunders Raid," 435; Mitchell, "Sanders Raid," 241.

293. McCartney, "Saunders Raid," 435; Tristam T. Dow, "Major Dow's Report," in *History of the 112th Regiment of Illinois Volunteer Infantry in the Great War of the Rebellion, 1862–1865*, ed. B. F. Thompson (Toulon: Stark County News, 1885), 44; Mitchell, "Sanders Raid," 241.

294. The city of Wartburg is located near Bird Mountain, Tennessee, elevation 3,142 feet. German and Swiss immigrants settled the area in the 1840's and named their town after Wartburg Castle, Germany, built in 1068. Wartburg Castle stands on a precipice which rises 1350 feet and overlooks the town of Eisenach, in the state of Thuringia, Germany. In Dyer, *Reminiscences*, 104 (see note 78).

295. Samuel C. Fry, "The Sanders Raid: A Brilliant Cavalry Exploit in East Tennessee," *National Tribune*, August 25, 1887: 1.

296. McCartney, "Saunders Raid," 435; Sanders Report, 386–87; Samuel Kelso, "Sanders's Raid: Destruction of the East Tennessee & Georgia Railroad," *National Herald* (May 14, 1885): 2; Chester, *Recollections*, 44–45.

297. McCartney, "Saunders Raid," 435; Mitchell, "Sanders Raid," 241; *OR*, ser. 1, vol. 19, ch. 31, pt. 2, 387; Kelso, "Sanders's Raid," 2 (see prev. note).

298. Another source identifies the crossing point as "Walden's Ferry." See Hewett, *Supplement to the Official Records*, 648.

299. Fry, "Sanders Raid," 1 (see note 295); Mitchell, "Sanders Raid," 240.

300. Fry, "Sanders Raid," 1.

301. NARA, *1870 United States Federal Census*, in *1790-1890 Federal Population Censuses—Part 5*, NARA Mf. public. M593, Record Group 29. District 2, Anderson, Tennessee, 553012, 8B, *Ancestry.com*, database on-line (Provo, UT, Ancestry.com Operations, Inc., 2009); NARA, *Compiled Service Records of Volunteer Union Soldiers Who Served in Organizations from the State of Tennessee, First Tennessee Infantry* [Reynolds, William S.], NARA Mf. public. 395. Catalog ID: 300398 (2010), *www.fold3.com*.

302. McCartney, "Saunders Raid," 435; Albert W. Mosey, *A Union Soldier's Diary* (Mansfield: Mansfield Board of Education, n.d.); Mitchell, "Sanders Raid," 241.

303. Widney, Diary (see note 240); Duke, Willcox, and Hines, "Morgan's Rough Riders," 317 (see note 247).

304. Private John Looney, of Kempton, Ford County, Illinois, served in Company G, 112th Illinois. In: McCartney, "Saunders Raid," 436–38.

305. Sheridan E. Vincent, comp., *Dr. Michael Vincent... and His Descendants* (Rochester: Vincent Family Record Publications, 1996), 109; Mitchell, "Sanders Raid," 241.

306. McCartney, "Saunders Raid," 437.

307. Tarrant, *Wild Riders*, 172–73.

308. *OR*, ser. 1, vol. 23, pt. 2, 436-37.

309. Ibid.; Wallace, *Kautz*, 39; Gause, *Four Years*, 125.

Chapter 8

310. W. P. Orms, "From the Raiders in East Tennessee," *Southern Confederacy* (June 24, 1863): 1. Accessed at: https://gahistoricnewspapers.galileo.usg .edu/lccn/sn82014677/1863-06-24/ed-1/

311. Dyer, *Reminiscences*, 104.

312. Sanders Report, 387; Fry, "Sanders Raid," 1; Dyer, *Reminiscences*, 104.

313. Sanders Report, 387; Dyer, *Reminiscences*, 104.

314. The term "the old harry" is of obscure origin, but it may be an archaic or childhood reference to Satan, who was supposed to have powerful legs. In: "The attack on Knoxville," The *Daily Dispatch* {Richmond}, June 24, 1863. Accessed at: Chronicling America, LOC, https://chronicling america.loc.gov/lccn/sn84024738/1863-06-24/ed-1/

315. "Federal raid in East Tennessee—immense destruction of railroad bridges and other property," The *Daily Dispatch* [Richmond], July 1, 1863. Accessed at: https://chroniclingamerica.loc.gov/lccn /sn84024738/1863-07-01/ed-1/

316. It sent 800 men to the Union Army. In: Groce, *Mountain Rebels*, 39.

317. Mitchell, "Sanders Raid," 242; R. Thomas Campbell, ed., *Southern Service on Land & Sea* (Knoxville: Univ. of Tennessee Press, 2002), 44.

318: Dyer, *Reminiscences*, 104.

319. Hesseltine, *Ramsey*, 158; Fisher, *War at Every Door*, 138; NARA, *Case Files of Applications from Former Confederates for Presidential Pardons* ["Amnesty Papers"], *1865–67,* Lenoir, William, Records of the Adjutant General's Office, Mf. 1003, Record Group 94, National

Archives, Washington, D.C. Accessed at: "Confederate Amnesty Papers," *Fold3* record no. 3656621, 3. https://www.fold3.com/title/59/confederate-amnesty-papers

320. The plantation included 2,700 acres. Despite their Confederate proclivities, the Lenoirs submitted a claim for more than $70,000 to compensate them for their alleged loss of livestock and goods during the war. In: "Attack on Knoxville" (see note 314); Hesseltine, *Ramsey*, 146, 158; Groce, *Mountain Rebels*, 18; Suzanne M. Pratt, "The Lenoir Family," in *Loudon County, Tennessee* (2004–6). Accessed at: www.tngenweb.org/loudon/family/lenoir.html; Civil War Traveler, "Lenoir Plantation. East Tennessee," *Lenoir City*, American Sesquicentennial Web Archive, LOC, lcwaN0005920 (Washington: U.S. Library of Congress, 2012). Accessed at: *CivilWarTraveler.com*, https://www.loc.gov/item/lcwaN0005920/; NARA, *Eighth Census of the United States, 1860* (Washington: U.S. Bureau of the Census, 1864) NARA Mf. public. no. M653, Record Group 29 [Roane County, TN]. Accessed at: *1860 U.S. Federal Census - Slave Schedules* (Lehi: Ancestry.com Operations, Inc., 2010), https://www.ancestry.com/search/collections/7668/ ; NARA, *1860 U.S. Federal Census - Population Schedule* [Roane County, TN, District 4] (Washington: NARA, n.d.), NARA Mf. public. no. M653, Record Group 29. *1860 United States Federal Census, Ancestry.com* (Provo: Ancestry.com Operations, Inc., 2009), 15. Accessed at: https://www.ancestry.com/search/collections/7667/.

321. "The attack on Knoxville; repulse of the enemy with heavy loss; Destruction of Bridges, &c. [First Dispatch]," *Daily Dispatch* [Richmond, VA], June 20, 1863.

322. Sanders Report, 387; Fry, "Sanders Raid," 1; Richard C. Rankin, "The Saunders Raid: Nice Work Done on a Flying Trip into East Tennessee," *National Tribune*, May 11, 1893: 4; Sperry, Frey, and Clark, *Battery D*, 84.

323. Hesseltine, *Ramsey*, 110.

324. Ibid.

325. Mark E. Neely, Jr., *The Civil War and the Limits of Destruction* (Cambridge: Harvard Univ. Press, 2007), 69, 108; Blair, *With Malice toward Some*, 122 (see note 53).

326. Hesseltine, *Ramsey*, 110.

327. Gideon M. Hart, "Military Commissions and the Lieber Code," *Military*

Law Review (Department of the Army Pamphlet 27-100-203 [Spring, 2010]), 10, n.62.

328. A year later, several local women, including at least one member of the Lenoir family, were jailed because they openly expressed sympathy for the Confederate cause. In: Fisher, *War at Every Door*, 108; Daniel E. Sutherland, ed., *A Very Violent Rebel: The Civil War Diary of Ellen Renshaw House* (Knoxville: Univ. of Tennessee Press, 1996), 9; George W. Cable, ed., "War Diary of a Union Woman in the South: 1860—63," *Strange True Stories of Louisiana* (New York: Charles Scribner's Sons, 1890), in *A Civil War Diary of a Union Woman in the South* (Whitefish: reprint, De Vinne Press, 2005), 74–75.

329. Daily Dispatch, "Attack on Knoxville."

330. Witt, *Lincoln's Code*, 154 (see note 166).

331. The Byrd mansion was located on a plantation along the Emory River, near the present-day town of Harriman, Tennessee, about twenty miles from Lenoir's Station. Byrd was thirty-nine at the time of the Sanders raid. In : Groce, *Mountain Rebels*, 18, 39; roanetnheritage.com, "Robert King BYRD (1823–1885)" (see note 64).

332. William G. McAdoo [Sr.], "Diary," entry of June 22, 1863, archival manuscript, no. 566, W. G. McAdoo [Sr.], (1820-1894) Diaries 1846-1894, Floyd-McAdoo Families Papers, Mf. 12,209-6N-6P, Reels 3-5, Items 27-63, Manuscript Div., LOC, Washington, D.C. Accessed at: https://lccn.loc.gov/mm80082277.

333. Since Sanders had not publicly embraced the Christian faith—he did not do so until he was on his deathbed six months later— he may not have been eligible for membership in the Masonic Order when the raid took place.

334. Neely, *Limits of Destruction*, 25–30 (see note 325).

335. Charles A. Dana, *Recollections of the Civil War* (New York: D. Appleton, 1898), 54; Groce, *Mountain Rebels*, 18; Neely, *Limits of Destruction*, 37–38; Hesseltine, *Ramsey*, 241; Seymour, *Divided Loyalties*, fn 87, 11; Masonic member, message to the author re Sanders, March 9, 2013. Accessed at: www.Masoniclodges.com; Dennis E. Haynes, *A Thrilling Narrative* (Fayetteville: Univ. of Arkansas Press, 2006), 14, fn140, 91.

336. Victor M. Hovis, Jr., *Union Lodge History* (Kingston: Union Lodge no.

38, Free & Accepted Masons of Kingston, Tennessee, 1996). Accessed at: http://union38.org/wordpress/?page_id=218; roanetnheritage.com, "Robert King BYRD (1823–1885)."

337. A section of its walls still stands today. See: Fry, "Sanders Raid," 1; McAdoo, Diary, June 21, 1863 (see note 332); Sanders Report, 387; Mitchell, "Sanders Raid," 242. On the Masonic connection, see Pratt, "Lenoir Family" (see note 320).

338. Mitchell, "Sanders Raid," 243; Kelso, "Sanders's Raid," 2.

339. Harvey Denney, "All About Saunder's Raid," *National Tribune* 35 (Sept. 9, 1915): 7.

340. Herman Melville, "Battle-Pieces," *The Oxford Book of Civil War Quotations*, comp. J. D. Wright (New York: Oxford Univ. Press, 2006), 317.

341. Denney, "All About Saunder's Raid," 7 (see note 339).

342. Rankin, *Seventh Ohio*, 6 (see note 219).

343. Ibid.; "The Raid into East Tennessee," *Holston Journal* [Knoxville], July 9, 1863; NARA, "Southern Claims Commission Approved Claims, 1871–1880: Tennessee, Knox County," *Fold 3.com* (2008). Accessed at: www.fold3.com/image/#258084156 .

344. These figures combine the value of real estate owned by Israel P. Lenoir, 35, a farmer, and Benjamin Ballard Lenoir, 39, a physician. In addition, William Lenoir, 47, a manufacturer, owned real estate valued at $28,000 and other property at $26,000. His holdings are not included in this estimation because they are assumed to be the Lenoir mills. William Lenoir may have owned part of the farm acreage, however. See: NARA, "1860 U.S. Federal Census - Population," Mf. public. M653, Rec. Gp. 29, Roane County, TN, District 4, 79 (see note 320).

345. Mitchell, "Sanders Raid," 243; Sperry, Frey, and Clark, *Battery D*, 86; *Holston Journal*, "Raid into East Tennessee," (see note 343).

346. NARA, "Southern Claims Commission, Tennessee, Jefferson County (1874)," NARA Mf. public. no. M1407, 34, 38; NARA, Southern Claims Commission Approved Claims, 1871–1880, www.fold3.com, 217.

347. Lt. Luttrell was an artillery officer who was temporarily attached to the cavalry. In: McKenzie, *Lincolnites and Rebels*, 127.

348. Luttrell actually requested reimbursement for the loss of two horses,

one in March and one during the Sanders raid. He asked for CS$400 each or CS$800 in total. According to a price schedule issued in the early summer of 1863, a prime artillery horse was valued at CS$400. In December, 1863, a Union cavalry captain stationed near Knoxville lost his horse and appraised the animal at US$75. In February, 1864, he sold two horses, for which he was paid US$50 and US$65. In: Hattaway and Beringer, *Davis*, 255; Maness and Combs, *Do They Miss Me At Home?* 144, 155, 175; NARA, "Compiled Service Records of Confederate Soldiers Who Served in Organizations from the State of Tennessee (1903-27)," and "Carded Service Records Showing Military Service of Soldiers Who Fought in Confederate Organizations: Capt. Burroughs's Co., Light Artillery (Rhett Artillery), Luttrell, James C.," NARA Mf. public no. M268. *Fold 3.com*, nos. 67708103, 67707836, 6770913, 6. Accessed at: www.fold3.com.

349. Daily Dispatch, "Attack on Knoxville."

350. "Kingston Pike," www.en.wikipedia.org/wiki/Kingston_Pike; Sam McDowell, ed. and comp., *East Tennessee History* (Hartford: McDowell Publications, 1978),13.

351. Civil War saboteurs liked to pile rails on top of a huge bonfire, because red-hot rails would bend under their own weight. If time permitted, rails could be twisted with special tools or bent around trees.

Chapter 9

352. Murderers' Hollow lay east of Lenoir and west of Bearden, Tennessee. In: NARA, 1863, "Confederate States Army Casualties: Lists and Narrative Reports, 1861–1865," Report of Siege, Tennessee: Knoxville, NARA Mf. public. no. M836, Roll 4, Rec. Gp. 109, image #272178231, #272178233; Jones, *Tennessee in the Civil War*, 18; Hesseltine, *Ramsey*, 117–19; Daniel E. Sutherland, *American Civil War Guerrillas* (Santa Barbara: Praeger, 2013), 16.

353. NARA, *Compiled Service Records of Confederate Soldiers Who Served in Organizations from the State of Tennessee (1863)*, NARA Mf. no. M268, R.G. 109, (Washington: NARA, n.d.), 5. *Fold 3.com*. Accessed at: www.fold3 .com; "Captain Wiggs," *Knoxville Register*, June 23, 1863: 1.

354. Earl J. Hess identifies the victim as James Harvey Baker, but in most

accounts, he is known simply as Harvey Baker, which is how he signed his name. A monument to Abner Baker, Harvey's son, stands today on the lawn of the Baker mansion, 9000 Kingston Pike. In: Hess, *Knoxville Campaign*, 7; Thompson, *112th Regiment*, 49; Sutherland, *Violent Rebel*, fn257, 361 (see note 328).

355. "The Murder of Doctor Harvey Baker by the Yankees," *Knoxville Register*, June 23, 1863: 1; E. Y. C., pseud., "Letter from E. Y. C.," *Knoxville Register* July 7, 1863: 1.

356. During the 1850's, his real estate climbed in value from $9,000 to $50,000, and his slave holdings increased from seventeen to twenty-one. If he had cleared all his assets in 1860, he could have purchased approximately one hundred average-sized Tennessee farms. See NARA, "1860 U.S. Federal Census - Population," Knox County (District 11), NARA Mf. no. M653, Rec. Gp. 29, Roll 1259 (Washington: NARA, n.d.), 951850; 1850 U.S. Federal Census, Record for Harvey Baker, NARA Mf. no. M432. Rec. Gp. 29, 76B (Washington: NARA, n.d.). *Ancestry.com*; NARA, 1850 United States Census [Slave Schedule], Tennessee, Knox County (Washington: NARA, n.d.), 26. *Ancestry.com*; "Dr. Harvey Baker," 1.

357. His sale of grain to the Confederate army was prosecutable as a violation of the *56th Article of War* (1806), which prohibits the sale of "victuals" to the enemy. In: Blair, *With Malice toward Some*, 57–58; E. P. Williams, "Certificate of Payment (1863)," and P. R. Grills, "Affidavit (1862)," both in NARA, *Confederate Papers Relating to Citizens or Business Firms, 1861–1865*," NARA Mf. no. M346, Rec. Gp. 109 (Washington: NARA, n.d.). *Fold3.com*. Accessed at: www.fold3.com; *Knoxville Register*, "The Murder of Doctor Harvey Baker by the Yankees," (see note 355); Hart, "Military Commissions," fn 10, 62 (see note 327).

358. At the time of the Sanders raid, Abner served with the 2nd Tennessee Cavalry and may have seen action in the "Loudon fight" on the day before his father was killed. Abner survived four years of hard fighting, but in September, 1865, suffered his own violent death. In a grisly after-shock to his father's demise, Abner evidently attempted to avenge his father's death and shot a Union veteran. That night he was lynched by a Unionist mob in Knoxville. On his military service, see: NARA, 1862, *Compiled military service records of Confederate soldiers from*

Tennessee units. Second Cavalry AND Second (Ashby's) Cavalry, NARA
Mf. M268 (Washington: NARA, n.d.), 109. *Fold 3.com*, at: www.fold3
.com. Accounts of Abner's death disagree, but Robert T. McKenzie's is
the most reliable. See: McKenzie, *Lincolnites and Rebels*, 184–87, 257;
Mary U. Rothrock, ed., *The French Broad-Holston Country* (Knoxville:
East Tennessee Historical Society, 1972), 145; Hess, *Knoxville Campaign*,
290; Sutherland, *Violent Rebel*, 184–85, 257fn.

359. Digby Gordon Seymour states that Baker was killed "just before trying
to escape to Knoxville." The *Knoxville Register* story does not report that
Baker was fleeing his home, but rather that he was proceeding to Knoxville
to participate in its defense. See: Seymour, *Divided Loyalties*, 234.

360. "Murder of Doctor Harvey Baker"; "Dr. Harvey Baker."

361. "Murder of Doctor Harvey Baker."

362. C. W. Charlton, "The Murder of Dr. Harvey Baker," *Holston Journal*
[Knoxville], July 9, 1863; Sutherland, *Violent Rebel*, 184; Seymour,
Divided Loyalties, 239.

363. *Holston Journal*, "Raid into East Tennessee."

364. McCartney, "Saunders Raid," 439.

365. Dow, "Major Dow's Report," 45 (see note 293); Thompson, *112th
Regiment*, 49–50; McCartney, "Saunders Raid," 438–39; Dyer,
Reminiscences; Groce, *Mountain Rebels*, 111.

366. Dow, "Major Dow's Report," 45; George W. Nicholas, "Capture, Prison
Life and Escape," in *History of the 112th Regiment of Illinois Volunteer
Infantry in the Great War of the Rebellion, 1862–1865*, ed. B. F. Thompson
(Toulon: Stark County News, 1885), 459.

367. McKenzie, *Lincolnites and Rebels*, 217; Hess, *Knoxville Campaign*, 7.

368. Groce, *Mountain Rebels*, 133–35; McCartney, "Saunders Raid," 438–39.

369. Indeed, even within the *Confederate* army, rank-and-file troops showed
resentment toward their upper-class comrades. In: Fred A. Bailey, *Class
and Tennessee's Civil War Generation* (Chapel Hill: Univ. of North
Carolina Press, 1987), 60–63.

370. Article III of the United States Constitution, states that the crime of treason requires an "overt act," but Civil War Unionists employed a looser
definition. In: Blair, *With Malice toward Some*, 57; "Treason Against the
United States," *New York Times*, Jan. 25, 1861.

371. Fisher, *War at Every Door*, 132.

372. Witt, *Lincoln's Code*, 130–31.

373. NARA, *1860 U.S. Federal Census - Population* [Knox County, District 11], M653, R.G. 29 (Washington: NARA, n.d.), 224. *Fold 3.com*, at: www.fold3.com.

374. Samuel P. Carter, "Message to Headquarters, Department of the Ohio," *Provost Marshal General Endorsements, Department of East Tennessee*, in NARA, *United States Army Continental Commands, 1821–1920* 29 (Washington: NARA, n.d.), 109. The affidavits were evidently forwarded to the Office of the Provost Marshal but have apparently been lost. Efforts to locate them have proved fruitless.

375. McCartney, "Saunders Raid," 439.

376. Nicholas, "Prison Life and Escape," 459 (see note 366).

Chapter 10

377. *OR*, ser. 1, vol. 23, pt. 2: 387; Reid, *Ohio in the War*, 799; Crow, *Storm in the Mountains*, 30.

378. Robert M. Rhea, "The Sanders Raid," *Sergeant Robert Rhea*. Accessed at: www.63rdtennessee.org/Veterans/Robert%20Rhea/robert-rhea.htm.

379. These included Colonel Gilmore's bonfires built near Big Creek Gap, augmented by reports of an attack on the salt works at Prestonburg, Kentucky, and other probes. In: Marvel, *Burnside*, 248–49.

380. Graf and Haskins, *Papers of Andrew Johnson, Vol. 6*, 245fn.

381. The Bell House was the newest but smallest of the three downtown hotels. It was located on the southwest corner of the intersection of State and Main Streets. Perhaps as punishment for its service to the rebels, the Army of the Ohio confiscated its mattresses when they occupied the city. In: Steve Cotham of the East Tennessee History Center, letter to the author, Apr. 12, 2012; Sutherland, *Violent Rebel*, 60.

382. Hesseltine, *Ramsey*, 106–7.

383. The line was also known as the Knoxville & Kentucky Rail Road.

384. Samuel Cooper to Buckner, June 17, 1863, *OR*, ser. 1, vol. 23, pt. 2: 875-76.

385. Maness and Combs, *Do They Miss Me At Home?* 234 fn, 135.

386. One Confederate account reported the number of defenders to be 1,000.

In: Milton A. Haynes, "Report of Lt. Col. Milton A. Haynes, Confederate
States Artillery, June 21st, 1863," *OR,* ser. 1, vol. 23, no. 1: 391. [Cited
hereinafter as Haynes Report.] Since Haynes consistently exaggerated
the numbers in his report, the lower figure is probably more accurate.
See also: "Communication to Atlanta Confederacy," *Knoxville Register,*
July 7, 1863: 2.

387. "Battle at Knoxville—Defeat of the Yankee Raiders," *Southern
Confederacy,* June 24, 1863, 2.

388. McKenzie, *Lincolnites and Rebels,* 146.

389. The main telegraph line which connected Loudon to Knoxville was out of
service, but Loudon reported the presence of the squadron to Richmond
by an alternate line. Richmond then relayed the news back to Knoxville.

390. *Southern Confederacy,* "Defeat of the Yankee Raiders," 1 (see note 387).

391. McAdoo [Sr.], Diary, June 20, 1863.

392. David Sullins, *Recollections of an Old Man* (Bristol: Lenoir Press, 1910),
5, 210, 217.

393. As an officer in the rebel army, Sullins fought at Shiloh. Ibid., 256–57.

394. Augustus Reichard, whose title was "Consul of His Majesty the King
of Prussia" in New Orleans, spelled Von Sheliha's name in the German
fashion: "Scheliha." In all Confederate records the "c" is missing. Von
Sheliha was commissioned a lieutenant in the Sixth Infantry, Prussian
Army, on Sept. 28, 1844. He was promoted to lieutenant colonel in the
Confederate Army on May 25, 1863. In: Augustus Reichard, letter of
certification, image # 74882793 (1861), *Fold3*.com, accessed at: www
.fold3.com. For more on Sheliha, see: James A. Seddon to Jefferson
Davis, August 23, 1863, in "Final Report, Court of Inquiry [Brig. Gen.
John W. Frazer]," NARA microfilm publications, R.G. 109.6, and NARA,
"Compiled Service Records of Confederate General and Staff Officers,
Sheliha, Victor," NARA Mf. no. M331, 586957. www.fold3.com; George B.
Davis, Leslie J. Perry, and Joseph W. Kirkley, eds., *The Official Military
Atlas of the Civil War* (Washington: Government Printing Office, 1895;
reprint, New York: Arno Press, 1978), plates 107–9; G. B. Hodge, "Report
to S. B. Buckner (June 22,1863)," in *Letters Received By the Confederate
Secretary of War, August to December, 1863,* and "Proceedings of the

Court of Inquiry, Knoxville, Tennessee, July 28, 1863." Both in: *War Department Collection of Confederate Records*, NARA no. M437, Roll 92, R.G. 109.6 (Washington: NARA, n.d.).

395. Victor S. Von Sheliha to Samuel Jones, June 5, 1863, *OR*, ser. 1, vol. 23, pt. 2: 864.

396. "Haynes Report," 391–92 (see note 386).

397. NARA, "Compiled Service Records of Confederate General and Staff Officers [Sheliha]," 3, 12.

398. "Col. Robert C. Trigg of Virginia," *Confederate Veteran* 17, no.2 (February, 1909): 65; U.S. Bureau of the Census, *Eighth Census of the United States, 1860*, NARA Mf. M653 (Washington: NARA, n.d.). Ancestry. com, *1860 U.S. Federal Census-Slave Schedules* [Christiansburg, Montgomery County, Virginia, Catharine L. Trigg] (Lehi: Ancestry.com Operations, Inc., 2010). Accessed at: https://www.ancestry.com/search /collections/7668; U.S. Bureau of the Census, *Eighth Census of the United States, 1860*, NARA Mf. M653, R.G. 29 (Washington: NARA, n.d.). Ancestry.com, *1860 U.S. Federal Census – Population* [Marianna, Jackson County, Florida] (Provo: Ancestry.com Operations, Inc., 2010), 733. Accessed at: www.Ancestry.com; "Jesse Johnson Finley," in *Biographical Directory of the United States Congress*, accessed at: http://bioguide.congress.gov/search/bio/F000134; "Lieut.-Gen. A.P. Stewart: B.L. Ridley's Journal" [Milton A. Haynes], *Confederate Veteran* 3, no. 9 (September, 1895): 260; Cullum, *Biographical Register*, 707 (see note 149); NARA, U.S. Bureau of the Census, *Eighth Census of the United States, 1860* [Slave Schedule, Western Division, Sevier County, Tennessee], NARA Mf. no. M653, (Washington: NARA, n.d.), 365. Ancestry.com, *1860 U.S. Federal Census—Slave Schedule*. Accessed at: www.Ancestry.com.

399. "Trigg [Virginia]," 65 (see note 398); Jeffery C. Weaver, *54th Virginia Infantry* (Lynchburg: H. E. Howard, 1993), 87–88.

400. *Biographical Directory of the United States Congress*, 1052-53.

401. David W. Hartman and David W. Coles, comps., *Biographical Rosters of Florida's Confederate and Union Soldiers, 1861–1865* (Wilmington: Broadfoot, 1995), 609; T. C. McCall, "Recollections of Florida History,"

Confederate Veteran 17, no. 7 (July, 1909): 344; Eicher and Eicher, *Civil War High Commands*, 235.

402. Eight of his fellow cadets became generals in the Confederate army, including one full general (P. G. T. Beauregard) and one lieutenant-general (W. J. Hardee). Five became generals in the Union army, one of whom was Major General Irvin McDowell. Cullum, *Biographical Register*, 707. NARA. in *U.S., Military and Naval Academies, Cadet Records and Applications, 1805–1908*, collection 1299 [database online], *Ancestry.com* (Lehi: Ancestry.com Operations Inc, 2008).

403. Haynes commanded a company in the 1st Tennessee Mounted Infantry, arriving in Mexico in April, 1847. NARA, "Compiled Service Records of Confederate Soldiers Who Served in Organizations Raised Directly by the Confederate Government" [state of Tennessee], NARA Mf. no. M258, War Department Collection of Confederate Records, R.G. 109 (Washington: NARA, n.d.), 3, 32. In: *U.S., Confederate Service Records, 1861-1865*, collection 1106 [database online], *Ancestry.com* (Provo: Ancestry.com Operations Inc, 2007); Jamie S. Linder and William B. Eigelsbach, eds. "To War With Mexico: A Diary of the Mexican-American War," *Journal of East Tennessee History*, No. 73 (2001): 95. In: East Tennessee Historical Society, "The Growth of the Republic Articles," *Teach Tennessee History*, PDF file, accessed at: http://teachtnhistory .org/index.cfm/m/231/dn/The_Growth_of_the_Republic/sectionId/0

404. While Haynes said there was no other choice, tens of thousands of his fellow Tennesseans and dozens of Southern-born West Pointers found one—they fought for the Union.

405. Tennessee's legislature approved a "Declaration of Independence" from the United States on May 6, 1861, and on the following day, May 7th, entered into a military league with the Confederacy. Haynes accepted his commission ten days later, on May 17th, 1861, which was three weeks before the voters of Tennessee approved the legislature's decision to secede. Technically, Haynes joined the "Provisional Army of the State of Tennessee." This unit was only nominally independent, for it was under Confederate control from the first and was soon absorbed into the Confederate army.

406. This was not for lack of effort, however. Haynes lobbied for promotion tirelessly, pulled every string imaginable, and watched in frustration while his classmates rose in grade. NARA, "Case Files of Applications from Former Confederates for Presidential Pardons, 1865-67 [Tennessee, Haynes, Milton A., 1865]" in *Confederate Amnesty Papers*, NARA Mf. no. M1003, R.G. 94, at: *Fold3 com*, title no. 59 (Aug. 2, 2007), 3. https://www.fold3.com/title/59/confederate-amnesty-papers.

407. NARA, "Compiled Service Records of Confederate Soldiers Who Served in Organizations [Tennessee]," 63 (see note 403); Dean Novelli, "On a Corner of Gay Street: History of the Lamar House-Bijou Theater, Knoxville, Tennessee, 1817–1985," *East Tennessee Historical Society's Publications* 56 (1984): 20.

408. Possibly First Lieutenant Robert B. Waddell, an artillery officer. Henry Heth, "General Orders, No. 29" (Knoxville: Headquarters, Department of East Tennessee, 1863), 1. www.fold3.com/image/#67096783.

409. Heth, "General Orders, No. 29," 2 (see prev. note).

410. Weaver, *54th Virginia*, 69–70 (see note 399); "Haynes Report," 391–92; "Trigg of Virginia," 64.

411. Probably Capt. Wiggs's company of the 1st Tennessee Cavalry CSA. This was the unit involved in the killing of Harvey Baker.

412. Six months later, Union General Ambrose Burnside used this cupola as an observation post to watch for approaching Confederates. In: *OR*, ser. 1, vol. 23, no.1: 391–92; *Holston Journal*, "Raid into East Tennessee."

413. *Knoxville Register*, "Communication to Atlanta Confederacy" (see note 386); Campbell, *Southern Service*, 58–59 (see note 317); Weaver, *54th Virginia*, 69–70.

414. Thomas W. Fisher, letter to father and mother, June 29, 1863, in "Civil War Letters of Pvt. Thomas Winton Fisher, CSA," Diane M. Gardner, comp., www.ted.gardner.org/603629.htm (see note 240); "Honor to Capt. Arnold," *Knoxville Register*, June 23, 1863: 1; *Knoxville Register*, "Communication to Atlanta Confederacy"; A Georgia Colonel, pseud., "Leaves from an Old Scrap Book," *Sunny South* [Atlanta, GA], Feb. 24, 1906: 2

415. Campbell, *Southern Service*, xii-xiii.

416. Ibid., 58; W. D. Blackman, "The Sanders Raid," *National Tribune*, Oct. 14, 1886: 4; *Southern Confederacy*, "Defeat of the Yankee Raiders," 2.

417. Sullins, *Recollections*, 256 (see note 392); Alexander M. Poe, "Defense of Knoxville," in *Battles and Leaders of the Civil War* 3, eds. Robert Underwood Johnson and Clarence C. Buel (New York: The Century Company, 1888), 734. Also see: The Ohio State University Department of History, *ehistory books*. Accessed at: https://ehistory.osu.edu/books /battles/vol3/734; *OR*, ser. 1, vol. 23, no.1; Campbell, *Southern Service*, 58.

418. Their location was described only as "Island Ford."

419. NARA, "Records of the U.S. Bureau of the Census," *Seventh Census of the United States, 1850* [Population], NARA Mf. no. M432, R.G. 29 (Washington: NARA, n.d.). At: *Ancestry.com, 1850 U.S. Federal Census - Population Schedule*, collection 8054 (Lehi: Ancestry.com Operations, Inc., 2009), 43A, Image 91. Accessed at: https://www.ancestry.com /search/collections/8054/; "Capt. Wyly's Company in the Fight at Knoxville," *Southern Confederacy*, June 29, 1863: 1; A Georgia Colonel, "Old Scrap Book," 2 (see note 414); William R. McIntire, "Affidavit, No. 28098" (Aug. 6, 1914), *Texas, Confederate Pension Applications, 1899- 1975 Vol.1*, 1–646 & 1–283 (Austin: Texas State Library and Archives Commission, 1914). In: *Alabama, Texas and Virginia, U.S., Confederate Pensions, 1884-1958*, collection 1677, *Ancestry.com* (Provo: Ancestry. com Operations, Inc., 2010); "Leyden Artillery," *Southern Confederacy*, June 24, 1863: 1; "Gallant Conduct of a Georgia Battery," *Southern Confederacy*, June 27, 1863: 1; J. H. Williams. "Letter to the editor," *Knoxville Register*, June 27, 1863: 1.

420. A Georgia Colonel, "Old Scrap Book," 2; "Wyly's Company," 1 (see note 419).

421. McEntire, "Affidavit" (see note 419); A Georgia Colonel, "Old Scrap Book," 2; "Leyden Artillery," 1 (see note 419); David C. Legg, ed., "Obituary of William Randolph McEntire," in Georgia Div., United Daughters of the Confederacy, comp., *9th Battalion Georgia Artillery Co. A* (Smyrna: Smyrna Historical Society, 1920); "Georgia Battery," 1 (see note 419).

422. The troops did not proceed on foot because they lacked a guide and were unarmed.

423. "Communicated," *Knoxville Register*, June 26, 1863: 1; Seymour, *Divided Loyalties*, 87—fn 9.

424. Civil War Centennial Commission of Tennessee, "Captain W. R. Browne's Tennessee Light Artillery Company, Formerly Captain H. Baker's Company" in *Tennesseans in the Civil War: A Military History of Union and Confederate Units, Vol. 1* (Nashville: Tennessee Civil War Centennial Commission, 1964). Republished by Tennessee Genweb Project, *tngenweb.org*, Tennessee and the Civil War (Nov. 26, 2016), 1. Accessed at: www.tngenweb.org/ civilwar/csaart/browne.html; NARA, *Compiled Service Records of Confederate Soldiers Who Served in Organizations from the State of Tennessee* (Carded Abstract of Service Records Showing Military Service of Soldiers Who Fought in Confederate Organizations). R.G. 109, M268 (Washington: NARA Microfilm Publications, n.d.). Fold3.com., Civil War Service Records (CMSR)—Confederate—Tennessee (May 14, 2008). https://www.fold3 .com/title/40/civil-war-service-records-cmsr-confederate-tennessee. Baker's birthplace and full name are unknown.

425. Captain Hugh L. W. McClung of the Tennessee Light Artillery was not the same person as Captain Hugh L. McClung of the 26th Tennessee Infantry. Hugh L. McClung was the son of Matthew McClung, a prominent Knoxville dry goods merchant. Hugh L. was killed at the battle of Fort Donelson in 1862. In: *Descendants of Moses White*. www .joepayne.org/white. Also see: "The McClung Family of Knoxville," unpublished essay, Calvin M. McClung Historical Collection, History & Genealogy Dept., East Tennessee History Center, Lawson McGhee Library [Knox County Public Library], Knoxville, TN, 169.

426. Ironically, Captain McClung was a distant cousin of Union general Samuel P. Carter who organized the raid, and his bridge-burning brothers. Civil War Centennial Commission of Tennessee, "Captain Hugh L. W. McClung's Tennessee Light Artillery Company: 'The Caswell Artillery,' 1st [Carter's] Tennessee Cavalry Regiment," in *Tennesseans in the Civil War: A Military History of Union and Confederate Units, Vol. 1* (Nashville: Tennessee Civil War Centennial Commission, 1964). Republished by Tennessee Genweb Project, tngenweb.org., Tennessee

and the Civil War (Nov. 26, 2016), *Confederate Artillery Units.* Accessed at: www.tngenweb.org/ civilwar/csacav/csa1carter.html.

427. Civil War Centennial Commission of Tennessee, "McClung's Tennessee Light Artillery" (see prev. note); Geoffrey R. Walden, comp. "Weapons Used in the Battle of Mill Springs," in *Mill Springs Battlefield History* (Nancy: Mill Springs Battlefield Association, 1998). Accessed at: www .cumberlandcreative.com/msba/weapons4.html.

428. NARA, *Compiled Service Records of Confederate Soldiers Who Served in Organizations from the State of Tennessee,* Carded Abstract, R.G. 109, M268 (Washington: NARA Microfilm Publications, n.d.). Fold3 .com, "Capt. Burroughs's Co., Light Artillery (Rhett Artillery)," Civil War Service Records (CMSR)—Confederate—Tennessee (May 14, 2008), image no. 67690259. Accessed at: https://www.fold3.com/title/40 /civil-war-service-records-cmsr-confederate-tennessee.

429. Sullins, *Recollections,* 256–57.

430. Volunteer, pseud., "Communication," *Knoxville Register,* June 26, 1863: 1.

431. Five months earlier, Longstreet and his artillerymen had participated in the battle of Gettysburg, in which Confederate troops assaulted powerful Union positions on Cemetery Ridge, an attack which Longstreet opposed and which ended in disaster. In Knoxville, Longstreet elected to assault a position on College Hill (which had been designated "Fort Sanders"). His men were smashed by a much smaller Union force. Alexander, *Fighting for the Confederacy,* 324.

432. Blake, a forty-six-year-old South Carolinian, was a member of the West Point class of 1847. He had the duty of enforcing conscription laws in the Department of East Tennessee. *Knoxville Register,* Nov. 8, 1862; Cullum, *Biographical Register,* 37.

433. McKenzie, *Lincolnites and Rebels,* 81.

434. Phillip D. Spence, "General Polk and His Staff," *Confederate Veteran* 9 (1901): 121; Sullins, *Recollections,* 252.

435. He had married a wealthy, slave-owning widow and now lived on a rice plantation in nearby Georgia called "Melora." McAdoo visited Knoxville regularly. Gordon B. McKinney, "East Tennessee Politics," *Journal of East Tennessee History* 48 (1976): 36.

436. In Job 1:1–3, Job curses the day he was born because his life has made him suffer. In cursing the Fourth of July, McAdoo implies that United States citizenship has given him nothing but misery. Ironically, McAdoo's son, William G. McAdoo, Jr. (1863-1941), served as United States Secretary of the Treasury, married the daughter of President Woodrow Wilson, and twice ran unsuccessfully for President of the United States.

437. McAdoo Diary, entries of June 20, July 9, 1863; McKinney, "McAdoo."

438. McKenzie, "Prudent Silence," 75–76.

439. No official muster roll has survived. Identities were cloaked for various reasons. Some participants were identified because they were not residents of the immediate area while others were merely "tender boys." Some volunteers masked their involvement so as not to appear boastful, while others hid it for reasons of self-protection. They feared arrest by rebel conscription agents or retribution by Unionists in the event that the Yankees regained the city.

440. William B. Hesseltine, "Four American Traditions," *Journal of Southern History* 27 (Feb. 1961): 3–31; Marvel, *Appomattox*, 110.

441. There were also some anomalies: five were born abroad (three in Switzerland, one in France, and one in Brazil)

442. Graf and Haskins, *Papers of Andrew Johnson, Vol. 6*, 327.

443. Kenneth W. Noe, "Who Were the Bushwackers?" *Civil War History* 49, no. 1 (March 2003): 12; McKenzie, "Prudent Silence," 77; Campbell, "East Tennessee," 65 (see note 86); Bailey, *Tennessee's Civil War Generation*, 21ff (see note 369).

444. See Appendix 3. Cf. McKenzie, *Lincolnites and Rebels*, 41–42.

445. McKenzie, *Lincolnites and Rebels*, 41–42.

446. John N. Fain, ed., *Sanctified Trial* (Knoxville: Univ. of Tennessee Press, 2004), 18; Madden, "Unionist Resistance," 24–25; Dirck, "Posterity's Blush," 247 (see note 54).

447. Verton M. Queener, "East Tennessee Sentiment and the Secession Movement, November, 1860—June 1861," *East Tennessee Historical Society's Publications* 20 (1964): 64; Madden, "Unionist Resistance," 24–25; Sutherland, *Violent Rebel,* 45; Graf and Haskins, *Papers of*

Andrew Johnson, Vol. 6, 328 fn; "Interesting Annual Memorial Service," *Confederate Veteran* 2 (1894): 323; McKenzie, *Lincolnites and Rebels*, 42.

448. "Rev. Joseph H. Martin, 1851–1863," *Historical Sermon, Second Presbyterian Church* (Knoxville: Second Presbyterian Church, n.d.), 5–8; Rhea, "The Sanders Raid" (see note 378).

449. Nancy Siker, "Lucien B. Woolfolk," *First Baptist Church* (Knoxville: First Baptist Church, 1992), 105–6.

450. Ibid.; William Rule, ed., *Standard History of Knoxville, Tennessee* (Chicago: Lewis Publishing, 1900), 428.; Wyatt-Brown, *Shaping of Southern Culture*, 168–78 (see note 60); W. Russell Briscoe, "Part 1: 1818–1876," in W. Russell Briscoe and Katherine B. Buehler, *"Her Walls Before Thee Stand: History of the Second Presbyterian Church, Knoxville, Tennessee,"* 1 ed. (Knoxville: private printing, 1968), 6. Accessed at: https://knoxcotn.org/old_site/churches/ 2ndpres/index .html; McKenzie, *Lincolnites and Rebels*, 35; "Rev. Joseph H. Martin"; Sullins, *Recollections*, 252; Dillan J. Carroll, "'The God Who Shielded Me Before, Yet Watches Over Us All,'" *Civil War History* 61 (Sept. 2015): 271–75.

451. Campbell, "East Tennessee," 65. Mark E. Neely, Jr., suggests in similar fashion that East Tennesseans may be divided between Traditionalists and Modernizers. The members of Knoxville's business and professional élite who mustered on June 19-20 would fall into the Modernizer category: "If it makes any sense to divide East Tennesseans into modernizers and traditionalists, then the modernizers may well have been the supporters of secession, whereas the supporters of the Union were in fact adherents of a pastoral life in what one of their leaders call America's Switzerland." Conversely, Robert Tracy McKenzie maintains that "it appears that Knoxville's Civil War was not solely, or even primarily, a class conflict." McKenzie, *Lincolnites and Rebels*, 126; Neely, *Southern Rights*, 127.

Chapter 11

452. Mitchell, "Sanders Raid," 243.

453. The Tazewell Road stretched north-northeast forty-five miles to the

village of Tazewell, Tennessee, then continued twelve miles northwest to the Cumberland Gap, which is approximately fifty-seven miles from Knoxville by road. The Tazewell section is now designated Tennessee State Highway 33.

454. William P. Sanders, "Sanders Report," 387; McCartney, "Saunders Raid," 439; Dow, "Major Dow's Report," 45; Kelso, "Sanders's Raid," 2; Hesseltine, *Ramsey*, 110–11; Haynes Report, 391–92; Rhea, "Sanders Raid," 5.

455. Mitchell, "Sanders Raid," 243.

456. Fry, "Sanders Raid," 1; Samuel C. Frey, Alfred Sperry, and Perez G. Clark, *Battered Destinies: Story of Battery D, Civil War, 1861-1865* (1908) (Pasadena: reis. Infotrans Press, 1996), 85. Internet Archive, digital copy, accessed at: http://web.archive.org/web/20030906170931 and http://www.infotran.com/BatteredDestinies.htm.

457. Tarrant, *Wild Riders*, 171. Lt. Humphrey survived the Sanders raid but was badly wounded near Hillsboro, Georgia, on July 31, 1864. Left in the hands of the enemy, he died on August 18, 1864. NARA, *Compiled Service Records of Volunteer Union Soldiers Who Served in Organizations from the State of Kentucky*, no. 300398, M397, "First Cavalry," 15.

458. McCartney, "Saunders Raid," 439–40.

459. The drummer was probably attached to the 7th Florida, which had arrived earlier that night.

460. Ibid.; Fry, "Sanders Raid," 1; Tarrant, *Wild Riders*, 171; Campbell, *Southern Service*, 58.

461. McCartney, "Saunders Raid," 440.

Chapter 12

462. Charles McClung McGhee, a vocal supporter of secession, was president of the East Tennessee & Georgia Railroad. During the war he supplied both sides, first selling provisions to the Confederate army, and then, after Knoxville was retaken, to the Union army. Hesseltine, *Ramsey*, 339; Groce, *Mountain Rebels*, 120.

463. *OR*, ser. 1, vol. 23, no.1: 392.

464. Mitchell, "Sanders Raid," 243; "We heard a gentleman . . .," Editorial, *Knoxville Register*, June 23, 1863: 2; Reid, *Ohio in the War*, 83.

465. Samuel C. Fry, "The Saunders Raid: An Ohio Light Artilleryman Corrects

Comrade R. C. Rankin," *National Tribune*, June 15, 1893: 3; Campbell, *Southern Service*, 58; Fry, "Sanders Raid," 1–2.

466. Fry, "Sanders Raid," 1–3 (see prev. note); Campbell, *Southern Service*, 58–59; Sullins, *Recollections*, 256.

467. McCartney, "Saunders Raid," 440; Volunteer, pseud., "Communication," 1; NARA, *Compiled Service Records of Confederate Soldiers . . . from the State of Tennessee*; *Knoxville Register*, "a gentleman," 2 (see note 464); "Captain William H. Burrough's Tennessee Light Artillery Company: 'Rhett Artillery,'" in *Tennesseans in the Civil War: Confederate Artillery Units*, Tennessee GenWeb Project (2004). Accessed at: www.tngenweb .org/civilwar/csaart/ burrough.html; "Captain Hugh L. W. McClung's Tennessee Light Artillery Company: 'The Caswell Artillery,'" in *Tennesseans in the Civil War: Confederate Artillery Units*, Tennessee GenWeb Project (2004). Accessed at: www.tngenweb.org/civilwar /csaart/mcclung.html.

468. Sperry, Frey, and Clark, *Battery D*, 85; McCartney, "Saunders Raid," 440; Kniffin, "Sanders" (see note 180); Volunteer, pseud., "Communication," 1.

469. Kelso, "Sanders's Raid," 3; Richard C. Rankin, *History of the Seventh Ohio Volunteer Cavalry*, (Ripley: J. C. Newcomb, 1881), 6.

470. Harriet Beecher Stowe, *The Key to Uncle Tom's Cabin*, 1 ed. (London: Thomas Bosworth and Clarke, Beeton and Co, 1853, 1898), 78; Wilbur Henry Siebert, *The Underground Railroad from Slavery to Freedom: A Comprehensive History*, 109, 308; Jacobson, *Borderland of Light*; Adams, *Neglected Period of Anti-Slavery*, 6 (see note 21); John Rankin, *Letters on American Slavery*, 2 ed. (Newburyport: Charles Whipple, 1836. reis. Andesite Press, 2017). www.bookdepository.com; Smith, *"Captain Richard Calvin Rankin,"* 781–3 (see note 20).

471. Briscoe, *"Her Walls Before Thee Stand,"* 6 (see note 450).

472. Pvt. Hosford is buried in the National Cemetery in Knoxville. Rankin, *History of the Seventh Ohio*, 6 (see note 469); Richard C. Rankin, "The Saunders Raid: Captain Rankin Considers . . . the Dispute Raised Against Him" [pt. 1], *National Tribune*, Aug. 3, 1893: 3; Hewett, gen., *Supplement to the Official Records*, vol. 49, pt. 2, ser. no. 61605; Mitchell, "Sanders Raid," 243–44; National Cemetery Administration, *Nationwide Gravesite Locator*. Ancestry.com, "U.S., Veterans' Gravesites, ca. 1775–

2019" (Provo: Ancestry.com Operations Inc., 2006). Accessed at: https://www.ancestry.com/search/collections/8750/; *1850 United States Federal Census* [Johnston, Trumbull County, Ohio] (Ancestry .com, 2009).

473. Kelso, "Sanders's Raid," 1; Rankin, "Rankin Considers Dispute [pt. 1]," 3 (see prev. note); E. Porter Alexander, *Military Memoirs of a Confederate* (Bloomington: Indiana Univ. Press, 1907), 451–52.

474. Sullins, *Recollections*, 296; McCartney, "Saunders Raid," 440; Haynes Report, 392–93.

475. Haynes's gun may have fired the shots that killed Pvt. Hosford or that knocked Lt. Mitchell unconscious. Sanders retired toward Strawberry Plains shortly thereafter, and Haynes may have concluded that this "retreat" was due to his good shooting. Haynes Report, 393; Tarrant, *Wild Riders*, 171.

476. Sanders Report, 387, 391; "Major Dow's Report," 45–46.

477. The 6th Florida was also known as the Magnolia State Guards. Hewett, *Supplement to the Official Records*, vol. 49, pt. 2, 605; "Major Dow's Report," 43–46; McAdoo, Diary, entry June 22, 1863.

478. The Asylum hospital became the City Hall. Two Georgians died: Corp. Thomas Caldwell and Pvt. W. R. Hodson. "Gallant Conduct," 1 (see note 419); Seymour, *Divided Loyalties*, 78; Hartman and Coles, *Florida's Confederate . . . Soldiers*, 634 (see note 401).

479. Blackman, "Sanders Raid" (see note 416); "Capt. Pleasant M. McClung," *Knoxville Register*, June 23, 1863: 1.

480. Sutherland, *Violent Rebel*, xxv; Seymour, *Divided Loyalties*, 16, 78; Sullins, *Recollections*, 256; McKenzie, *Lincolnites and Rebels*, 147; McAdoo, Diary, entry June 22, 1863.

481. "Pig-headed" may be "big-headed." McAdoo, Diary, entry June 22, 1863.

482. Smith and Cooper, *Union Woman*, 11 (see note 149).

483. Sullins, *Recollections*, 259.

484. Ibid., 258.

485. Their estimate was by 2,600 to 1,000. Ibid.; Haynes Report, 393.

486. Hesseltine, *Ramsey*, 114.

487. McAdoo, Diary, entry June 27, 1863; Hesseltine, *Ramsey*, 106, 111–12, 117–18.

488. McAdoo, Diary.

Chapter 13

489. "Major Dow's Report," 46; "Progress of the Yankee Raiders," *Knoxville Register*, June 23, 1863: 2; Mitchell, "Sanders Raid," 244.

490. Edmiston, "Fighting at Philadelphia," 2 (see note 142); Rankin, "Saunders Raid," 4 (see note 322); McCartney, "Saunders Raid," 441; Rankin, *Seventh Ohio*, 6; *Knoxville Register*, "Progress," 2 (see note 489).

491. Fisher, *War at Every Door*, 54, 56, 70, 164; McKenzie, *Lincolnites and Rebels*, 103; Pilgrim, pseud., "Abolitionists at Strawberry Plains—Bridge Burning—House Pillaging—Official Vandalism," *Holston Journal*, July 9, 1863; Madden, "Unionist Resistance," 32; Groce, *Mountain Rebels*, 20, 79, 82; George W. Randolph to Daniel Leadbetter, *OR*, ser. 1, vol. 11, pt. 3: 626; Mitchell, "Sanders Raid," 242; Thomsen, *Rebel Chief*, 200.

492. Fry's name is occasionally misspelled as "Frey." Samuel Jones, "Holding Burnside in Check in East Tennessee," in *Battles and Leaders of the Civil War, Vol. 5* (1882), ed. Peter Cozzens (Urbana: Univ. of Illinois Press, 2002), 439; W. L. Nicholson and A. Lindenkohl, comps., *The Mountain Region of North Carolina and Tennessee* [1863], map, Josh Hawley Map Collection, no. 43.5, Library of Congress Geography and Map Div., (Washington: U.S. Coast and Geodetic Survey, 1863). https://www.loc.gov/item/79696027/. Fold3.com., *Civil War Maps, 1861–1865*, Southern States Region (May 20, 2010), 1, image no. 260558364. Accessed at: https://www.fold3.com/image/260558364?terms=war ,tennessee,us,mountain,civil,region,of; Frey, Sperry and Clark, *Battered Destinies*, 85 (see note 456); Rankin, "Saunders Raid," 4.

493. McMillan's Station was also spelled *McMilan's* Station. James McMillan, a very staunch Unionist, may have resided there, although the connection is uncertain. The settlement was located near present day Mascot, Tennessee. See: McKenzie, *Lincolnites and Rebels*, 151; John R. Branner, "Mossy Creek" [letter to brother, June 22, 1863], *Knoxville Register*,

June 23, 1863: 1; "Damages Done By the Enemy," *Knoxville Register*, June 23, 1863: 1; *Knoxville Register*, "Progress," 2.

494. Dow, "Major Dow's Report," 46; McCartney, "Saunders Raid," 441; Mitchell, "Sanders Raid," 244; Sperry, Frey, and Clark, *Battery D*, 85; *OR*, ser. 1, vol. 23, pt. 2: 387.

495. Despite his known opposition to the rebellion, Mayor Luttrell remained in office throughout the war.

496. Two of his sons entered the Confederate army, and the eldest, John, died. It would have been difficult to remove an official whose eldest son had given his life for the Confederate cause. Mayor Luttrell also sold corn and hay to the Confederate army, although he later claimed to have done so involuntarily. His youngest son, Samuel, joined the Union army. NARA, *Confederate Papers Relating to Citizens or Business Firms, 1861–65. Quartermaster's Receipt, 1862*, M346, image no. 43282376. www.fold3 .com; McKenzie, *Lincolnites and Rebels*, 127, 135.

497. Weaver, *54th Virginia*, 1; Tarrant, *Wild Riders*, 172; William P. Sanders, "Sanders Report," 385, 393.

498. The confluence of Flat Creek and the Holston River was probably located on the south side of present-day Mascot, Tennessee.

499. A "Howe truss" used inexpensive materials and was cheap to build because it eliminated the need for skilled carpenters. Tennessee Department of Transportation, "Existing Covered Bridges in Tennessee," *Historic Bridges* (Nashville: Tennessee Dept. of Transportation, n.d.), 2. Accessed at: https://www.tn.gov/tdot/structures-/historic-bridges /existing-covered-bridges.html.

500. Sanders Report, 387; Denney, "All About Saunder's Raid," 7; McCartney, "Saunders Raid," 441; Mitchell, "Sanders Raid," 244; Mosey, *Diary*, 19 (see note 302); Rankin, *Seventh Ohio*, 6.

501. Walden, "Weapons Used" (see note 427).

502. Frey, Sperry and Clark, *Battered Destinies*, 85; William R. Trotter, *Bushwhackers!* 2: *The Mountains* (Greensboro: Signal Research, 1988), 83; Harvey Denney, "Over the Mountains," *National Tribune* 20 (Feb. 21, 1901): 2; Denney, "All About Saunder's Raid," 7; Mitchell, "Sanders Raid," 242; Fry, "Sanders Raid," 1; Rankin, *Seventh Ohio*, 6; McCartney, "Saunders Raid," 441.

503. Sanders Report, 388.

504. In 1863 high explosives had yet to be invented, and therefore destroying a bridge was surprisingly time consuming. In this case, six hours elapsed.

505. Ibid.; Mitchell, "Sanders Raid," 244; Sperry, Frey, and Clark, *Battery D*, 86; *Knoxville Register*, "Progress."

506. McCartney, "Saunders Raid," 442; Mitchell, "Sanders Raid," 244.

Chapter 14

507. Ibid.

508. John T. Levi, "Special Requisition," in *Compiled Service Records of Confederate Soldiers . . . from the State of North Carolina* [John T. Levi]," NARA, M270, 9.

509. Mossy Creek was also occasionally spelled "Mossey Creek." The town changed its name to "Jefferson City" forty years later. While it lies in Jefferson County, Dandridge is the seat.

510. Strawberry Plains is eighteen miles east of Knoxville, and New Market is seven miles east of Strawberry Plains. Pilgrim, pseud., "Abolitionists," 1.

511. However, by the time its prediction hit the newsstands, the timbers were already ablaze. Hesseltine, *Ramsey*, 107–12; "The Raids! The Raids!" *Southern Confederacy*, June 22, 1863: 1; Pilgrim, pseud., "Abolitionists."

512. McCartney, "Saunders Raid," 451–52; Mitchell, "Sanders Raid," 244.

513. John R. Branner to James A. Seddon, June 22, 1863, *Telegrams Received By the Secretary of War*. M437, Roll 15, R. G. 109.6 (Washington: NARA Microfilm Publications, n.d.); Branner, "Mossy Creek," 1 (see note 493); Pilgrim, pseud., "Abolitionists," 1; *OR*, ser. 1, vol. 23, pt. 2: 881.

514. Sanders Report, 388.

515. Denney, "All About Saunder's Raid," 7; Kniffin, "Sanders," 1.

516. Brents, *Patriots and Guerrillas*, 13.

517. *1860 United States Federal Census: Population Schedule, Jefferson, Tennessee*, 189. Ancestry.com., Family History Library Film no. 805258. www.ancestry.com; Harvey Hubbard, "Vandalism," *Southern Confederacy*, July 3, 1863: 1.

518. Hubbard, "Vandalism" (see prev. note) 1; *Knoxville Register*, "Progress," 2; Branner, "Mossy Creek," 1.

519. Bailey, *Tennessee's Civil War Generation*, 76.

520. Hubbard, "Vandalism," 1.

521. Ibid.

522. In 1865 the U.S. District Attorney charged both Branners with treason. Branner, "Mossy Creek," 1; *Knoxville Register*, "Progress," 2; Ancestry. com. [NARA], *1860 United States Federal Census— Slave Schedules*, NARA Mf. no. M653, Roll (Provo: Ancestry.com Operations, Inc., 2009). Accessed at: https://www.ancestry.com/search/collections/7667/; Vernon H. Crow, "The Justness of Our Cause," *Journal of East Tennessee History* 56–57 (1984-85): 71–101; Ancestry.com [NARA], Ancestry.com [NARA], *1860 United States Federal Census* [Population Schedule, Jefferson, Tennessee], Family History Library, Film no. 805258 (Provo: Ancestry.com Operations, Inc., 2009), 187-88. Accessed at: https://www .ancestry.com/search/ collections/7667/; William W. Stringfield, "Notes for a speech, 1861," Stringfield Papers, Special Collections, Hunter Library, Western Carolina University, Cullowhee, NC; Stringfield, "Memoirs of the Civil War," 16.

523. Hubbard, "Vandalism," 1.

524. McCartney, "Saunders Raid," 442.

525. "Major Dow's Report," 46; McCartney, "Saunders Raid," 441–42; Sanders Report, 388; Mitchell, "Sanders Raid," 244–45.

526. Sanders Report, 388; Denney, "Saunder's Raid," 7; Rankin, "Saunders Raid," 4; Rankin, *Seventh Ohio*, 7.

527. Sanders Report, 388; "Major Dow's Report," 46.

528. Victor S. Von Sheliha to Samuel Jones, June 20, 1863, *OR*, ser. 1, vol. 23, pt. 1: 391.

529. The rear guard were members of the 2nd and 7th Ohio. Mitchell, "Sanders Raid," 245; Rankin, *Seventh Ohio*, 7.

530. Sanders Report, 388; "Major Dow's Report," 46; McCartney, "Saunders Raid," 442.

531. McCartney, "Saunders Raid," 442; "Major Dow's Report," 46; Mitchell, "Sanders Raid," 245; Rankin, *Seventh Ohio*, 9.

532. Mitchell, "Sanders Raid," 245.

533. "Major Dow's Report," 46–47; McCartney, "Saunders Raid," 443.

534. McCartney, "Saunders Raid," 443.

535. Richard S. Hartigan, *Lieber's Code and the Law of War* (Chicago: Precedent, 1983), 45, 48, 120–24.

536. Sanders Report, 388.

537. Rankin, *Seventh Ohio*, 7.

538. Ibid; Mitchell, "Sanders Raid," 244–46.

539. Passes through Cumberland Mountain were named colloquially and often changed over the years. Sanders reported that he and his men made their way through "Smith's Gap," but the portal through which they actually escaped was identified on Civil War-era maps (as well as by some participants) as "Childer's Gap." This designation, sometimes spelled "Childre's Gap," disappeared from most later renditions. Mitchell, "Sanders Raid," 246.

540. Nicholas, "Prison Life and Escape," 459.

541. Rankin, *Seventh Ohio*, 7.

542. Mitchell, "Sanders Raid," 246.

543. Ibid., 241.

544. Sanders Report, 388.

545. Libby Prison was located in Richmond. Only Union officers were confined there, under notoriously bad conditions.

546. Rankin, *Seventh Ohio*, 7–8.

547. Dow, "Major Dow's Report," 47.

548. McCartney, "Saunders Raid," 433–52.

549. U.S. Geological Survey, *Jellico East Quadrangle,* Topographic Map (Reston: U.S. Geological Survey, 1970); Campbell, *Southern Service,* 47.

550. Sanders Report, 388.

551. *OR,* ser. 1, vol. 23, pt. 2: 13, 385, 389.

Chapter 15

552. "Federal Raid Into East Tennessee—Immense Destruction of Railroad Bridges and Other Property," *Knoxville Register,* July 5, 1863: 2.

553. Ibid.

554. Rankin, *Seventh Ohio*, 8; "Immense Destruction," 2 (see note 552).

555. Bradley, *Tullahoma,* 86; Eicher and Eicher, *Civil War High Commands,* 496.

556. The Charlotte and Wilmington routes were 822 and 892 miles long, respectively. Black, *Railroads*, 185.

557. Burnside's estimate was reasonable. Under Civil War conditions, a two-month period for repairs of this nature was normal. In the winter of 1864, Union engineers required about three months to repair the bridges and track between Chattanooga and Knoxville

558. *OR*, ser. 1, vol. 23, pt. 2: 390.

559. Seddon to Engineer Bureau, June 26, 1863, *OR*, ser. 1, vol. 23, pt. 1: 390; Black, *Railroads*, 83.

560. "James L. Cooley," in *Tennessee Civil War Veterans' Questionnaires 2*, eds. Gustavus W. Dyer and John T. Moore (Easley: Southern Histories Press, 1985), 2, 550–52; Black, *Railroads*, 223.

561. "Immense Destruction," 2.

562. Foster, *War Stories*, 126–27 (see note 65); O.K., pseud., "Dispatch [Abingdon, VA], Sept. 22, 1863," *Richmond Dispatch*, Sept. 25, 1863.

563. Smith, *Campaign to Nowhere*, 34, 143 (see note 45).

564. Black, *Railroads*, 198–99.

565. The Floridian was probably Pvt. Leonard Anderson of Co. A, 7th Florida Infantry. "Lucien" has not been identified. In: L. J. A. [Leonard Anderson?], letter to the editors, *Southern Confederacy*, July 3, 1863: 2; and also: Lucien, "Letter to Mr. Sperry," *Knoxville Register*, June 27, 1863: 1.

566. Crist, Dix and Williams, *Davis Papers, Vol. 9*, 265.

567. Younger, *Inside the Confederate Government*, 80.

568. Crist, Dix and Willams, *Davis Papers, Vol. 9*, 243–45.

569. Buckner's westernmost outpost was located near Jamestown, Tennessee, and was under the command of Brigadier General John Pegram. Sanders's path lay about twenty-five miles to the *east* of Pegram's position, while Bragg's nearest men were at least an additional twenty miles farther *west*. Duke, Willcox, and Hines, "Morgan's Rough Riders," 327; Orlando B. Willcox, "The Escape," in *Famous Adventures and Prison Escapes of the Civil War*, ed. George W. Cable (New York: Century Co., 1913), 115. Also see: Gutenberg Project (July 6, 2006), Ebook no. 18765. Accessed at: https://www.gutenberg.org/files/18765/18765-h/18765-h.htm; Younger, *Inside the Confederate Government*, 81.

570. August V. Kautz, "Memoirs, 1861–65," 1, entry June 9, 1863, Kautz Papers, LOC.

571. Cooper, *Jefferson Davis*, 456–57.

572. A native Tennessean, Frazer was a member of the U.S.M.A. class of 1849. Arthur W. Bergeron, Jr., "John Wesley Frazer," in *The Confederate General 2*, 1 ed., eds. William C. Davis and Julie Hoffman (Harrisburg: National Historical Society, 1991), 146–47.

573. The court recorder was Capt. O. H. Prince, 3rd Alabama Cavalry. "Col. Thomas Claiborne," *Confederate Veteran*, June, 1913; Alexander, *Fighting for the Confederacy*, 506; O. H. Prince, recorder, "Proceedings of the Court of Inquiry [Brig. Gen. John W. Frazer, July 28, 1863]," in *Letters Received By the Confederate Secretary of War, Aug. to Dec., 1863*, NARA, R.G. 109.6, M437, Roll 92. (Washington: NARA Microfilm Publications, n.d.); Lewellyn A. Shaver, *A History of the Sixtieth Alabama Regiment, Gracie's Alabama Brigade* (Montgomery: Barrett & Brown, 1867), 12.

574. The 65th Georgia was commonly known as Fain's Regiment. Hodge, Report to Maj. Gen. S. B. Buckner, June 22, 1863 (see note 394).

575. Prince, "Proceedings of the Court of Inquiry [Frazer]" (see note 573).

576. Buckner to Seddon, April 22, 1863, *Letters Received by the Confederate Secretary of War.*

577. Prince, "Proceedings of the Court of Inquiry [Frazer]."

578. Seddon to Davis, Aug. 23, 1863, *Letters Sent by the Confederate Secretary of War*

579. Seddon to Buckner, July 24, 1863, *Letters Sent by the Confederate Secretary of War.*

580. Crist, *Davis Papers*, vol. 9, 390, 403; Alexander, *Fighting for the Confederacy*, 286; Byron G. McDowell, "Report to Major [W. W.] Stringfield," Sept. 16, 1863, *OR*, ser. 1, vol. 30, pt. 2: 637; Marvel, *Burnside*, 279.

581. Sally B. Putnam, *Richmond During the War* (Lincoln: Univ. of Nebraska Press, 1996), 258; McDowell, "Report to Major Stringfield," 637; Alexander, *Fighting for the Confederacy*, 286; Crist, *Davis Papers, Vol. 9*, 390, 403.

582. Davis's inability to remember either Frazer's full name or how to spell it weakened his apologia. He spelled it "I. W. Frazier." Jefferson Davis, *The*

Rise and Fall of the Confederate Government 2 (New York: D. Appleton, 1881), 428; Stickles, *Buckner*, 227.

583. Kate Livingston, "Diary of Kate Livingston, 1859–1868," comp. Mrs. Arlie Turner, *Records of Hamblen County* (U.S. Works Progress Administration, 1938), 78. Accessed at: https://jefferson.tngenealogy.net/research-aids.

584. Graf and Haskins, *Papers of Andrew Johnson, Vol. 5*, 85.

585. Ibid., *Vol. 6*, 514.

586. McKenzie, *Lincolnites and Rebels*, 147.

587. Graf and Haskins, *Papers of Andrew Johnson, Vol. 6*, 295–fn96.

588. John Hervey Crozier (1812–1889), a lawyer, represented Knoxville as a Whig in the U.S. House of Representatives, 1845-49. He would certainly have been acquainted with Abraham Lincoln who was also a Whig congressman at the time. Yet, while Lincoln became a Republican, in 1856 Crozier joined the Democratic Party. Although Crozier was charged with cowardice, Confederate records report that he presented himself for duty. Ibid.; McKenzie, *Lincolnites and Rebels*, 147.

589. Graf and Haskins, *Papers of Andrew Johnson*, vol. 6, 295–96n.

590. L. J. A. [Leonard Anderson?], "Letter to the editors," 2 (see note 565).

591. Guerrant, *Bluegrass Confederate*, 312 (see note 66); Putnam, *Richmond*, 248 (see note 581); Fain, *Sanctified Trial*, 74, 88 (see note 446).

592. Luttrell was openly in sympathy with the Union. McAdoo Diary, entries of July 1 and 6, 1863.

593. McAdoo Diary, entries of June 27, Sept. 3, 1863.

594. Ibid., entry of June 9, 1863.

595. E. Y. C., pseud., "Letter from E. Y. C.," 1 (see note 355).

596. After resigning from the U.S. Navy, Hodge won election to the Kentucky state legislature. He then enlisted in the Confederate Army as a private. Sanders's men actually passed within about eleven miles of Clinton, where Frazer had his headquarters. Clinton lies eighteen miles from Knoxville, and is also eleven miles closer to Wartburg than is Knoxville. Boatner, *Civil War Dictionary*, 403–4; G. B. Hodge, report to Buckner, June 22, 1863.

597. He also commended the service of three of his captains and two of his lieutenants. Sanders Report, 388.

598. Ibid., 389.

599. McCartney, "Saunders Raid," 434–35.

600. He was identified as "E. Y. C." but has not been identified. "The Railroads and the Mails," *Knoxville Register*, June 26, 1863: 2; E. Y. C., pseud., "The Escape of the Yankee Raiders," *Knoxville Register*, July 7, 1863: 1.

601. "The Union Men," *New York Times*, Sept. 25, 1863 [repr., *Richmond Examiner*, Sept. 7, 1863]; "Railroads and the Mails," 2; "The Raiders Not Gone Yet," 2 (see note 73);

602. Both slaves and white women routinely aided fugitives. Lorien Foote, *The Yankee Plague* (Chapel Hill: Univ. of North Carolina Press, 2016), 22–24.

Chapter 16

603. Duke, Willcox, and Hines, "Morgan's Rough Riders," 316–17.

604. Ibid., 322, 332.

605. A witness later asserted that one of the prisoners whom Sanders greeted (and subsidized generously) was his future brother-in-law, one "Richard Guthridge." Unfortunately, however, no record of a Confederate soldier by that name (or anything similar) can be found. The person who was so identified may have been Pvt. Richard Gutridge (or Gutterridge) of the 2nd Ohio Cavalry, a farmer who resided in Concord, Ohio. Gutridge had a sister, Eliza, age 21, but he was a *Union* soldier and could not have been a prisoner of war. The incident took place on July 19, 1863, shortly after the 2nd Ohio participated in the battle of Buffington Island. Hot and tired, both the Ohioans and their prisoners went swimming. Since none were in uniform, their affiliations may well have been mistaken. While it is not impossible that, on that day, Sanders was engaged to be married, three months later he was very actively seeking a bride.

He never wed. Grover S. Wormer, "The Morgan Raid," in *War Papers Read Before the Commandery of the State of Michigan, Military Order of the Loyal Legion of the United States* (Detroit: James H. Stone, 1898), 206; Lester V. Horwitz, *The Longest Raid of the Civil War: Little-Known & Untold Stories of Morgan's Raid into Kentucky, Indiana & Ohio* (Cincinnati: Farmcourt Publishing, 1999), 13; William P. Sanders ["Doc"], letter to Cousin May [Sanders?]; Brown, "Sanders found romance in Knoxville amid Civil War."

606. August V. Kautz, "Reminiscences," 1.

607. Marvel, *Burnside*, 298; Stewart Sifakis, "William Price Sanders," *Who Was Who in the Civil* War (New York: Facts on File, Inc., 1988), 568–69; Eicher and Eicher, *Civil War High Commands*, 609–10; Cullum, *Biographical Register 2*, 668; William P. Sanders, US Army Service Record.

608. John R. Wright [J. R. W.], "Letter From the 107th, Dec. 6th, 1863," *Clinton* [IL] *Public*, Jan. 14, 1864. https://dewitt.illinoisgenweb.org/civil-war -news-1864.htm; Poe, "Defense of Knoxville," 737.

609. Poe had formerly been selected for promotion to brigadier general of volunteers, but his promotion was not approved. For a time, he reverted to his permanent rank of captain in the regular army. He later won promotion.

610. Poe, "Defense of Knoxville," 737.

611. Ibid; Cox, *Military Reminiscences 2*, 31.

612. Alexander, *Fighting for the Confederacy*, 319; Alexander, "Longstreet at Knoxville," 749 (see note 271).

613. Hess, *Knoxville Campaign*, 90.

614. *Richmond Dispatch*, Nov. 24, 1863; McKenzie, *Lincolnites and Rebels*, 160; Cox, *Reminiscences*, 31; Hess, *Knoxville Campaign*, 89–90.

615. Hess, *Knoxville Campaign*, 92; Kelly, *GENERAL WHO?* (see note 153); Benjamin B. French, *Witness to the Young Republic: A Yankee's Journal, 1828–1870*, eds. Donald B. Cole and John J. McDonough (Hanover: Univ. Press of New England, 1989), 435–36; Briscoe, *"Her Walls Before Thee Stand,"* 6.

616. That evening, eight Union generals assembled at the Second Presbyterian Church, then located near the center of Knoxville, for a funeral service for General Sanders. The Second Presbyterian was a hotbed of rebellion, and its pastor, the Reverend Joseph Martin, was an ardent secessionist. When the city was occupied by the Union army, it compelled the Second Presbyterian to permit a pro-Union pastor to conduct services in its sanctuary. After a graveside service, William P. Sanders was buried in the church cemetery. Ninety-three years later, after its warring factions reconciled, the congregation constructed a new church. The Second Presbyterian now stands atop the hill where

Sanders was mortally wounded. General Sanders's remains now lie in the Chattanooga National Cemetery, Chattanooga, TN, grave no. 1601.

Appendix 2

617. Mark Grimsley, *The Hard Hand of War* (New York: Cambridge Univ. Press, 1995), 13–15.

618. Paludan, *Victims*, 87.

619. Hart, "Military Commissions," 15ff; Sutherland, *Guerrillas*, 52.

620. Grimsley, *Hard Hand of War*, 151; Witt, *Lincoln's Code*, 193–95; Sutherland, *Guerrillas*, 52.

621. Noncombatant status offered Baker some protection, since U.S. military law did not normally permit Union troops to kill noncombatants, but there were exceptions. Baker qualified as a "disloyal citizen" under the Lieber code because he was known to have given verbal and material support to the rebellion. "Disloyal citizens" could be arrested and prosecuted for a variety of infractions, and Article 156 amplified the concept by specifying that military authorities were permitted to subject "disloyal citizens" to a "stricter police." This meant that as a "disloyal citizen," Baker was not entitled to an ordinary citizen's presumption of innocence. The regulations granted soldiers the right to be suspicious of civilians whom they knew to be disloyal and to act appropriately. Even if Baker had been not been armed or if he had not jeopardized his non-combatant status, his slayers could still not be prosecuted if his death was "incidentally unavoidable" during an "armed contest." Also, a person who presented a "peculiar danger to the captor" could be slain without penalty. In short, it was permissible to kill Baker if he was classified as a combatant, but even if he was not strictly a combatant, killing him was still legally allowable if his death came as an ancillary consequence of a legitimate military operation. Witt, *Lincoln's Code*, 234, 293.

622. Witt, *Lincoln's Code*, 394; Grimsley, *Hard Hand of War*, 173.

623. Even under Confederate law, Baker's action was impermissible. The Confederate Army adhered to the Articles of War of 1806, which recognized the "customs of war." Under this provision, a guerrilla could be summarily executed if caught in the act. The Confederacy's Partisan Ranger Act also provided an individual a legal means of engaging the

enemy without joining a regular unit of the Confederate Army, but he was required to sign up with a recognized partisan band and also to display a badge of identification. Baker had done neither. Witt, *Lincoln's Code*, 4, 180–2, 223

624. "The Murder of Doctor Harvey Baker by the Yankees," *Southern Confederacy*, June 27, 1863: 1; "Dr. Harvey Baker," 1.

BIBLIOGRAPHY

Abbreviations

FHS   Filson Historical Society, Louisville,KY

HL   Hunter Library, Western Carolina University, Cullowhee, NC.

ISL   Illinois State Library, Springfield

LOC   Library of Congress

NARA   National Archives and Records Administration

OR   *The War of the Rebellion: A Compilation of the Official Records of the Union and Confederate Armies.* 128 vols. Washington, DC; Government Printing Office, 1880–1901.

SOR   *Supplement to the Official Records of the Union and Confederate Armies.* 100 vols. Wilmington, NC: Broadfoot Publishing Co.

USMAL   U.S. Military Academy Library, West Point, NY.

USAMHI   U.S. Army Military History Institute, Carlisle, PA.

UTK   Special Collections, University of Tennessee, Knoxville.

WHC   Wheaton History Center, Wheaton, Illinois.

WRHS   Western Reserve Historical Society, Cleveland, Ohio.

Archival Sources

James D. Barnett Papers. WRHS.

H. W. Chester Papers. WHC.

Compiled Service Records of Confederate Soldiers Who Served in Organizations [from the State of North Carolina]. R.G. 109.6, M270, 9. Washington: NARA, n.d.

Confederate Papers Relating to Citizens or Business Firms. R.G. 109.6, M346. Washington: NARA, n.d.

Final Report, Court of Inquiry [Brig. Gen. John W. Frazer]. NARA Microfilm Publications, R.G.109.6., Washington, DC.

Thomas Jefferson Henderson Papers. ISL.

Loudon Bridge/Civil War Collection. UTK.

August V. Kautz Papers. LOC.

August V. Kautz Papers. USAMHI.

Felix Kirk Letter. MS-2152. UTK.

Robert Neville Letter. UTK.

Sanders Family Papers. FHS.

Records of William P. Sanders, Record and Pension Office, R.G. 94. Washington: NARA, n.d.

William W. Stringfield Papers. HL.

Records of the Adjutant General's Office, Records relating to the U.S. Military Academy, R.G. 94.2.6. USMAL.

U.S. War Department. Collection of Confederate Records. R.G. 109.6. Washington: NARA, n.d.

Governmental Documents and Electronic Records

Bowery, Charles R., Jr., and Brian D. Hankinson, eds. Letter of Jefferson Davis to Totten, Jan. 24, 1853. In *United States Military Academy Superintendent's Letter Book No. 2 and No. 3: The Daily Correspondence of Brevet Colonel Robert E. Lee, Superintendent, United States Military Academy September 1, 1852, to March 24, 1855.* United States Military Academy Library Occasional Papers #5, USMAL (West Point, NY, 2003).

Branner, John R. Telegram to James A. Seddon, June 22, 1863. *Telegrams Received by the Secretary of War.* M437, Roll 15, R. G. 109.6. Washington: NARA Microfilm Publications.

Bright, David L. *Confederate Railroads* (2002–6). www.csa-railroads.com.

Buckner, Simon B. *Abstract from field return of the Department of East Tennessee . . . May 31, 1863.* Comp. Calvin D. Cowles. *OR*, ser. 1, vol. 23, pt. 2: 855. Washington: U.S. War Department, Government Printing Office, 1889.

——. *Abstract from field return of the Department of East Tennessee . . . July 31, 1863. OR*, ser. 1, vol. 23, pt. 2: 945.

——. Letter to James A. Seddon, April 22, 1863. In *Letters Received by the Confederate Secretary of War.* M437, Roll 82, R.G. 109.6. Washington: NARA Microfilm Publications.

Burnside, Ambrose E. *Abstract from return of the Army of the Ohio . . . June, 1863. OR*, ser. 1, vol. 23, pt. 2: 489. Washington: U.S. Department of War, Government Printing Office.

Burt, David J. Letter to wife, July 11, 1863. In Francis Burt Barrett Papers,

Archives of the Park Historian, Chickamauga National Military Park, Fort Oglethorpe, GA. www.izzy.net/-michaelg/65ga-vi.htm.

Byrd, Robert K. Letter to Henry J. Welcker, Oct. 24, 1862. In Roane County TN Records. www.roanetn.com/cwletter.htm.

Civil War Centennial Commission of Tennessee. "Captain Hugh L. W. McClung's Tennessee Light Artillery Company: 'The Caswell Artillery.'" In *Tennesseans in the Civil War: Confederate Artillery Units* (2004). www.tngenweb.org/civilwar/ csaart/mcclung.html.

———. "Captain William H. Burroughs's Tennessee Light Artillery Company: 'Rhett Artillery.'" In *Tennesseans in the Civil War: Confederate Artillery Units* (2004). www.tngenweb.org/civilwar/csaart /burrough.html.

———. "Federal Cavalry Units: 3rd Tennessee Mounted Infantry Regiment, U.S.A." In *Tennesseans in the Civil War*, vol. 1. http://www.tngenweb .org/civilwar/usacav/ usa3minf.html.

The Civil War Home Page. *Results from the 1860 Census.* http://www.civil-war .net/ pages/1860_census.html.

Confederate States Army, Adjutant-General and Inspector General, Special Orders No. 136, Paragraph 21 (1863). *OR*, ser. 1, vol. 23, pt. 2.

Cowdon, James S., and James D. Holman. "Statistical Map of the United States of America [1865]," *Library of Congress Civil War Maps* 2ed. Geography and Map Div., LOC. Washington: M. Joyce, Eng., 1888. Image #260557673, www.fold3.com.

Davis, George B., Leslie J. Perry, and Joseph W. Kirkley, eds. *Atlas to Accompany the Official Records of the Union and Confederate Armies.* Washington: U.S. Government Printing Office, 1891–95.

Descendants of Moses White, Genealogy Page, Joe Payne's Webworks. www .joepayne.org/white.html.

Fisher, Thomas W. Letter to father and mother, Mar. 23, 1863. In *Civil War Letters of Pvt. Thomas Winton Fisher, CSA*. Diane McGinley Gardner, comp. www.ted.gardner.org/603629.htm.

Grills, P. R. "Receipt for Services, May 29, 1862." In *Confederate Papers Relating to Citizens or Business Firms.* M346, NARA. www.fold3 .com.

Hart, Gideon M. "Military Commissions and the Lieber Code: Toward a
    New Understanding of the Jurisdictional Foundations of Military
    Commissions," in *Military Law Review* 203 (Spring 2010). Captain
    Evan R. Seamone, ed. Department of the Army Pamphlet 27-100-
    203. Charlottesville: Judge Advocate General's Legal Center and
    School, U.S. Army, 2010. http://www.jagcnet.army.mil/MLR

Heth, Henry. GENERAL ORDERS, No. 29, Jan. 11, 1863, Headquarters,
    Department of East Tennessee, Knoxville. www.fold3.com
    /image/#67096783.

Hewett, Janet B., gen. ed. *Supplement to the Official Records of the Union and
    Confederate Armies, Vol. 49, Part 2—Record of Events.* Serial No. 61.
    Wilmington: Broadfoot Publishing Co., 1997.

——, gen. ed. *Supplement to the Official Records of the Union and Confederate
    Armies, Vol. 50, Part 1—Record of Events.* Serial No. 62. Wilmington:
    Broadfoot Publishing Co., 1997.

——, gen. ed. *Supplement to the Official Records of the Union and Confederate
    Armies, Vol. 65, Part 2-Record of Events.* Serial No. 77. Wilmington,
    NC: Broadfoot Publishing Co., 1998.

Hodge, G. B. "Report to Maj. Gen. S. B. Buckner." *Letters Received by the
    Confederate Secretary of War, August to December, 1863.* R.G.
    109.6, M437, Roll 92. Washington: National Archives Microfilm
    Publications.

Hovis, Victor M., Jr. *Union Lodge History* (1996). Union Lodge #38, Free
    & Accepted Masons of Kingston, Tennessee. http://union38.org
    /wordpress/?page_id=218.

Kelly, Dorothy E. *GENERAL WHO? William P. Sanders.* Knoxville: Knoxville
    Civil War Roundtable, 1999. www.discoveret.org/kcwrt/history
    /sanders99

Lawton, A. R. "Corn for Lee's Army (1863)." *Confederate Railroads*, comp.
    David L. Bright. www.csa-railroads.com/Essays/Original.

Livingston, Kate. "Diary of Kate Livingston, 1859–1868," comp. M. A.
    Turner.

McIntire, William R. *Confederate Pension Applications 1899—1975, Vol. 1,*
    1-646 & 1-283. Affidavit #28098, August 6, 1914. Austin: Texas State

Library and Archives Commission. www.Ancestry.com. https://
www.ancestry.com/search/ collections/1677/

Morris, Andrew H. Letter to Jane [Mrs. A. H. Morris], July 11, 1863.
Records of the 65th Georgia Volunteer Infantry. http://www.izzy.net
/~michaelg/65ga-vi.htm.

Myers, Abraham C. "Trouble in Knoxville" Telegram to Gen. Felix K.
Zollicoffer, in *Confederate Railroads,* comp. David L. Bright. www
.csa-railroads.com/ Essays/Original.

——. "Wallace to Run East Tennessee & Virginia." Telegram to C. Wallace,
Sept. 18, 1861, in *Confederate Railroads,* comp. David L. Bright. www
.csa- railroads.com/ Essays/Original.

Newman, Kate, et al. "History of Strawberry Plains." Unpublished essay, Rush
Strong High School, Strawberry Plains, TN, 1936. http://jefferson
.tngenealogy.net/ about-jeff/20-history/23-history-strawberry
-plains.

Nicholson, W. L., and A. Lindenkohl, comps. *The Mountain Region of North
Carolina and Tennessee* [1863]. Map. LOC Geography and Map
Division, Washington, DC. Image #260558364, www.fold3.com.

Pleasanton, Alfred. *Operations in Loudon County [Virginia], etc. OR,* ser. 1,
vol. 19, pt. 2.

——. *The Maryland Campaign. OR,* ser. 1, vol. 19, pt. 1.

——. *The Peninsular Campaign, March 17-September 2, 1862. OR,* ser. 1, vol.
11, pt. 2.

The Political Graveyard. "Lewis Sanders, Jr." (2009). *www.politicalgraveyard
.com.*

Pratt, Suzanne M. "The Lenoir Family." In *Loudon County, Tennessee* (2004–
6). www.ngenweb.org/loudon/family/lenoir.html.

Prince, O. H, recorder. "Proceedings of the Court of Inquiry [Brig. Gen. John
W. Frazer]. *"Letters Received by the Confederate Secretary of War,
August to December, 1863.* R. G. 109.6, M437, Roll 92. Washington:
NARA Microfilm Publications.

Proceedings of the Court of Inquiry, Knoxville, Tennessee, July 28, 1863. R. G.
109.6, M437, Roll 92. War Department Collection of Confederate
Records. Washington: NARA Microfilm Publications, n.d.

Reichard, Augustus. "Letter of certification, 1861." Image # 74882793. www
.fold3.com.

Rhea, Robert M. "The Sanders Raid." *Sergeant Robert Rhea.* www.63rd
tennessee.org/ Veterans/Robert%20Rhea/robert-rhea.htm.

Robbins, Don K., trans. 1860 Federal Census Roane, TN (2004). ftp://ftp
.us-census.org/ pub/usgenweb/census/xtn/roane/1860/.

Robert King BYRD (1823–1885). www.roanetnheritage.com/research
/assembley/17.htm

Sanders, William P. U.S. Army Service Record. OFF352063, March 13 –
November 19, 1863. Records of William P. Sanders. U.S., Department
of War, Record and Pension Office, R.G. 94. Washington: NARA.

———. Letter to the Secretary of War, Dec. 22, 1851. *Records of the Adjutant
General's Office,* R.G. 94.2.6: Records relating to the U.S. Military
Academy, USMAL.

———. "Reports of Col. William P. Sanders . . . Commanding Expedition." *OR,*
ser, 1, vol. 23, pt. 1.

Seddon, James A. Letter to Jefferson Davis, August 23, 1863. *Final Report,
Court of Inquiry* [Brig. Gen. John W. Frazer]. R.G. 109.6. Washington:
NARA Microfilm Publications.

Smith, Mrs. A. E. Letter to husband, May 26, 1863. Civil War Letters from
Mrs. A. E. Smith to her husband. UTK, Special Collections. www
.utk.edu/spcoll.

Tennessee Department of Transportation. Existing Covered Bridges in
Tennessee. *Covered Bridges in Tennessee.*

Tennesseans in the Civil War. "Confederate Artillery Units. Formerly
Captain H. Baker's Company." *Captain W. R. Browne's Tennessee
Light Artillery Company.* ww.tngenweb.org/ civilwar/csaart/browne
.html.

U.S., Congress, *Biographical Directory of the United States Congress, 1774–
2005* (2005). U.S., Geological Survey. *Jellico East Quadrangle.*
Topographic Map, 7.5 minute, 1970.

U.S., Military Academy. *Official Register of the Officers and Cadets of the U.S.
Military Academy, West Point, New York* (1853–56).

———. *Register of Cadet Applications, 1819–1867.* No. 24: 1851–52. M2037,
Roll 3. Records of the Adjutant General's Office, 1780's–1917, R.G.

94. Washington: NARA, n.d. Ancestry.com. *U.S. Military and Naval Academies, Cadet Records and Applications, 1805–1908*, Record for William P. Sanders (2008). Lehi: Ancestry.com Operations, Inc., 2008. https://www.ancestry.com/search/collections/1299/.

——. *Register of Cadet Applications, 1819–1867*. No. 26: 1853–54. M2037, Roll 3. Records of the Adjutant General's Office, 1780's-1917, R.G. 94. Washington: NARA, n.d. Ancestry.com. *U.S. Military and Naval Academies, Cadet Records and Applications, 1805–1908*, Record for William P. Sanders (2008). Lehi: Ancestry.com Operations, Inc., 2008. https://www.ancestry.com/search/collections/1299/.

——. *Register of Cadets, 1803–1866*, M2124. Records of the Adjutant General's Office, 1762–1984, R. G. 94. National Archives, Washington, D.C. Ancestry.com. "Roll of the Cadets, According to Merit in Conduct, for the Year Ending, June 15th, 1853." *U.S. Military and Naval Academies, Cadet Records and Applications, 1805–1908*. Lehi: Ancestry.com Operations, Inc., 2008. https://www.ancestry.com /search/collections/1299/.

U.S., NARA. *Case Files of Applications from Former Confederates for Presidential Pardons {"Amnesty Papers"), 1865–1867* [Milton A. Haynes, Tennessee]. M1003, R.G. 94. Fold3.com. Confederate Amnesty Papers (August 02, 2007). Applications for pardon submitted to President Andrew Johnson by former Confederates excluded from earlier amnesty proclamations. https://www.fold3 .com/title/59/confederate-amnesty-papers.

——. *Case Files of Applications from Former Confederates for Presidential Pardons, 1865–1867* [Lenoir, William]. M1003, R.G. 94. Fold3.com. Confederate Amnesty Papers (August 02, 2007). Record no. 3656621. https://www.fold3.com/title/59/ confederate-amnesty-papers.

——. *Compiled Service Records of Volunteer Soldiers Who Served During the Mexican War in Organizations from the State of Tennessee* [Company C, Byrd, Robert K.]. M638, R.G. 94, 1–7. Washington: NARA Microfilm Publications, n.d. Fold3.com. Mexican War Service Records— Tennessee (August 18, 2011). https://www.fold3.com/title/772 /mexican-war-service-records-tennessee.

——. *Compiled Service Records of Confederate Soldiers Who Served in*

Organizations from the State of Tennessee [Capt. Burroughs's Co., Light Artillery (Rhett Artillery), Luttrell, James C.]. R.G. 109, M268. Washington: NARA Microfilm Publications. Carded Abstract of Service Records Showing Military Service of Soldiers Who Fought in Confederate Organizations. Fold3.com. Civil War Service Records (CMSR)—Confederate—Tennessee (May 14, 2008). https://www.fold3.com/title/40/civil-war -service-records-cmsr-confederate-tennessee.

——. *Compiled Service Records of Volunteer Union Soldiers Who Served in Organizations from the State of Kentucky* [First Cavalry], R.G. 109, M397. Washington: NARA Microfilm Publications, 1963. Fold3.com. *Civil War Service Records (CMSR)—Union—Kentucky* (March 4, 2009), 300398. https://www.fold3.com/title/50 /civil-war-service-records-cmsr-union-kentucky.

——. *Compiled Service Records of Confederate Soldiers Who Served in Organizations from the State of Tennessee.* R.G. 109, M268. Washington: NARA Microfilm Publications, 1960. Fold3. com. *Civil War Service Records (CMSR)—Confederate— Tennessee* (May 14, 2008). https://www.fold3.com/title/40 /civil-war-service-records-cmsr-confederate-tennessee.

——. *Compiled Service Records of Confederate Soldiers Who Served in Organizations from the State of Tennessee.* R.G. 109, M268. Washington: NARA Microfilm Publications, 1960. Fold3.com. "Second Cavalry AND Second (Ashby's) Cavalry," *Civil War Service Records (CMSR)—Confederate—Tennessee* (May 14, 2008). Compiled military service records of Confederate soldiers from Tennessee units. https://www.fold3.com/title/40 /civil-war-service-records-cmsr-confederate-tennessee.

——. *Compiled Service Records of Confederate General and Staff Officers* [Sheliha, Victor]. M331. Washington: NARA Microfilm Publications, 1962. Fold3.com. *Civil War Service Records (CMSR)— Confederate— Officers* (May 14, 2008), 586957. https://www.fold3.com/title/38 /civil-war-service-records-cmsr-confederate-officers

——. *Confederate States Army Casualties: Lists and Narrative Reports, 1861–1865* [Report of Siege: Tennessee, Knoxville], R. G. 109,

M836, Roll 4. War Department Collection of Confederate Records, Microfilm Publications Library, National Archives, Washington, D.C. Fold3.com. *Confederate Casualty Reports* (Aug. 17, 2011), Images no. 272178231 and 272178233. https://www.fold3.com/title/770/ confederate-casualty-reports

———. *Confederate Papers Relating to Citizens or Business Firms, 1861–65* [Quartermaster's Receipt]. R. G. 109, M346. War Department Collection of Confederate Records, Microfilm Publications Library, National Archives, Washington, D.C. Fold3.com. *Confederate Citizens File* (December 28, 2007), Image no. 43282376. https://www.fold3 .com/title/60/confederate-citizens-file.

———. *Returns from U.S. Military Posts, 1800–1916* [Camp Floyd], M617. Records of the Adjutant General's Office 1780s—1917, R.G. 94. National Archives, Washington, D.C. Ancestry.com. *U.S., Returns from Military Posts, 1806—1916* (Provo, UT, USA: Ancestry .com Operations Inc, 2009). https://www.ancestry.com/search /collections/ 1571/.

———. *Records of the Accounting Officers of the Department of the Treasury, 1775–1978*, R.G. 217. NARA, National Archives Microfilm Publications Library, Washington, D.C. Fold3.com. *Southern Claims Commission Approved Claims, 1871–1880* [Tennessee, Knox County]. Southern Claims Commission, Civil War Collection (October 10, 2008), image # 258084156. https://www.fold3.com/title/473 /southern-claims-commission-approved-claims-1871–1880.

———. *Seventh Census of the United States, 1850* [Mississippi: Free Schedules, Adams County, City of Natchez]. Records of the Bureau of the Census, R.G. 29. Washington: NARA Microfilm Publications, National Archives, n.d. M432B, Roll 368.

———. *Seventh Census of the United States, 1850* [Mississippi: Slave Schedules, Adams County, City of Natchez]. Records of the Bureau of the Census, R.G. 29. Washington: NARA Microfilm Publications, National Archives, n.d. M432B, Roll 363.

———. *Seventh Census of the United States, 1850*. M432, 43A. Records of the U.S., Bureau of the Census, R.G. 29. Washington: NARA Microfilm Publications, n.d. Ancestry.com. *1850 United States Federal Census*

[Population Schedule]. Lehi: Ancestry.com Operations, Inc., 2009), image 91. https://www.ancestry.com/search/ collections/8054/

——. *Seventh Census of the United States, 1850* [U.S., Bureau of the Census]. R.G. 29, M432, 43A. Washington: NARA, 1850. Ancestry.com. *1850 United States Federal Census—Slave Schedules* [Tennessee: Knox County]. Lehi: Ancestry.com Operations, Inc., 2004. R.G. 29, M432, 43A. https://www.ancestry.com/search/collections/8055/.

——. *Eighth Census of the United States, 1860,* M653. Records of the Bureau of the Census, R.G. 29. NARA Microfilm Publications Library, NARA, Washington, D.C. Ancestry.com. *1860 United States Federal Census* [Population Schedule: Jefferson, Tennessee]. Provo: Ancestry.com Operations, Inc., 2009. Family History Library Film: 805258. https:// www.ancestry.com/search/ collections/7667/

——. *Eighth Census of the United States, 1860,* M653. Records of the Bureau of the Census, R.G. 29. NARA Microfilm Publications Library, NARA, Washington, D.C. Ancestry.com. *1860 United States Federal Census—Slave Schedules.* Lehi: Ancestry.com Operations, Inc., 2010. https:// www.ancestry.com/search/collections/7668/.

——. U.S., *OR.* "Operations in Kentucky and Tennessee, July 1 to November 19, 1861." ser. 1, vol. 4, ch. 12.

——. "Operations in Kentucky, Tennessee, Northern Alabama, and West Virginia, November 19, 1861, to March 4, 1862," ser. 1, vol. 7, ch. 17.

——. "Operations in Kentucky, Tennessee, Northern Alabama, and Southwest Virginia, March 4-June 10, 1863," ser. 1, vol. 10, pt. 2, ch.22.

——. "Operations in Northern Virginia, West Virginia, Maryland, and Pennsylvania, September 3 to November 14, 1862: Reports...," ser. 1, vol. 19, pt. 2, ch.31.

——. "Correspondence... January 21 to August 10, 1863," ser. 1, vol. 23, pt. 2.

——. "Reports... January 21 to August 10, 1863: Report of Lt. Col. Milton A. Haynes, Confederate States Artillery, June 21st, 1863," ser. 1, vol. 23, pt. 1: 391–93.

——. "Correspondence, Orders, etc., from December 20, 1860 to June 30, 1862," ser. 4, vol. 1.

——. *Southern Claims Commission Approved Claims, 1871–1880* [Tennessee, Knox County]. www.fold3.com/image/#258084206.

——. *Southern Claims Commission Approved Claims, 1871–1880* [Tennessee, Knox County]. www.fold3.com/image/#258084225.

U.S. Works Progress Administration, *Records of Hamblen County, TN*, 1938. http://jefferson.tngenealogy.net/research-aids.

Books

Adams, Alice D. *The Neglected Period of Anti-Slavery in America (1808–1831)*. Boston: Atheneum, 1908.

Alexander, Edward P. *Military Memoirs of a Confederate*. Bloomington: Indiana Univ. Press, 1962. First published 1907.

——. *Fighting for the Confederacy: The Personal Recollections of General Edward Porter Alexander*. Chapel Hill: Univ. of North Carolina Press, 1989.

Ash, Stephen V., ed. *Secessionists and Other Scoundrels: Selections from "Parson" Brownlow's Book*. Baton Rouge: Louisiana State Univ. Press, 1999.

Bailey, Fred A. *Class and Tennessee's Civil War Generation*. Chapel Hill: Univ. of North Carolina Press, 1987.

Bates, Alfred E. "The Second Regiment of Cavalry, I (1836–65)." In *The Army of the United States*, comp. T.F. Rodenbough. New York: Maynard, Merrill, & Co, 1896, 173–79.

Black, Robert C., III. *The Railroads of the Confederacy*. Chapel Hill: Univ. of North Carolina Press, 1952.

Blair, William A. *With Malice toward Some: Treason and Loyalty in the Civil War Era*. Chapel Hill: Univ. of North Carolina Press, 2014.

Boatner, Mark, III. *The Civil War Dictionary*. New York: David McKay Company, 1959.

Bohrnstedt, Jennifer C., ed. *While Father Is Away: The Civil War Letters of William H. Bradbury*. Lexington: Univ. Press of Kentucky, 2003.

Bonekemper, Edward H., III. *The Myth of the Lost Cause: Why the South Fought and Why the North Won*. Washington: Regnery History, 2015.

Bradley, Michael R. *Tullahoma: The 1863 Campaign for the Control of Middle Tennessee*. Shippensburg: Burd Street Press, 2000.

Brewer, James D. *The Raiders of 1862*. Westport: Praeger Publishers, 1997.

Brownlee, Richard S. *Gray Ghosts of the Confederacy: Guerrilla Warfare in the West, 1861–1865*. Baton Rouge: Louisiana State Univ. Press, 1958.

Burlingame, Michael, ed. *Lincoln Observed: Civil War Dispatches of Noah Brooks*. Baltimore: Johns Hopkins Univ. Press, 1998.

Byrd, Marvin. *A Unionist in East Tennessee: Captain William K. Byrd and the Mysterious Raid of 1861*. Charleston: History Press, 2011.

Cable, George W., ed. *A Civil War Diary of a Union Woman in the South*. Kessinger Publishing Legacy Reprints Series. Whitefish: De Vinne Press, 2010. First published 1885.

Campbell, Mary E. R. *The Attitude of Tennesseans Toward the Union, 1847–1861*. New York: Vantage Press, 1961.

Campbell, Richard T., ed. *Southern Service on Land & Sea: The Wartime Journal of Robert Watson CSA/CSN*. Knoxville: Univ. of Tennessee Press, 2002.

Carter, William R. *History of the First Regiment of Tennessee Volunteer Cavalry in the Great War of the Rebellion . . . 1862–1865*. Johnson City: Overmountain Press, 1992.

Carwardine, Richard. *Lincoln: A Life of Purpose and Power*. New York: Alfred A. Knopf, 2003.

Chester, Henry W. *Recollections of the War of the Rebellion: A Story of the 2nd Ohio Volunteer Cavalry, 1861–1865*, ed. A. R. Adamson. Wheaton: Wheaton History Center, 1996.

Coffman, Edward M. *The Old Army: A Portrait of the American Army in Peacetime, 1784–1898*. New York: Oxford Univ. Press, 1986.

Connelly, Thomas L. *Army of the Heartland: The Army of Tennessee, 1861–1862*. Baton Rouge: Louisiana State Univ. Press, 1967.

———. *Autumn of Glory: The Army of Tennessee, 1862–1865*. Baton Rouge: Louisiana State Univ. Press, 1971.

Conover, Charlotte R. *The Patterson Log Cabin*. Dayton: Press of the National Cash Register Co., 1906.

Cooper, William. J., Jr. *Jefferson Davis, American*. New York: Alfred A. Knopf, 2000.

Cox, Jacob D. *Military Reminiscences of the Civil War, Vol. I: November 1863–June 1865*. New York: Charles Scribner's Sons, 1900.

Crawford, Martin. *Ashe County's Civil War*. Charlottesville: Univ. Press of Virginia, 2001.

Crist, Linda L., ed. *The Papers of Jefferson Davis*, Vol. 5: 1853–1855. Baton Rouge: Louisiana State Univ. Press, 1985

——, *The Papers of Jefferson Davis*, Vol. 9: January-September, 1863. Baton Rouge: Louisiana State Univ. Press, 1997.

Crow, Vernon H. *Storm in the Mountains: Thomas' Confederate Legion of Cherokee Indians and Mountaineers.* Cherokee: Press of the Museum of the Cherokee Indian, 1982.

Cullum, George W., comp. and ed. *Biographical Register of the Officers and Graduates of the United States Military Academy at West Point, N.Y.* Boston: USMA Assoc. of Graduates,Houghton, Mifflin, 1891.

Current, Richard N. *Lincoln's Loyalists: Union Soldiers from the Confederacy.* Boston: Northeastern Univ. Press, 1992.

Dana, Charles A. *Recollections of the Civil War: With the Leaders at Washington and in the Field in the Sixties.* New York: D. Appleton, 1898.

Davis, Jefferson. *The Rise and Fall of the Confederate Government* 2, 1Ed. New York: D. Appleton, 1881.

Davis, William C. *An Honorable Defeat: The Last Days of the Confederate Government.* New York: Harcourt, 2001.

——. *Look Away! A History of the Confederate States of America.* New York: Free Press, 2002.

Davis, William C., and Meredith Swentor-Barwick, eds. *Bluegrass Confederate: The Headquarters Diary of Edward O. Guerrant.* Baton Rouge: Louisiana State Univ. Press, 1999.

Dirck, Brian R. *Lincoln and Davis: Imagining America, 1809–1865.* Lawrence: Univ. Press of Kansas, 2001.

Duke, Basil W. *Reminiscences of General Basil W. Duke.* West Jefferson: Genesis Publishing, 1998.

Dyer, John W., and Amelia W. Dyer. *Reminiscences; or, Four Years in the Confederate Army.* Evansville: Keller Printing and Publishing Co., 1898.

Dyer, Thomas G. *Secret Yankees: The Union Circle in Confederate Atlanta.* Baltimore: Johns Hopkins Univ. Press, 1999.

Eicher, David J. *Dixie Betrayed: How the South Really Lost the Civil War.* New York: Little, Brown, 2006.

Eicher, John H., and David J. Eicher. *Civil War High Commands*. Stanford: Stanford Univ. Press, 2001.

Fain, John N., ed. *Sanctified Trial: The Diary of Eliza Rhea Anderson Fain, A Confederate Woman in East Tennessee*. Knoxville: Univ. of Tennessee Press, 2004.

Fisher, Noel C. *War at Every Door: Partisan Politics and Guerrilla Violence in East Tennessee, 1860–1869*. Chapel Hill: Univ. of North Carolina Press, 1997.

Foote, Loren. *The Yankee Plague: Escaped Union Prisoners and the Collapse of the Confederacy*. Chapel Hill: Univ. of North Carolina Press, 2016.

Foster, John W. *War Stories for My Grandchildren*. Washington: Privately printed, 1918.

French, Benjamin B. *Witness to the Young Republic: A Yankee's Journal, 1828–1870*. Ed. D. B. Cole and J. J. McDonough. Hanover: Univ. Press of New England, 1989.

Fullencamp, Leonard J., ed. and comp. *An Overview of the Gettysburg Campaign*. Carlisle Barracks: U.S. Army War College, 2006.

Gause, Isaac. *Four Years with Five Armies*. New York: Neale Publishing, 1908.

Gienapp, William E., and Erica L. Gienapp, eds. *The Civil War Diary of Gideon Welles, Lincoln's Secretary of the Navy*. Urbana: Univ. of Illinois Press, 2014.

Godbold, E. Stanley, Jr., and Mattie U. Russell. *Confederate Colonel and Cherokee Chief: The Life of William Holland Thomas*. Knoxville: Univ. of Tennessee Press, 1990.

Graf, Leroy P., and Ralph W. Haskins, eds. *The Papers of Andrew Johnson*. Vol. 5, 1861–1862. Knoxville: Univ. of Tennessee Press, 1979.

———, *The Papers of Andrew Johnson:* Vol. 6, 1862–1864. Knoxville: Univ. of Tennessee Press, 1983.

Griggs, Walter S., Jr. *General John Pegram C.S.A.* Lynchburg: H. E. Howard, 1993.

Grimsley, Mark. *The Hard Hand of War: Union Military Policy toward Southern Civilians, 1861–1865*. New York: Cambridge Univ. Press, 1995.

———. *Mountain Rebels: East Tennessee Confederates and the Civil War, 1860–1870*. Knoxville: Univ. of Tennessee Press, 1999.

Guerrant, Edward O. *Bluegrass Confederate: The Headquarters Diary of*

Edward O. Guerrant. Eds. William C. Davis and Meredith Swinton-Barwick. Baton Rouge: Louisiana State Univ. Press, 1999.

Hamilton, William D. *Recollections of a Cavalryman of the Civil War After Fifty Years.* Columbus: F. J. Heer, 1915.

Harrison, Lowell H. *The Civil War in Kentucky.* Lexington: Univ. Press of Kentucky, 1975.

Hartigan, Richard S. *Lieber's Code and the Law of War.* Chicago: Precedent Publishing, Inc., 1983.

Hartman, David W., and David W. Coles, comp. *Biographical Rosters of Florida's Confederate and Union Soldiers, 1861–1865.* Wilmington: Broadfoot, 1995.

Hattaway, Herman, and Richard E. Beringer. *Jefferson Davis, Confederate President.* Lawrence: Univ. Press of Kansas, 2002.

Hattaway, Herman, and Archer Jones. *How the North Won: A Military History of the Civil War.* Urbana: Univ. of Illinois Press, 1983.

Haynes, Dennis E. *A Thrilling Narrative: The Memoir of a Southern Unionist.* Fayetteville: Univ. of Arkansas Press, 2006.

Hess, Earl J. *The Rifle Musket in Civil War Combat.* Lawrence: Univ. Press of Kansas, 2008.

———. *The Knoxville Campaign: Burnside and Longstreet in East Tennessee.* Knoxville: Univ. of Tennessee Press, 2012.

Hesseltine, William B., ed. *Dr. J. G. M. Ramsey: Autobiography and Letters.* Nashville: Tennessee Historical Commission, 1954.

Horwitz, Lester V. *The Longest Raid of the Civil War: Little-Known & Untold Stories of Morgan's Raid into Kentucky, Indiana & Ohio.* Cincinnati: Farmcourt Publishing, 1999.

Hsieh, Wayne W. *West Pointers and the Civil War: The Old Army in War and Peace.* Chapel Hill: Univ. of North Carolina Press, 2009.

Humes, Thomas W. *The Loyal Mountaineers of Tennessee.* Knoxville: Ogden Bros., 1888.

Ingersoll, Henry H., et al., eds. *Joshua William Caldwell: A Memorial Volume.* Nashville: Brandon Printing, 1909.

Inscoe, John C., and Gordon B. McKinney. *The Heart of Confederate Appalachia: Western North Carolina in the Civil War.* Chapel Hill: Univ. of North Carolina Press, 2000.

Jacobson, Donna B. *Borderland of Light: Reverend John Rankin and Ripley, Ohio, 1820–1850*. Uncasville: Privately Printed, 2011.

James, James R. *To See the Elephant: The Civil War Letters of John A. McKee (1861–1865)*. Leawood: Leathers Publishing, 1998.

Jones, James B., Jr., comp. *Tennessee in the Civil War: Selected Contemporary Accounts of Military and Other Events, Month by Month*. Jefferson: McFarland, 2011.

Kamphoefner, Walter D., and Wolfgang Helbich, eds. *Germans in the Civil War: The Letters They Wrote Home*. Chapel Hill: Univ. of North Carolina Press, 2006.

Leonard, Elizabeth D. *Lincoln's Avengers: Justice, Revenge, and Reunion After the Civil War*. New York: W. W. Norton, 2004.

Livermore, Thomas L. *Numbers and Losses in the Civil War*. Civil War Centennial Series. Bloomington: Indiana Univ. Press, 1957. First published 1900.

Longacre, Edward G. *Lincoln's Cavalrymen: A History of the Mounted Forces of the Army of the Potomac, 1861–1865*. Mechanicsburg: Stackpole Books, 2000.

Longacre, Glenn V., and John E. Hass, eds. *To Battle for God and the Right: The Civil War Letterbooks of Emerson Opdycke*. Urbana: Univ. of Illinois Press, 2003.

Lonn, Ella. *Salt as a Factor in the Confederacy*. Tuscaloosa: Univ. of Alabama Press, 1965.

Mackey, Robert R. *The Uncivil War: Irregular Warfare in the Upper South, 1861–1865*. Norman: Univ. of Oklahoma Press, 2004.

Maness, Donald C., and H. Jason Combs, eds. *Do They Miss Me at Home? The Civil War Letters of William McKnight, Seventh Ohio Cavalry*. Athens: Ohio Univ. Press, 2010.

Marvel, William. *Burnside*. Chapel Hill: Univ. of North Carolina Press, 1991.

———. *The Battles for Saltville: Southwest Virginia in the Civil War*. Virginia Civil War Battles and Leaders Series. Lynchburg: H. E. Howard, 1992.

———. *A Place Called Appomattox*. Chapel Hill: Univ. of North Carolina Press, 2000.

Massey, Mary E. *Ersatz in the Confederacy: Shortages and Substitutes on the Southern Homefront*. Columbia: Univ. of South Carolina Press, 1993.

Mathews, Gary R. *Basil Wilson Duke, CSA: The Right Man in the Right Place.* Lexington: Univ. Press of Kentucky, 2005.

McCammon, Charles S., ed. and comp. *Loyal Mountain Troopers, the Second and Third Tennessee Volunteer Cavalry in the Civil War; reminiscences of Lieutenant John W. Andes and Major Will A. McTeer.* Maryville: Blount County Genealogical and Historical Society, 1992.

McDonough, James L. *War in Kentucky: From Shiloh to Perryville.* Knoxville: Univ. of Tennessee Press, 1994.

McDowell, Samuel, comp. and ed. *East Tennessee History.* Hartford: McDowell Publications, 1978.

McIntosh, James T., ed. *The Papers of Jefferson Davis, Vol. 2: June 1841–July 1846.* Baton Rouge: Louisiana State Univ. Press, 1974.

McKenzie, Robert T. *One South or Many? Plantation Belt and Upcountry in Civil War-Era Tennessee.* New York: Cambridge Univ. Press, 1994.

———. *Lincolnites and Rebels: A Divided Town in the Civil War.* New York: Oxford Univ. Press, 2006.

McKinney, Gordon B. *Zeb Vance: North Carolina's Civil War Governor and Gilded Age Political Leader.* Chapel Hill: Univ. of North Carolina Press, 2004.

McKnight, Brian D. *Contested Borderland: The Civil War in Appalachian Kentucky and Virginia.* Lexington: Univ. Press of Kentucky, 2006.

McLachlan, Sean. *American Civil War Guerrilla Tactics.* New York: Osprey Publishing, 2009.

McPherson, James M. *Battle Cry of Freedom: The Civil War Era.* New York: Oxford Univ. Press, 1988.

———. *For Cause and Comrades: Why Men Fought in the Civil War.* New York: Oxford Univ. Press, 1997.

———. *Tried by War: Abraham Lincoln as Commander in Chief.* New York: Penguin, 2008.

Mobley, Joe A., ed. *The Papers of Zebulon Baird Vance.* Raleigh: Office of Archives and History, North Carolina Department of Cultural Resources, 2013.

Murray, Melba L. *Bradley Divided: Bradley County, Tennessee During the Civil War.* Collegedale: College Press, 1992.

Neely, Mark E., Jr. *Southern Rights: Political Prisoners and the Myth of*

Confederate Constitutionalism. Charlottesville: Univ. Press of
Virginia, 1999.

———. *The Civil War and the Limits of Destruction.* Cambridge: Harvard Univ.
Press, 2003.

Ness, George T., Jr. *The Regular Army on the Eve of The Civil War.* Baltimore:
Toomey Press, 1990.

Nevins, Allen. The War for the Union, vol. 1: *The Improvised War, 1861–1862.*
New York: Charles Scribner's Sons, 1959.

———. The War for the Union 2: *The Organized War, 1863–1864.* New York:
Charles Scribner's Sons, 1971.

Nicolay, John G. *The Outbreak of Rebellion* [1881]. Facsimile reprint. In
Thomas Yoseloff, Campaigns of the Civil War, Vol. 1. Ser. New York:
Thomas Yoseloff/A. S. Barnes & Co., 1963.

Nicolay, John G., and John Hay. *Abraham Lincoln: A History.* New York:
Century Co., 1890.

Paludan, Phillip S. *Victims: A True Story of the Civil War.* Knoxville: Univ. of
Tennessee Press, 1981.

Parker, Anna V. *The Sanders Family of Grass Hills.* Madison: Coleman Printing,
1966.

Piston, William G. *Carter's Raid: An Episode of the Civil War in East Tennessee.*
Johnson City: Overmountain Press, 1989.

Porter, Horace. *Campaigning with Grant.* New York: Bantam, 1991.

Putnam, Sally B. *Richmond During the War: Four Years of Personal Observation.*
Lincoln: Univ. of Nebraska Press, 1996. First published 1867 by G. W.
Carleton & Company.

Rankin, John. *Letters on American Slavery: Addressed to Mr. Thomas Rankin,
merchant at Middlebrook, Augusta Co., Va.*, 2ed. reis. Andesite Press,
2017. First published 1836 by Charles Whipple. www.bookdepository
.com.

Rankin, Richard C. *History of the Seventh Ohio Volunteer Cavalry.* Ripley:
J. C. Newcomb, 1881.

Reid, Whitelaw. *After the War: A Tour of the Southern States, 1865–1866.* New
York: Harper & Row, 1866.

———. *Ohio in the War: Her Statesmen, Her Generals, and Soldiers, Vol. 2: The*

History of Her Regiments. Cincinnati: Moore, Wilstach & Baldwin, 1868.

Robertson, James I., Jr., ed. *Soldier of Southwestern Virginia: The Civil War Letters of Captain John Preston Sheffey*. Baton Rouge: Louisiana State Univ. Press, 2004.

Rothrock, Mary U., ed. *The French Broad-Holston Country: A History of Knox County, Tennessee*. Knoxville: East Tennessee Historical Society, 1972.

Rule, William, ed. *Standard History of Knoxville, Tennessee*. Chicago: Lewis Publishing, 1900.

Scott, Robert G., ed. *Forgotten Valor: The Memoirs, Journals, & Civil War Letters of Orlando B. Willcox*. Kent: Kent State Univ. Press, 1999.

Scott, Samuel W., and Samuel P. Angel. *History of the Thirteenth Regiment, Tennessee Volunteer Cavalry, U.S.A.* Philadelphia: P. W. Ziegler, 1903 [Reprint, Alpha Editions, 2019].

Sensing, Thurman. *Champ Ferguson, Confederate Guerrilla*. Nashville: Vanderbilt Univ. Press, 1970.

Seymour, Digby G. *Divided Loyalties: Fort Sanders and the Civil War in East Tennessee*. Knoxville: Univ. of Tennessee Press, 2002.

Shaver, Lewellyn A. *A History of the Sixtieth Alabama Regiment, Gracie's Alabama Brigade*. Montgomery: Barrett & Brown, 1867.

Siebert, William H. *The Underground Railroad from Slavery to Freedom: A Comprehensive History*. New York: Macmillan, 1898.

Singer, Jane. *The Confederate Dirty War: Arson, Bombings, Assassination and Plots for Chemical and Germ Attacks on the Union*. Jefferson: McFarland, 2005.

Smith, David C. *Campaign to Nowhere: The Results of General Longstreet's Move into Upper Tennessee*. Strawberry Plains: Strawberry Plains Press, 1999.

Smith, John D., and William J. Cooper, eds. *A Union Woman in Civil War Kentucky: The Diary of Frances Peter*. Lexington: Univ. Press of Kentucky, 2000.

Sperry, Alfred, Samuel C. Fry, and Perez G. Clark. *A Military Record of Battery D, First Ohio Veteran Volunteers, Light Artillery*. Oil City: Derrick Publishing, 1908.

Starr, Stephen Z. *The Union Cavalry in the Civil War* 3: *The War in the West, 1861–1865*. Baton Rouge: Louisiana State Univ. Press, 1985.

Stickles, Arndt M. *Simon Bolivar Buckner: Borderland Knight*. Chapel Hill: Univ. of North Carolina Press, 1940.

Stout, Harry S. *Upon the Altar of the Nation: A Moral History of the Civil War*. New York: Viking Press, 2006.

Stowe, Harriet B. *The Key to Uncle Tom's Cabin*. London: Thomas Bosworth and Clarke, Beeton and Co, 1853.

Sullins, David. *Recollections of an Old Man: Seventy Years in Dixie, 1827–1897*. Bristol: Lenoir Press, 1910.

Sutherland, Daniel E. *A Savage Conflict: The Decisive Role of Guerrillas in the American Civil War*. Chapel Hill: Univ. of North Carolina Press, 2009.

——, ed. *A Very Violent Rebel: The Civil War Diary of Ellen Renshaw House*. Knoxville: Univ. of Tennessee Press, 1996.

——. *American Civil War Guerrillas: Changing the Rules of Warfare*. Santa Barbara: Praeger Press, 2013.

Tarrant, Eastham. *The Wild Riders of the First Kentucky Cavalry: A History of the Regiment in the Great War of the Rebellion, 1861–1865*. Lexington: Henry Clay Press, 1969.

Tatum, Georgia L. *Disloyalty in the Confederacy*. Chapel Hill: Univ. of North Carolina Press, 1934.

Taylor, Amy M. *The Divided Family in Civil War America*. Chapel Hill: Univ. of North Carolina Press, 2005.

Temple, Oliver P. *East Tennessee and the Civil War*. Cincinnati: Robert Clarke, 1899.

Thompson, Bradford F. *History of the 112th Regiment of the Illinois Volunteer Infantry in the Great War of the Rebellion, 1862–1865*. Toulon: Stark County News, 1885.

Thomsen, Paul A. *Rebel Chief: The Motley Life of Colonel William Holland Thomas, C.S.A.* New York: Tom Doherty Associates, 2004.

Trotter, William R. *Bushwhackers! The Civil War in North Carolina 2: The Mountains*. Greensboro: Signal Research, 1988.

Vincent, Sheridan E., comp. *Dr. Michael Vincent . . . and His Descendants, Including the Civil War Letters of . . . Corporal Martin Luther*

Vincent, 112th Illinois Infantry. Rochester: Vincent Family Record Publications, 1996.

Wagner, Margaret E., Gary W. Gallagher, and Paul Finkelman, eds. *The Library of Congress Civil War Desk Reference*. New York: Simon & Schuster, 2002.

Wallace, Andrew. *General August V. Kautz and the Southwestern Frontier*. Tucson: Privately Printed, 1967.

Wayne, Michael. *The Reshaping of Plantation Society: The Natchez District, 1860–1880*. Baton Rouge: Louisiana State Univ. Press, 1983.

Weaver, Jeffery C. *54th Virginia Infantry*. Virginia Regimental Histories Series. Lynchburg: H. E. Howard, 1993.

White, Jonathon W. *Abraham Lincoln and Treason in the Civil War*. Baton Rouge: Louisiana State Univ. Press, 2011.

Williams, David, Teresa C. Williams, and David Carlson. *Plain Folk in a Rich Man's War: Class and Dissent in Civil War Georgia*. Gainesville: Univ. Press of Florida, 2002.

Wilson, Clyde N., ed. *The Papers of John C. Calhoun*. Charleston: Univ. of South Carolina Press, 1986.

Witt, John F. *Lincoln's Code: The Laws of War in American History*. New York: Free Press, 2012.

Wood, Mayme P. *Hitch Hiking Along the Holston River from 1792–1962*. Nashville: Richland Press, 1964.

Woodbury, Augustus. *Major General Ambrose E. Burnside and the Ninth Army Corps*. Providence: Sidney S. Rider, 1867.

Woodward, C. Vann, ed. *Mary Chesnut's Civil War*. New Haven: Yale Univ. Press, 1981.

Woodworth, Steven E. *Jefferson Davis and His Generals: The Failure of Confederate Command in the West*. Lawrence: Univ. Press of Kansas, 1990.

Wyatt-Brown, Bertram. *The Shaping of Southern Culture: Honor, Grace, and War, 1760s–1890s*. Chapel Hill: Univ. of North Carolina Press, 2001.

Younger, Edward, ed. *Inside the Confederate Government: The Diary of Robert Garlick Hill Kean, Head of the Bureau of War*. New York: Oxford Univ. Press, 1957.

Articles

Alexander, Edward P. "Longstreet at Knoxville." In *Battles and Leaders of the Civil War, Vol. 3*, eds. R. U. Johnson and C. C. Buel, 745–52. New York: Thomas Yoseloff, 1956.

Bates, Alfred E. "The Second Regiment of Cavalry, 1. (1836–65)." In *The Army of the United States*, comp. T. F. Rodenbough, 173–79. New York: Maynard, Merrill, 1896.

Bergeron, Arthur W., Jr. "John Wesley Frazer." In *Confederate General 2*, eds. W. C. Davis and J. Hoffman, 146–47. Harrisburg, PA: National Historical Society, 1991.

Bible, Donahue. "The Hangings of the Greene County Bridge Burners." *Tennessee Ancestors* 21, no. 2 (August 2005): 130–38.

———. "Further Insight into the Life and Military Service of Captain David Fry." *Tennessee Ancestors* 22, no. 2 (2006): 121–23.

Boynton, J. H. "Army Correspondence." Reprint. *Athens* [TN] *Union Post*, Sept. 2, 1863. In *History of the 112th Regiment of the Illinois Volunteer Infantry in the Great War of the Rebellion, 1862–1865*, ed. B. F. Thompson, 81–92. Toulon, IL: Stark County News, 1885.

Brown, Fred. "Sanders found romance in Knoxville amid Civil War." *News Sentinel* [Knoxville], April 10, 2011.

Bryan, Charles F., Jr. "'Tories' Amidst Rebels: Confederate Occupation of East Tennessee, 1861–1865." *East Tennessee Historical Society's Publications* 60 (1988): 3–22.

Burns, Robert C. "General and Admiral Too." *East Tennessee Historical Society's Publications* 48 (1976): 29–34.

Campbell, James B. "East Tennessee During the Federal Occupation, 1863–1865." *East Tennessee Historical Society's Publications* 19 (1947): 64–80.

Carroll, Dillan J. "'The God Who Shielded Me Before, Yet Watches Over Us All': Confederate Soldiers, Mental Illness, and Religion." *Civil War History* 61 (Sept. 2015): 252–80.

Carter, William H. "The Sixth Regiment of Cavalry." In *The Army of the United States: Historical Sketches of Staff and Line with Portraits of Generals-in-Chief*, 232–50. New York: Maynard, Merrill, 1896.

Confederate Veteran. "Col. Robert C. Trigg of Virginia." 17 (1909): 64.

———. "Col. Thomas Claiborne." 21 (1913): 302.

———. "General Polk and His Staff." 9 (1901):121.

———. "Milton A. Haynes." 3 (1895): 260.

———. "Interesting Annual Memorial Service." 2 (1894):323.

"James L. Cooley." In *Tennessee Civil War Veterans' Questionnaires* 2, eds. George W. Dyer and Joseph T. Moore, 550–52. Easley: Southern Histories Press, 1985.

Copeland, James. "Secession and the Union in Tennessee and Kentucky: A Comparative Analysis." In *Border States: Journal of the Kentucky-Tennessee American Studies Association*, 11 (1997). http://spider .georgetowncollege.edu/htallant/border/bs11/fr-cope.

Crow, Vernon H. "The Justness of Our Cause: The Civil War Diaries of William W. Stringfield." *East Tennessee Historical Society's Publications* 56–57 (1984–85): 71–101.

Cullum, George W. "George L. Hartsuff." In *Biographical Register of the Officers and Graduates of the U.S. Military Academy . . .*, 484–90. Boston: Houghton, Mifflin, 1891.

———. "William P. Sanders." In *Biographical Register of the Officers and Graduates of the U.S. Military Academy . . .* 2, nos. 1001 to 2000,668. Boston: Houghton, Mifflin, 1891.

Dirck, Brian R. "Posterity's Blush: Civil Liberties, Property Rights, and Property Confiscation in the Confederacy." *Civil War History* 48, no. 3 (Sept. 2002): 237–56.

Dow, Tristam T. "Major Dow's Report." In *History of the 112th Regiment of Illinois Volunteer Infantry in the Great War of the Rebellion, 1862–1885*, ed. B. F. Thompson, 42–48. Toulon: Stark County News, 1885.

Duke, Basil W., Orlando B. Willcox, and Thomas H. Hines. "A Romance of Morgan's Rough Riders." In *Battles and Leaders of the Civil War, Vol. 6*, ed. Paul Cozzens, 315–46. Urbana: Univ. of Illinois Press, 2004.

Fisher, Noel C. "Definitions of Victory: East Tennessee Unionists in the Civil War and Reconstruction." In *Guerrillas, Unionists, and Violence on the Confederate Home Front*, ed. Daniel E. Sutherland, 58–88. Fayetteville: Univ. of Arkansas Press, 1999.

Fremantle, A. J. L. "The Gettysburg Campaign: From the Diary of A. J. L. Fremantle [1863]." In *Two Witnesses at Gettysburg*, 2 ed., ed. Gary W. Gallagher, 79–149. Malden: Wiley-Blackwell, 2009.

Green, Jennifer R., and Patrick Kirkwood. "Reframing the Antebellum Democratic Mainstream: Transatlantic Diplomacy and the Career of Pierre Soulé." *Civil War History* 61 (Sept. 2015): 212–51.

Groce, W. Todd. "The Social Origins of East Tennessee's Confederate Leadership." In *The Civil War in Appalachia: Collected Essays*, eds. Kenneth W. Noe and Shannon H. Wilson, 30–54. Knoxville: Univ. of Tennessee Press, 1997.

Hart, Gideon M. "Military Commissions and the Lieber Code: Toward a New Understanding of the Jurisdictional Foundations of Military Commissions." *Military Law Review*. Department of the Army Pamphlet 27–100–203 (Spring, 2010).

Hayes, Phillip. C. "Campaigning in East Tennessee." In *Military Essays and Recollections, Vol. 4*, 318–47. Chicago: Illinois Commandery, MOLLUS, 1907.

Hess, Earl J. 2014. "Where Do We Stand? A Critical Assessment of Civil War Studies in the Sesquicentennial Era." *Civil War History* 60, no. 4 (Dec. 2014):371–403.

Holston Journal [Knoxville, TN]. Charlton, C. W. "The Murder of Dr. Harvey Baker." July 9, 1863.

———. "Pilgrim," pseud., "Abolitionists at Strawberry Plains—Bridge Burning—House Pillaging—Official Vandalism." July 9, 1863.

———. "The Raid into East Tennessee." July 9, 1863.

Inscoe, John C. "Mountain Unionism, Secession, and Regional Self-Image: The Contrasting Cases of Western North Carolina and East Tennessee." In *Looking South: Chapters in the Story of an American Region*, ed. W. B. Moore, Jr. and J. F. Tripp, 115–32. Westport: Greenwood Press, 1989.

———. "Highland Households Divided: Family Deceptions, Diversions, and Divisions in Southern Appalachia's Inner Civil War." In *Enemies of the Country: New Perspectives on Unionists in the Civil War South*, eds. John C. Inscoe and Robert C. Kenzer, 54–72. Athens: Univ. of Georgia Press, 2001.

Jones, Archer. "Tennessee and Mississippi, Joe Johnston's Strategic Problem."
    Tennessee Historical Quarterly 18, no. 2 (1959): 134–47.

Jones, Samuel. "Holding Burnside in Check in East Tennessee." In *Battles
    and Leaders of the Civil War, Vol. 5* [1882], ed. Paul Cozzens, 429–49.
    Urbana: Univ. of Illinois Press, 2002.

Kelly, Dorothy. "The Bridge Burnings and Union Uprising of 1861." *Tennessee
    Ancestors* 21, No. 2 (Aug. 2005): 123–29.

Kelso, Samuel. "Sanders's Raid: Destruction of the East Tennessee & Georgia
    Railroad." *National Herald*, May 14, 1885: 3.

———. "The Saunders Raid: Sketch of the Part Taken by Two Guns of Battery
    D, 1st Ohio L.A." *National Herald*, May 22, 1893: 3.

Kniffin, Gilbert C. "General Wm. P. Sanders," *National Intelligencer*, May 6,
    1882: 1.

———. "Manoevering Bragg Out of Tennessee." In *Battles and Leaders of the
    Civil War, Volume 2: The Tide Shifts*, eds. R. U. Johnson and C. C.
    Buel, 635–37. Secaucus: Castle, 1887.

Kochi, Tarik. "The Partisan: Carl Schmitt and Terrorism." *Law Critique* 17
    (2006): 267–95.

Konkle, Andrew J. "Report to Col. James Barnett, June 29th, 1863." In *A
    Military Record of Battery D, First Ohio Veteran Volunteers, Light
    Artillery*, eds. Alfred Sperry, Samuel C. Fry, and Perez Clark, 94–95.
    Oil City, PA: Derrick Publishing, 1908.

Knoxville Register. Branner, John R. "Mossy Creek" [letter to brother, June 22,
    1863]. June 23, 1863: 2.

———. "Captain Pleasant M. McClung." June 23, 1863: 1.

———. "Captain Wiggs." June 23, 1863:1.

———. "Communicated." June 26, 1863:1.

———. "Communication to Atlanta Confederacy." July 7, 1863.

———. "Damages Done By the Enemy." June 23, 1863: 1.

———. "Dr. Harvey Baker." June 23, 1863.

———. E. Y. C., pseud. "The Escape of the Yankee Raiders." July 1, 1863.

———. "Federal Raid Into East Tennessee—Immense Destruction of Railroad
    Bridges and Other Property." July 5, 1863: 2.

———. "Honor to Capt. Arnold." June 23, 1863: 1.

———. Lucien [Woolfolk?]. "Letter to Mr. Sperry." June 27, 1863.

———. "The Murder of Doctor Harvey Baker by the Yankees." June 23, 1863: 2.

———. "Progress of the Yankee Raiders." June 23, 1863: 2.

———. "The Raiders Not Gone Yet." July 4, 1863: 2.

———. "The Railroads and the Mails." June 26, 1863: 2.

———. Editorial. "We heard a gentleman." June 23, 1863: 2.

———. Williams, J. H. "Letter to the editor." June 27, 1863.

Legg, David C., comp. "Obituary of William Randolph McEntire." In *9th Battalion Georgia Artillery, Co. A.* Smyrna: Smyrna Historical Society, 1920.

Linder, Jamie S., and William B. Eigelsbach, eds. "To War With Mexico: A Diary of the Mexican-American War." *Journal of East Tennessee History*, no. 73 (2001): 74–100.

Longstreet, James. "Lee's Invasion of Pennsylvania." In *Battles and Leaders of the Civil War: The Tide Shifts*, eds. R. U. Johnson and C. C. Buel, 244–51. New York: Century Magazine, 1884–88.

Madden, David. "Unionist Resistance to Confederate Occupation: The Bridge Burners of East Tennessee." *East Tennessee Historical Society's Publications* 52 (1980): 22–39.

McKenzie, Robert T. "Prudent Silence and Strict Neutrality: The Parameters of Unionism in Parson Brownlow's Knoxville, 1860–1863." In *Enemies of the Country: New Perspectives on Unionism in the Civil War South*, eds. John C. Inscoe and Robert R. Kenzer, 73–96. Athens: Univ. of Georgia Press, 2001.

———. "Contesting Secession: Parson Brownlow and the Rhetoric of Proslavery Unionism, 1860–1861." *Civil War History* 48 (Dec. 2002): 294–312.

McKinney, Gordon B. "East Tennessee Politics: An Incident in the Life of William Gibbs McAdoo, Sr." *East Tennessee Historical Society's Publications* 48 (1976): 34–39.

Melville, Herman. "Battle-Pieces." In *The Oxford Book of Civil War Quotations*, comp.

J. D. Wright. New York: Oxford Univ. Press, 2006,

Moffatt, Charles G. "East Tennessee, the Railroad and the Bridge Burners." *Confederate Chronicles of Tennessee* 1 (1986): 17–24.

Morgan, George W. "Cumberland Gap." In *Battles and Leaders of the Civil*

War, Vol. 3: The Tide Shifts, eds. R. U. Johnson and C. C. Buel, 62–69. Secaucus: Castle, 1956.

Morgan, Jonathan. "Letter Written by 'Pottertown' Potter . . . Concerning the 'Bridge-burning,'" [1897]. In *Their Eyes Have Seen the Glory: East Tennessee Unionists in the Civil War*, ed. and comp. Donahue Bible, 1–4. Mohawk: Dodson Creek Publishers, 1997.

Mitchell, Charles D. "The Sanders Raid Into East Tennessee, June, 1863." In *Sketches of War History, 1861–1865*, vol. 6, ed. Ohio Commandery, MOLLUS, 238–51. Wilmington: Broadfoot, 1992.

National Tribune [Washington, D.C.]. Blackman, W. D. "The Sanders Raid." (Oct. 14, 1886): 4.

——. Denney, Harvey. "Over the Mountains: Strawberry Plains and Other Events of Campaigning." 20 (Feb. 21, 1901): 2.

——. Denney, Harvey. "All About Saunder's Raid [*sic*]." 35 (Sept. 9, 1915):7.

——. Edmiston, D. W. "Fighting at Philadelphia," 14 (Feb. 7, 1895): 2

——. Fry, Samuel C. "The Saunders Raid: A Brilliant Cavalry Exploit in East Tennessee [*sic*]." (Aug. 25, 1887): 1–2.

——. Rankin, Robert C. "The Saunders Raid: Captain Rankin Considers . . . the Dispute Raised Against Him [pt. 1]." (Aug. 3, 1893): 3.

——. "The Saunders Raid: An Ohio Light Artilleryman Corrects Comrade R. C. Rankin." (June 15, 1893): 3.

——. "The Saunders Raid: Nice Work Done on a Flying Trip into East Tennessee." (May 11, 1893): 2.

——. "The 2d and 7th Ohio Cavalry." (Sept. 22, 1887): 3.

New York Times. "The Germans in Hooker's Battles—The National Spirit of our Adopted Citizens." June 4, 1863.

——. "Treason Against the United States." Jan. 25, 1861.

——. "The Union Men." Sept. 25, 1863. Reprint from *Richmond Examiner*, Sept. 7, 1863. UTK.

Nicholas, George W. "Capture, Prison Life and Escape." In *History of the 112th Regiment of Illinois Volunteer Infantry in the Great War of the Rebellion, 1862–1865*, ed. B. F. Thompson, 456–71. Toulon: Stark County News, 1885.

Noe, Kenneth W. "Who Were the Bushwackers? Age, Class, Kin, and Western

Virginia's Confederate Guerrillas, 1861–1862." *Civil War History* 49, no. 1 (Mar. 2003): 5–31.

Patman, Richard F. "46 Years Ago No. 1." *Calhoun Times* [Calhoun, GA], April 7, 1910.

Poe, Orlando M. "The Defense of Knoxville." In *Battles and Leaders of the Civil War, Vol. 3*, eds. R. U. Johnson and C. C. Buel, 731–45. New York: Thomas Yoseloff, 1956.

Queener, Verton M. "East Tennessee Sentiment and the Secession Movement, November, 1860—June 1861." *East Tennessee Historical Society's Publications* 20 (1948): 59–83.

"Rev. Joseph H. Martin, 1851–1863." In *Historical Sermon, Second Presbyterian Church*. Knoxville: Second Presbyterian Church, n.d.

Richmond Dispatch. O.K. [pseud]. "Dispatch, Abingdon, Virginia, Sept. 22, 1863." Sept. 25, 1863.

——. "The attack on Knoxville; repulse of the enemy with heavy loss; Destruction of Bridges, &c. [First Dispatch]." June 20, 1863.

——. "The attack on Knoxville." June 24, 1863.

——. "Federal raid in East Tennessee—immense destruction of railroad bridges and other property." July 1, 1863.

Sanders, Lewis. "History of Kentucky Cattle." *The Cultivator* [Albany, NY], March, 1849.

Scarborough, William K. "Lords or Capitalists? The Natchez Nabobs in Comparative Perspective." *Journal of Mississippi History* 54, no. 3 (Aug. 1992): 239–68.

Sifakis, Stewart. "William Price Sanders." In *Who Was Who in the Civil War*, 568–69. New York: Facts on File, Inc., 1988.

Siker, Nancy. "Lucien B. Woolfolk." In *First Baptist Church*, 105–6. Knoxville: First Baptist Church, 1992.

Silber, Nancy. "When Charles Francis Adams Met Robert E. Lee: A Southern Gentleman in History and Memory." In *Inside the Confederate Nation: Essays in Honor of Emory M. Thomas*, eds. Lesley J. Gordon and John C. Inscoe, 349–60. Baton Rouge: Louisiana State Univ. Press, 2005.

Smith, Joseph P. "Captain Richard Calvin Rankin, 1821–1899." In *History of the Republican Party in Ohio*, 780–83. Chicago: Lewis Publishing, 1898.

Southern Confederacy [Atlanta, GA]. "Battle at Knoxville—Defeat of the
    Yankee Raiders." June 2, 1863.

——. "Capt. Wyly's Company in the Fight at Knoxville." June 29, 1863.

——. "Gallant Conduct of a Georgia Battery." June 27, 1863.

——. Hubbard, Henry H. "Vandalism." July 3, 1863.

——. L. J. A. [Leonard Anderson?]. Letter to the editors. July 2, 1863.

——. "The Murder of Doctor Harvey Baker by the Yankees." June 27, 1863.

——. "The Raids! The Raids!" June 22, 1863.

——. Wyly, Benjamin F. "Leyden Artillery." June 24, 1863: 1.

——. "The Yankee Raid." June 24, 1863.

——. "Yankee Trick with the Telegraph." July 6, 1863.

Stealey, John E., III. "West Virginia's Constitutional Critique of Virginia: The
    Revolution of 1861–1863." *Civil War History* 57, no. 1 (Mar. 2011):
    66–88.

Strasser, William A. "A Terrible Calamity Has Befallen Us": Unionist Women
    in Civil War East Tennessee." *Journal of East Tennessee History* 71
    (1999): 66–88.

Sunny South [Atlanta, GA]. A Georgia Colonel, pseud. "Leaves from an Old
    Scrap Book," Feb. 24, 1906.

Sutherland, Daniel E. "Memories of a Rooted Sorrow: The Legacy of the
    Guerrilla War." *Civil War History* 62 (Mar. 2016): 8–35.

Thomas, Horace H. "Personal Reminiscences of the East Tennessee Campaign:
    August, 1863, to December, 1864." In *Military Collections and
    Recollections, Vol. 4*, comp. and ed. Illinois Commandery, MOLLUS,
    284–300. Wilmington: Broadfoot, 1992.

Wallenstein, Peter. "'Helping to Save the Union': The Social Origins, Wartime
    Experiences, and Military Impact of White Union Troops from East
    Tennessee." In *The Civil War in Appalachia: Collected Essays*, eds.
    Kenneth W. Noe and Samuel H. Wilson, 1–29. Knoxville: Univ. of
    Tennessee Press, 1997.

Warner, Ezra J. "George Lucas Hartsuff." In *Generals in Blue: Lives of the Union
    Commanders*, 212–13. Baton Rouge: Louisiana State Univ. Press, 1964.

——. "William Price Sanders." In *Generals in Blue: Lives of the Union
    Commanders*, 419–20. Baton Rouge: Louisiana State Univ. Press,
    1964.

Wilshire, Joseph W. "A Reminiscence of Burnside's Knoxville Campaign." In *Sketches of War History, 1861–1865: Papers & Index, Vol. 9*, ed. Ohio Commandery, MOLLUS, 3–22. Wilmington: Broadfoot, 1993.

Wormer, Grover S. "The Morgan Raid." In *War Papers Read Before the Commandery of the State of Michigan Military Order of the Loyal Legion of the United States*, 191–216. Detroit: James H. Stone, 1898.

Kean, Robert G.); civilian supporters, 130

Confederate military units

—Department of East Tennessee, 65–68, 122, 151, 186, 195; 6th Alabama Infantry, 12; 1st Florida Cavalry, 186; 6th Florida Infantry, 147; 7th Florida Infantry, 125; Florida Volunteer Coast Guard, 125; 5th Georgia Cavalry, xi, 167; 9th Georgia Artillery, 126, 145; 65th Georgia Infantry, 61, 187–89; 1st Louisiana Cavalry, 78, 85, 165 (see also Scott, Col. John S.); 5th Missouri Infantry, 127; 2nd Tennessee Cavalry, 129; 54th Virginia Infantry, 123

—Tennessee Corps of Artillery, 124

—Tennessee Light Artillery, 128

Congress of Vienna, 14

conscription (CSA), 16, 131

Cooper, William J., 13

Corps of Engineers (CSA), 182

Cox, Major General Jacob D., USA, 21–22

Crawford, Brigadier General Robert A., USA, 25, 32

Crittenden, John J., 28

Crozier, John H., 133, 192

Cumberland Gap, ix, 26, 29, 67–69, 118, 129, 136, 185, 191

Cumberland River, ix, 53, 62–65, 75, 81, 173, 176

currency, Confederate, 165

Davis, Jefferson: assigns Lt. Sanders to California, 42; assists Cadet William Sanders, 40; and Brigadier General John W. Frazer, 190–91; as micromanager, 13, 67, 184; military strategy, 196; orders occupation of East Tennessee, 9; political activity, 2, 38–39, 44; suspends habeas corpus, 16, 19; as US Secretary of War, 40–41; at USMA, 13, 41; warns Cadet William Sanders, 40–41

Davis, William C., 15

Democratic Party, 38

Denney, Private Henry, USA, 159–60

Digby, Gordon S., 2

District of Central Kentucky, USA, 46, 48

District of the Gulf (CSA), 67

Donelson, Major General Daniel S., CSA, 67

Dow, Captain John, USA, 175

Dow, Major Tristram T., USA, ix, 56, 151, 163, 167, 170, 175–77, 197

Ducktown, TN, 6–7

Duke, Brigadier General Basil W., CSA, 39

Dutton's Hill, KY, battle of, 12, 48–49, 51, 205

Dye, Private Isaiah C., USA, 81–82

East Tennessee: agriculture,
124, 163; military value, 6–7;
topography, 31, 67–68, 73, 79;
votes against secession, 5–6
East Tennessee & Georgia RR, 8,
33, 57, 94
East Tennessee & Kentucky RR,
118
East Tennessee & Virginia RR,
8, 59, 125, 136–39, 151, 159,
162, 183
Edwards, Lieutenant J. R., USA,
28–29
Elizabethton, TN, 114
Emory Creek, TN, ix

Fain, Eliza, 194
Finley, Colonel Jesse J., CSA, 123
Flat Creek, TN, x, 86, 152–53
Fleming, John M., 192
Florida, population of, 6
Fort Donelson, TN, 123
Fort Laramie, WY, 42
Foster, Colonel John W., USA, 183
Frankfort, KY, 2, 37
Franklin House, Knoxville, TN, 124
Frazer, Brigadier General John W.,
CSA: court-martialed, 186–91;
fails to detect Sanders, 195;
ordered to hold Cumberland
Gap "to the last," 191; ordered
to march to Jacksborough
Gap, 118; Seddon recommends
censure, 190; surrenders

Cumberland Gap, accused of
cowardice, 191
Freehling, William W., 199
Fry, Captain David W., USA, 15. *See
also* bridge burning
Fry, Captain Samuel C., USA, 152
Fullington, Sergeant Alexander,
USA, 75–76. *See also* revenge

gallows, 15
Gettysburg, PA, battle of, 2, 205
Ghent, KY, 37
Gilbert, Colonel Samuel A., USA,
75–76
Gillmore, Brigadier General
Quincy A., USA, 48
Grant, Lieutenant General Ulysses
S., USA, 1, 23, 53, 66, 69, 127
"Grass Hills," KY, 37
Greeneville, TN, 9, 15, 70
guerrillas, 13–14

Hanover Court House, VA, battle
of, 46
Haggin, James Ben Ali, 46
Haggin, Mrs. Eliza Sanders, 40–41
Halleck, Major General Henry W.,
USA, 1–2, 24, 26, 36, 88, 177
Hamilton, Major William D., USA,
75
Harris, Isham G., 9
Hartsuff, Major General George L.,
USA, 35, 51, 75
Haynes, Lieutenant Colonel